A BRIEF HISTORY OF THE EPISCOPAL CHURCH

A BRIEF HISTORY OF THE EPISCOPAL CHURCH

*with a chapter on the Anglican Reformation
and an appendix on the quest for an
annulment of Henry VIII*

DAVID L. HOLMES

TRINITY PRESS INTERNATIONAL
Valley Forge, Pennsylvania

Trinity Press International, P.O. Box 851, Valley Forge, PA 19482-0851

Library of Congress Cataloging-in-Publication Data

Holmes, David Lynn
    A brief history of the Episcopal Church : with a chapter on the
Anglican Reformation and an appendix on the quest for an annulment of
Henry VIII / David L. Holmes.
        p.   cm.
    Includes bibliographical references and index.
    ISBN 1-56338-060-9
    1. Episcopal Church — History.   2. Anglican Communion — United
States — History.   I. Title.
    BX5880.H74   1993
    283'.73 — dc20   93-31234
                                                                          CIP

Printed in the United States of America

    94   95   96   97   98   99   10   9   8   7   6   5   4   3   2

To Carolyn

CONTENTS

ILLUSTRATIONS

MAP

FOREWORD

The evolution of the Anglican communion in America entails a record of considerable complexity. For what we know today as the Episcopal Church was, originally, the Church of England in the Colonies. And the English Church achieved its post-Reformation identity in the reigns of Henry VIII, Edward VI, and Elizabeth. So the history of the English Church, as it reaches across more than two hundred years from the Elizabethan Settlement to the time late in the eighteenth century when at last an American episcopate was securely established, is by force of circumstances inherently a part of the history of the Episcopal Church. Moreover, like all other provinces of the Anglican communion, the American church has over the last hundred and fifty years reflected the deep tensions between the high church movement and those of an evangelical persuasion. And, like the Christian enterprise generally, the Episcopal Church has had to reckon with the many intellectual challenges of modernity and with the ever increasing complications of a technological culture. It all forms a tangled and fascinating story, and one marvels at David Holmes having managed not to neglect any important phase of it in so relatively brief a chronicle.

There are, of course, other books that review the history of the Episcopal Church in a more closely detailed and comprehensive way — such as, for example, James Thayer Addison's classic of a generation ago *The Episcopal Church in the United States* (1951) or Robert Prichard's recent volume, *A History of the Episcopal Church* (1991). But the generality of readers, I suspect, will find Mr. Holmes's work to be the most attractive and absorbing presentation of its subject in the currently available literature. At every point it is marked by freedom from partisan bias and judiciousness of perspective; the prose is brisk and immaculate; and I am confident that the book will have a long and useful life.

NATHAN A. SCOTT, JR.

William R. Kenan Professor Emeritus of Religious Studies and Professor Emeritus of English
The University of Virginia

ACKNOWLEDGMENTS

The author expresses his heartfelt thanks to two graduates of the College of William and Mary, David Carlson and Janet Singletary Thomas, for their assistance in the research and typing of this book. Readers will find the contributions of Mr. Carlson and Ms. Thomas in style and content on virtually every page, and the book would be substantially less interesting without them. He acknowledges the valuable readings given to the manuscript at two stages by John F. Woolverton, editor of *Anglican and Episcopal History*, and in the final stage by David Hein.

He also expresses his gratitude to the faculty research committee of the College of William and Mary, to the Virginia Foundation for the Humanities, and to the Episcopal Theological Seminary of the Southwest, whose fellowships allowed him to research and write in the field of Episcopal church history. His colleagues in the Department of Religion at William and Mary have unstintingly supported his requests for leave.

The staffs of many libraries — especially those of the Archives of the Episcopal Church, the Swem Library of the College of William and Mary, and the Alderman Library of the University of Virginia — were invariably helpful and available.

Portions of this history appeared in condensed form in the *Encyclopedia of the American Religious Experience,* edited by Charles H. Lippy and Peter W. Williams (New York: Charles Scribner's Sons, 1988), and are reprinted with the permission of the publisher.

Finally, individual thanks go to Nathan A. Scott, Jr., Laura G. Barrett, George Gallup, Jr., Thomas C. Reeves, Ray W. Frantz, Jr., Elinor S. Hearn, Charles H. Long, Jr., Harold Rast, Charles F. Rehkopf, David A. Scott, Frank E. Sugeno, Jerry Van Voorhis, Robert Vaughan, and Peter W. Williams for suggestions and support on the manuscript.

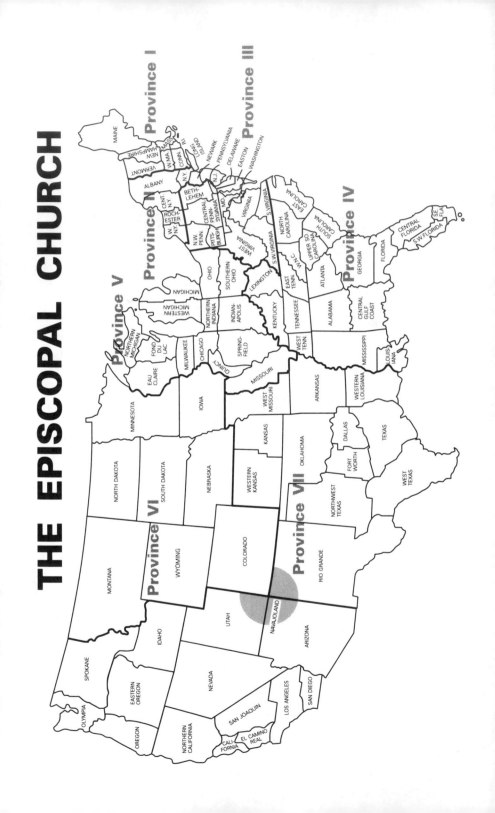

THE OFFICE OF THE SUFFRAGAN BISHOP
FOR THE ARMED FORCES
Under the direction of the Presiding Bishop

THE EPISCOPAL CHURCH IN MICRONESIA
Under the jurisdiction of the Presiding Bishop

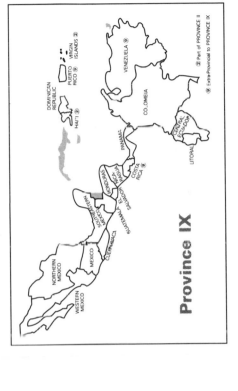

Province IX

DOMINICAN
REPUBLIC

HAITI ②

PUERTO
RICO ⑨

VIRGIN
ISLANDS ②

VENEZUELA ⑨

COLOMBIA

NORTHERN
MEXICO

WESTERN
MEXICO

MEXICO

CUERNAVACA

SOUTHEASTERN
MEXICO

GUATEMALA

EL SALVADOR

HONDURAS

NICARAGUA

COSTA
RICA ⑨

PANAMA

CENTRAL
ECUADOR

LITORAL

② Part of PROVINCE II

⑨ Extra-Provincial to PROVINCE IX

CONVOCATION OF AMERICAN CHURCHES IN EUROPE
Under jurisdiction of the Presiding Bishop (part of Province II)

Brussels
Paris
Frankfurt
Wiesbaden
Munich
Geneva
Florence
Rome

Province VIII

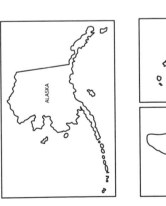

ALASKA

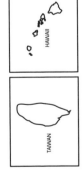

HAWAII

TAIWAN

1

THE ANGLICAN
REFORMATION

THE CONTINENTAL REFORMATION

The Anglican Reformation that emerged from Henry VIII's break with
Roman Catholicism was the most complex, prolonged, and in many ways
conservative of the Christian movements that arose during the period of
the Protestant Reformation.

In sixteenth-century Europe, the religious pluralism Americans accept
today as a birthright was unknown. Virtually everywhere the religion of
the ruling authority determined the religion of the people. If the king
remained loyal to papal teachings during the conflicts of the Reformation, then his land remained Roman Catholic. If the ruler accepted the
teachings of one of the principal Protestant Reformers — Martin Luther,
John Calvin, and Ulrich Zwingli (whose brief reformation in Switzerland
was continued and largely replaced by Calvinism) — then his people also
followed Luther, Zwingli, or Calvin.

Politics, economics, and social considerations played a role, but the
Reformation was overall a distinctly religious movement. Ironically, although it arose in reaction to the worldliness and corruption of late
medieval Roman Catholicism, it nevertheless emerged out of the spiritual
riches of precisely the same church it was attempting to reform.

By the time the Reformation's storms had quieted on the continent
of Europe, France, parts of Germany, and most of central and southern Europe (led by Spain) remained loyal to the teaching of Roman
Catholicism that Christ had entrusted his church to the care of the papacy. The Scandinavian lands and many of the German states had become
Lutheran. Calvinism had won the Netherlands and some of the Swiss can-
tons, and taken root in parts of Germany, France, and Hungary. Roman
Catholic and Protestant governments alike had persecuted almost out of

existence the small number of Christians who had embraced the more thoroughgoing reformation of the Anabaptists (the forerunners of today's Mennonite, Amish, and Hutterite churches).

Initially positive and meaning "to assert (or stand) for" something, the term "Protestant" came from a protest issued in 1529 by six princes and fourteen cities when a diet of the German Holy Roman empire revoked an earlier decision to allow religious toleration to Lutheran and Zwinglian churches. Few of the continental churches used the term for themselves (the Lutherans preferring "Evangelical" and the Zwinglians and Calvinists favoring "Reformed"), but the name stuck. Although the various churches subsequently called "Protestant" varied, they were united in certain central affirmations.

Above all, Protestants maintained that they were not teaching new doctrines but rather restoring (an important word in Protestantism) the Christianity described in the New Testament and in the writings of the early church fathers. Calvin, for example, claimed that he could have written his landmark *Institutes of the Christian Religion* (first edition, 1536) out of the writings of the fourth- and fifth-century church father Augustine of Hippo. Roman Catholicism required reforming, Protestants asserted, because it had not only departed from the true faith of early Christianity but also added a substantial body of man-made religion to it.

All Protestants — whether Lutheran, Reformed, or Anabaptist — believed that the Holy Scripture was the sole source of revealed truth, that its reading nourished Christians, and that individual conscience could interpret it. They rejected the concept of a hierarchical and intermediary priesthood, believed that all baptized believers formed a universal priesthood with direct access to God, emphasized the role of the laity, viewed clergy as laypeople set aside to witness full-time for Jesus Christ, and on biblical grounds supported the marriage of clergy.

Stressing the sovereign transcendence of God and the sinfulness of humankind, Protestants taught that men and women were powerless to save themselves through so-called good works. They taught that salvation comes only through the loving mercy of God, which the Christian receives through his or her total commitment of trustful faith and not (as Roman Catholicism then taught) through a combination of faith, good works that earn merits, and the dispensations of the church. The Reformation taught that the Christian's good works — the love of God and neighbor over the self — then flow from this new relationship out of gratitude, but are in no way meritorious. Called "justification by grace through faith," this central teaching of Protestantism is articulated in such hymns as "A Mighty Fortress is Our God," "Ah, Holy Jesus," and "Just as I Am."

For most early Protestants the belief in God's sovereignty and human sinfulness also led to a belief in predestination — the teaching that God had selected some persons for salvation while allowing or ordaining all others to follow their own ways to sin and damnation. Although most early Protestants found the biblical support for the doctrine compelling, other Protestants challenged it (as did the Roman Catholics) and argued that God allowed Christians to accept or reject salvation. Although the teaching is embedded in such popular hymns as "Amazing Grace" and "Rock of Ages," belief in predestination steadily declined until only a small number of Protestants asserted it by the twentieth century.

In matters of liturgy, most Protestants — Lutheranism was a partial exception — believed that a return to the doctrine and practices of early Christianity carried with it a simplification of worship. On the basis of Scripture and the teachings of the church fathers, Protestants reduced the seven sacraments of the medieval church to the two they believed Jesus Christ had instituted — baptism and the Lord's Supper or eucharist; unlike Roman Catholicism, they insisted that the laity receive not only the bread but also the wine in the eucharist. All Protestants taught that the preaching of the Word was God's chosen means of spreading the gospel, opposed any subordination of preaching to the sacraments, advocated that worship be in the language of the people (the "vernacular") rather than Latin, and objected to the role Roman Catholicism had given over the centuries to the person and work of the Virgin Mary.

Protestants rejected monasticism and the medieval distinction between the higher calling of the clergy and the lower life of the laity. They held that all honest forms of work could be a divine vocation. On New Testament grounds, however, they imposed an almost monastic standard of personal morality on church members — a standard that proved easier to achieve in Anabaptism and Calvinism than in Lutheranism.

Implicit in Protestantism from the beginning was what came to be known as the Protestant Principle: the assertion that all attempts by Christianity to capture the Word of God fail, for the simple reason that the finite cannot express the infinite. Because creeds, doctrines, edicts of popes, proclamations of councils of bishops, and even books of the Bible are human expressions, they can distort or fall short of divine truth. Because they emerge from the limitations of human existence, they can err. For most Protestants of the Reformation era, it simply did not please the Most High God to make Christianity infallible by overriding human limitations. One sees this Protestant Principle enunciated as early as 1521, when Luther made the momentous assertion to the Diet of Worms that popes and general councils of bishops could err and had erred. The axiom *Ecclesia reformata sed semper reformanda* ("a church reformed but always open to further reformation") expresses the Protestant refusal to absolutize a church structure.

The Protestant Principle has allowed Protestants to break without fear of damnation with their denominations and to form new ones that they believe better represent the teaching of Scripture. Protestants have also divided over doctrinal questions, principally concerning predestination, church government, the presence or absence of the body and blood of Christ in the eucharist, and the age at which a Christian may be baptized. From the beginning, the finely wrought theology of Calvinism proved impossible to reconcile with that of Lutheranism, even though Calvin viewed Luther as his mentor and the two interpretations of Christianity agreed on doctrine after doctrine.

Anglicanism is not necessarily Protestant. But readers can gain a good sense of the differences between Roman Catholic and Protestant teachings by comparing the decrees of the Council of Trent (1545–1563), which aimed both at renewing Roman Catholicism and at refuting Protestant teachings, to the Confession of Augsburg (1530), which, though Lutheran, embodied most of the central beliefs of other Protestants.

THE PENDULUM SWING OF THE
CHURCH OF ENGLAND

From the 1520s on, the number of Christians in England who were influenced by the teachings of the Protestant Reformation grew. As Lutheran and Reformed (or Calvinist) state churches supported by taxes and the power of the government began to dot the landscape of Europe, the question was whether English Christianity would remain Roman Catholic, accept one of the continental forms of Protestantism, or follow yet a third option. And the crucial figure in the answer to the question was the English monarch.

The reigns through 1688 of the Tudor kings and queens (Henry VIII, Edward VI, Mary, Elizabeth I) and the Stuart monarchs (James I, Charles I, Charles II, and James II) witnessed a pendulum swing of Anglicanism in terms of religious loyalty. Under Henry VIII the Church of England became a kind of autonomous Catholicism, independent of Rome, like Eastern Orthodoxy or the apparently indigenous British Catholicism of the earliest Christian centuries. An English translation of the Bible was made accessible in each church, and men of Protestant inclinations began to be appointed bishops. Doctrinally and to a large extent liturgically, however, the Church of England appeared unchanged (the mass, for example, remained in Latin). But Henry entrusted the education of his two heirs — Edward VI, his son by Jane Seymour, and Elizabeth I, his daughter by Anne Boleyn — to Protestant tutors. Since he clearly knew that the Protestant upbringing of his heirs could have momentous consequences for English history, Henry's decision may indicate that he was less opposed to the Reformation than historians have often assumed.

During the reign of the sickly, precocious boy-king Edward VI (1547–1553), Anglicanism moved closer theologically to continental Calvinism. Under Henry VIII, Thomas Cranmer, the archbishop of Canterbury, had been obliged to bridle his Protestant instincts. But under Edward's Calvinist advisors Cranmer was allowed to move the Church of England firmly into the Reformation camp. Protestant in teaching, his Forty-Two Articles of Religion (1553) were intended as a confession of faith required of all clergy, schoolmasters, and Oxford and Cambridge faculty and students. Never enforced because of Mary Tudor's accession to the throne, these articles formed the foundation of the later Thirty-Nine Articles.

Concerned with reforming not only doctrine but also worship, Cranmer issued two versions (1549 and 1552) of what became the official service book of the Church of England, the Book of Common Prayer. Worship in England now changed to the vernacular, the language of the people — a sign of Protestantism. A monument of English prose style, written both for the ear and for the eye, the Book of Common Prayer contained the orders for daily and Sunday services, for administering the sacraments, and for other rites of the Church of England. Its sources lay in the medieval Roman Catholic mass, in the Eastern Orthodox liturgies of St. John Chrysostom and St. Basil, in Lutheran liturgies, and in other liturgies of the Christian churches, revised to conform to what Cranmer believed to be biblical teaching. All were blended and shaped by the genius of Cranmer. The first version of the Book of Common Prayer (1549) included more medieval ceremonial than the second (1552).

Although brief, the Edwardian reformation became the basis for the emergence of a genuine Anglicanism under Elizabeth I.[1] When Cranmer buried Edward with Protestant ceremonies in 1553, the dead king's half-sister, Mary Tudor, Henry's daughter by Catherine of Aragon, had a private Latin mass said for his soul — a portent of the swing of the pendulum soon to occur. During her brief rule from 1553 to 1558, Mary

5

Archbishop Thomas Cranmer (1489–1556).

courageously returned the country to papal obedience and to Latin masses. More than eight hundred clergy and laity of the Church of England — the "Marian Exiles" — fled to Geneva and to other centers of Reformed Protestantism in Europe. When they returned during the reign of Mary's successor, they would bring with them ideas about Christianity that are now called "Calvinist," "Zwinglian," or "Reformed."

Although the evidence seems to indicate that Mary might have won the majority of England's people back to Roman Catholicism, she made many political blunders, such as marrying the king of Spain (one of England's principal rivals) and thus raising the spectre of Spanish control of England. In a nation that found the burning of heretics distasteful, she also martyred such an exorbitant number of Protestants (including Archbishop Cranmer) that she acquired the name of "Bloody Mary." In 1555, when the fires flamed up around them at the execution spot in Oxford, one of those Protestant heretics, a former bishop of Worcester named Hugh Latimer, cried out to his companion at the stake, a former bishop of London named Nicholas Ridley, and said words that would become famous:

> Be of good comfort, Master Ridley, and play the man. We shall this day light such a candle by God's grace in England as I trust shall never be put out.

The words were also prophetic. During Mary's reign the Reformation spread from the ground up, and the English people were made ready for religious peace and for some form of national Catholicism or Protestantism.

THE ELIZABETHAN SETTLEMENT

When Mary died childless and largely discredited in 1558, her half-sister Elizabeth I (ruled 1558–1603) succeeded her. Cool in temperament, authoritative in manner, skillful in politics, but possessed of her share of human failings, Elizabeth had a distaste for the fanaticism and religious persecution she had witnessed in England from childhood on. Her private religious views are somewhat unclear. Although raised in the Henrician Catholicism of her father's reign, she had not only been tutored by Protestants but had also experienced six years of Calvinist influence in the national church during the reign of her half-brother. Like the later Stuart kings, however, she opposed Calvinism because its republican thrust tended to make life uneasy for monarchs as well as their bishops.

During her half-sister Mary's reign, Elizabeth had conformed outwardly to Roman Catholicism. Yet she opposed Roman Catholicism, not only on religious grounds but also because the pope had excommunicated her father and ruled that she herself was the illegitimate offspring of a concubine. Privately she seems to have preferred a high church form of Anglicanism, though her prayers show a more distinct Protestant orientation. "Unbelligerent Protestantism" perhaps best describes her religious views.

Had Elizabeth been able to impose her private views and still maintain national unity, the Church of England probably would have kept ritualistic worship and celibate clergy. It would have added such Protestant teachings as justification by grace through faith. In addition, it would have included communion in both kinds (the giving of both bread and wine to the laity in the eucharist, one of the hallmarks of Reformation Protestantism). But Elizabeth imposed her private views only to a point. Desirous of national unity and confronted by a nation that may have been (there can be no exact figures) one-third Protestant, one-third Catholic, and one-third much like herself in desiring an end to doctrinal contention, she attempted to create a national church that could blend Catholic and Protestant elements and steer a middle course between theological extremes.

Elizabeth wished to avoid the mistakes of her half-brother and half-sister. On the one hand, Edward's Calvinist model had proved too Protestant for many English citizens. Yet Elizabeth knew that an increasing number of earnestly religious people in England (later to be called "Puritans" because of their desire to purify the Church of England from what they considered medieval accretions in belief, government, garb, and worship) advocated Calvinism as the original religion of the New Testament. Many of their leaders were Marian Exiles who had returned to England wanting to conform the Church of England to the Protestantism they had experienced in the Reformed centers of Europe. On the other hand, Mary's Roman Catholic model had failed in England because it had seemed too bloody, too foreign, and too medieval and magical. Yet a substantial part of the population, including many people living in rural areas, still favored it.

Elizabeth's desire was to forge a national church that could unite all Catholic-minded English men and women who were willing to stop short of recognizing the authority of the pope and all Protestant-minded citizens who were willing to accept bishops. Those who were inclined toward Protestantism (which on the whole rejected rule by bishops as untrue to the New Testament) had to accept bishops, for the Elizabethan church continued the threefold ministry of bishops, priests, and deacons, and hence could be viewed as having kept the apostolic succession.

This hierarchical structure seemed to place the national church in the camp of Roman Catholicism. But in the disputed doctrinal and liturgical questions of the Reformation era, Elizabeth wished the Church of England to take a different tack — the *via media,* or "middle way" —

between Rome and Geneva. The church would adhere to the first four Ecumenical Councils. But within the broad unity of worship according to a trinitarian, incarnational Book of Common Prayer that combined Protestant understandings with Catholic form and structure, the church would still leave room for a wide spectrum of emphases. It would not be among the Christian traditions whose members agreed to think exactly alike.

Although this consolidation of contending elements called the "Elizabethan Settlement" or "Reformation Settlement" took time, the Church of England's hold on the English people steadily increased during Elizabeth's reign. Five aspects of the settlement deserve discussion.

THE BOOK OF COMMON PRAYER

If the Anglican reformers very early gave up enforcing common theological belief upon England, they emphasized in its place the unity Christians could attain through common prayer. It was characteristic of the settlement that Elizabeth and her advisors established the norms for the Church of England's worship before they turned to its theological standards.

The principal instrument of the settlement became Cranmer's accomplished product, the second (1552) Book of Common Prayer, which Elizabeth reissued in 1559 with minor changes in the medieval direction. Not a theological confession to subscribe to but a living book to worship by, its creeds, sacraments, offices, prayers, psalmody, canticles, use of Scripture, and liturgical directives set the standard of doctrine and worship for Anglicanism. It claimed to reproduce the worship and teachings of the early Christian church. Elizabeth's Act of Uniformity (1559) required clergy to use the revised Book of Common Prayer in all public worship; it also required laity to attend church under penalty of fines and censures.

As it did during Edward's time, the Elizabethan Prayer Book had opponents who felt it moved too far from medieval Catholicism and others who felt it did not move far enough. As late as 1608, an Anglican parson complained that his congregation, believing that the old Latin prayers carried more weight with God than English prayers, disregarded the Prayer Book and used such half-remembered words from the mass as "Creezum zuum patrum onitentem ejus amicum, Dominum nostrum qui sum sops, Virgini Mariae, crixus fixus, Ponchi Pilati audubiticus, morti by Sunday. . . . "[2]

The Puritan party, which desired biblical warrant for all beliefs, practices, and offices of a Christian church, viewed the Prayer Book as a half-way house to true reform and objected that it retained practices that were unscriptural. Its original list of practices lacking explicit scriptural warrant included using godparents and the sign of the cross in baptism, a ring in the marriage service, the kneeling posture at the holy communion, and a surplice (or white linen gown) for clergy. These relatively mild complaints increased as the century went on and came to include attacks on episcopal government as unfaithful to Scripture. A Puritan party was in the making that would shake the nation in the next century, but the disturbances would also lead to constitutional government for the English people.

In time, however, the Book of Common Prayer became widely loved. Reissued with some modifications in 1662, it remained essentially unchanged until the twentieth century. Its prayers, rhythms, and phrases became embedded into the minds of the English people. Hear, for example, the words of the General Confession said at Morning and Evening Prayer:

> Almighty and most merciful Father; We have erred, and strayed from thy ways like lost sheep. We have followed too much the devices and desires of our own hearts. We have offended against thy holy laws. We have left undone those things which we ought to have done; And we have done those things which we ought not to have done; And there is no health in us. . . .

And the last collect (or short prayer) in the service of Evening Prayer caught the mood of that hour:

> Lighten our darkness, we beseech thee, O Lord; and by thy great mercy defend us from all perils and dangers of this night. . . .

The phrasing of the General Thanksgiving (added in 1662) likewise expressed the feelings of many:

> Almighty God, Father of all mercies, we thine unworthy servants do give thee most humble and hearty thanks for all thy goodness and loving-kindness to us, and to all men. . . .

In the holy communion service, the opening to the *Sanctus* caught the spirit of duty and joy:

> It is very meet, right, and our bounden duty that we should at all times, and in all places, give thanks unto thee, O Lord, Holy Father, Almighty Everlasting God.

The invitation for the people to come forward to receive the consecrated bread and wine was also intended as a "fencing of the table" against unworthy communicants:

Ye that do truly and earnestly repent you of your sins, and are in love and charity with your neighbours, and intend to lead a new life, following the commandments of God, and walking from henceforth in his holy ways; Draw near with faith, and take this holy Sacrament to your comfort, and make your humble confession to Almighty God. . . .

The words said when the priest delivered the bread to the people blended two understandings of the eucharistic presence:

The Body of our Lord Jesus Christ, which was given for thee, preserve thy body and soul unto everlasting life. Take and eat this in remembrance that Christ died for thee, and feed on him in thy heart by faith with thanksgiving.

Like other words from the pages of the Book of Common Prayer, phrases from the burial service became part of the common language:

Man that is born of a woman hath but a short time to live, and is full of misery. . . . In the midst of life we are in death. . . .

Forasmuch as it hath pleased Almighty God of his great mercy to take unto himself the soul of our dear sister here departed, we therefore commit her body to the ground; earth to earth, ashes to ashes, dust to dust; in sure and certain hope of the Resurrection to eternal life.

The majestic prayers, the slow cadences, the doublets of words and phrases, the crescendo of clauses in tension, the dramatic moves from moods of penitence to moods of confidence, and the doctrines embodied in the Elizabethan Prayer Book embedded themselves in the hearts and minds of Anglicans.[3] More than four hundred years passed before its language or structure changed in any substantial way. And when Prayer Book revision was proposed in the Church of England, the Episcopal Church, and other Anglican churches in the twentieth century, the Elizabethan Prayer Book had staunch defenders.

THE THIRTY-NINE ARTICLES

Holy Scripture and the Book of Common Prayer became the fundamental theological documents of Anglicanism. The principal doctrinal statement of the Elizabethan Settlement appeared later, twelve years after the reissuance of the Book of Common Prayer. Patterned upon the Forty-Two Articles of Edward's reign and consisting of a series of brief paragraphs, the Thirty-Nine Articles (1571) laid down in broad terms the Anglican approach on matters of Christian doctrine and practice in dispute during the Reformation period.

11

Some of the articles affirmed such traditional teachings as the Trinity, the incarnation, the resurrection, and original sin. Others specifically rejected such Roman Catholic teachings as purgatory, sacrificial masses, and the adoration of the eucharistic host, and affirmed such Protestant teachings as the authority of Holy Scripture, justification by grace through faith, worship in the vernacular, communion in both kinds, the fallibility of general councils, and the marriage of clergy. Several articles rejected such Anabaptist teaching as baptism only of believing adults and ministry by unordained people.

The distinctiveness of Anglicanism from continental Protestantism emerged in the articles that dealt with the threefold ministry of bishops, priests, and deacons, with the authority of the church over rites and ceremonies, and with the treatment of the Apostles', Nicene, and Athanasian creeds as authoritative for Christians precisely because they are held to be true to Scripture. The *via media* is clearly exhibited in Article 20, which declares that "the Church hath . . . authority in Controversies of Faith" but limits that authority by adding "it is not lawful for the Church to ordain anything that is contrary to God's Word written. . . . "

Though reflecting the early Calvinist influence on the English Reformation, the articles reject some alternatives that, if included, would have moved Anglicanism further from Roman Catholicism and placed it more clearly in the Lutheran or Calvinist ranks. Avoiding narrow definitions, they display in places the common Anglican concern that overprecision in the definition of the mysteries of God will only prove divisive. Thus Article 17, "Of Predestination and Election," which deals with a controversial subject that had exercised Christians from Paul to Augustine to Bonaventure to Aquinas to Calvin to the Puritans, is masterfully ambiguous. Article 28, "On the Lord's Supper," is clear and direct when rejecting the medieval teaching of transubstantiation and the Zwinglian interpretation of a memorial feast, but is unclear in its description of whether and how the body and blood are present.

Such ambiguity and parsimony of words on controverted topics was purposeful, for the goal was to unite rather than to divide English Christians. The drafters of the Thirty-Nine Articles followed one of the prime rules of diplomacy, which is not to ask for too much precision. Confronted with the dogmatism of three interpretations of Christianity — Roman Catholic, Lutheran, and Reformed — that were striving for mastery across the English Channel, some Anglican writers came to believe that the mysteries of God could not be encapsulated in a theological blueprint.

The Thirty-Nine Articles were not intended to be a creedal statement paralleling such Reformation confessions of faith as the Augsburg Confession (Lutheranism), the Helvetic Confessions (Calvinism), or the edicts of the Council of Trent (Roman Catholicism). With the exception of members of Oxford and Cambridge universities, the articles have never been required of laity in England or the United States. Their authority among the clergy in both countries has steadily declined since the Oxford Movement of the nineteenth century, though many evangelicals have continued to view them as a summation of Anglican belief.

Today the American Book of Common Prayer places the Thirty-Nine Articles in the section entitled "Historical Documents of the Church." The Apostles' and Nicene creeds (which "may be proved by most certain warrants of Holy Scripture," in the words of the Thirty-Nine Articles) remain the Episcopal Church's principal doctrinal symbols. Upon ordination Episcopal clergy must affirm only that they "believe the Holy Scripture of the Old and New Testaments to be the Word of God, and to contain all things necessary to salvation."

THE BOOKS OF HOMILIES

In addition to the Book of Common Prayer and the Thirty-Nine Articles, the Books of Homilies provided a third doctrinal repository for the *via media*. Recommended by Article 30 of the Thirty-Nine Articles as containing "a godly and wholesome Doctrine . . . necessary for these times," they were intended for reading aloud by clergy in churches as a means of inculcating the theological foundations for the Reformation Settlement. In addition, they were issued to assure that congregations did hear sermons on Sunday, for preaching was infrequent and often uninformed in the pre-Reformation Church of England.

The first Book of Homilies, issued during Edward VI's reign, contained twelve sermons, most probably written by Archbishop Cranmer. The second book, issued early in Elizabeth's reign, contained twenty-one additional homilies, the majority by John Jewel, bishop of Salisbury. More Protestant in content than the Book of Common Prayer or the Thirty-Nine Articles, the homilies covered such subjects as faith, good works, prayer, holy communion, swearing and perjury, fear of death, contentiousness, and adultery. With their reading in the churches enforced by many bishops into the following century, they proved an effective means of spreading the doctrine of the *via media*. Although occasionally advocated in the nineteenth century by Anglican evangelicals, their language and form has led to their disuse in recent centuries.

THEOLOGIANS OF THE ELIZABETHAN SETTLEMENT

Three theologians of the Elizabethan Settlement merit discussion. In 1562, Bishop John Jewel wrote his *Apology for the Church of England,* the first systematic defense of the Church of England against Roman Catholicism. Steeped in the writings of the church fathers, Jewel argued that the Church of England had the right to reform itself to conform to "the primitive Church of the ancient Fathers and Apostles." He pledged to become a Roman Catholic again if anyone could show that papal doctrine agreed with the teachings of the early Christian church:

> If all the learned men that be alive be able to bring any one sufficient sentence, out of any old catholic doctor, or father: Or out of any old general council: Or out of the holy scriptures . . . Or . . . [out] of the primitive Church whereby it may be clearly and plainly proved, that there was any private mass in the whole world . . . for the space of six hundred years after Christ. . . . Or that the bishop of Rome was then called . . . head of the universal Church. . . . Or that the people was then taught to believe that Christ's body is . . . carnally, . . . in the sacrament. . . . [I will] give over and subscribe unto him.[4]

A second theologian was William Perkins, a Cambridge scholar, gifted teacher, and pastor of wide abilities. Perkins was a predestinarian Calvinist (precisely the kind of English Christian the carefully worded Article 17 of the Thirty-Nine Articles wanted to retain within the national church) and an opponent of medievalist ritual. Yet he considered himself a "Reformed Catholic" — the title of one of his books (1597) — and a loyal member of the Church of England. He tolerated episcopacy, believed in a real presence in the eucharist, but wished the theology and the deportment of the established church's clergy to be more in tune with the biblical norm. Though many of the students he taught at Cambridge ultimately separated themselves from the Church of England, Perkins remained an example of the Puritan Anglicans who were content to accept the main lines of the Elizabethan Settlement and only wished to improve and enrich the church's spiritual life.

The premiere theologian of Elizabeth's reign — though one whose influence was not strong until the seventeenth century — was Richard Hooker, whose *Treatise of the Laws of Ecclesiastical Polity* (1594–1597, with posthumous additions) emerged as the first work of systematic theology

14

written from a specifically Anglican standpoint. Calm, deliberate, insightful, unpolemic, a classic of Tudor prose style, Hooker's work systematically set forth the teachings of the Church of England in contrast to those of Puritanism on the left and Roman Catholicism on the right. Arguing that Roman Catholics had added too much to traditional Catholicism and that Puritans had subtracted too much, the *Laws* affirmed Anglicanism's continuity with the Catholic Church of the fathers. By holding the foundation of the Church of England to rest in Scripture, reason, and tradition — "a threefold cord not quickly broken," with Scripture as paramount authority and ultimate appeal — he gave Anglicanism a theological method. And rooting his thought in natural law, Hooker constructed a broad theory of ecclesiastical and civil government.

So charitable to other Christians that Pope Clement VIII declared that the *Laws* contained "seeds of eternity" within it, Hooker declared that Anglicanism differed from Roman Catholicism only in so far as Rome was in error. Denying the Puritan assertion that the Bible provides answers to all questions, he defended developments in church institutions and practices as long as those developments were not opposed to Scripture. In contrast to the Puritans, he found episcopacy supported by Scripture, but as opposed to the Roman Catholics he held that episcopacy exists for the good of the church and is not of its essence. Thus to Hooker, a parish priest himself, the ministries of continental Protestants were valid. "The judicious Hooker" died at the age of forty-seven, having already made substantial contributions to the theology of the Elizabethan *via media*.

THE EMERGENCE OF ANGLICANISM

The Elizabethan, or Reformation, Settlement marks the real beginning of the Church of England. Unlike much of continental Protestantism, Anglicanism cannot be traced to a single founder. But if popular history insists, the name should be that of Elizabeth, and clearly not that of her father.

Elizabeth died in 1603 unmarried and with no heir. Although her policy had spared England the wars that ravaged Reformation Europe, the period of the Stuart sovereigns that followed was one of civil and ecclesiastical turmoil. The policies of James I (ruled 1603–1625), Charles I (ruled 1625–1649), and William Laud (archbishop of Canterbury, 1633–1645) forced out large numbers of Puritans. The two subsequent monarchs — Charles II (ruled 1660–1685) and James II (ruled 1685–1688) — converted to Roman Catholicism; and Puritans ruled during the Commonwealth period of 1649–1660. Yet during this chaotic period Anglicanism produced the stately translation of the Bible known as the "King James" or "Authorized" Version (1611). It also produced such exponents of the *via media* as the eloquent and saintly bishop Lancelot Andrewes, the noted preacher and devotional writer Jeremy Taylor, and the winsome poet-priest George Herbert.

Thus the English Reformation was not a static event, but continued to develop at least until the start of the Commonwealth period in 1649. The political reestablishment of the Church of England during the Restoration Settlement of 1662 and the reissuing of a revised Book of Common Prayer in the same year may be viewed as a second foundation for Anglicanism. Nevertheless, Elizabeth's forty-five years of rule placed an indelible stamp on the national church's life and worship. Catholic but independent under Henry VIII, Calvinist under Edward VI, and Roman Catholic under Mary, the Church of England became Anglican under Elizabeth I. Ever since the Reformation Settlement, the Church of England has been neither Roman Catholic, nor Lutheran, nor Reformed. Its central thrust has been toward a unique, distinctive interpretation of the Christian Gospel now called "Anglican." After the Roman Catholic James II was removed from the throne in 1688, the reign of William and Mary (ruled 1689–1702) stopped the English ecclesiastical pendulum from swinging wildly. Since the time of Queen Anne (ruled 1702–1714), all monarchs of England have been Anglican, and the Church of England has become increasingly open to a wider latitude of belief and practice.

CHURCH PARTIES

From the time of Elizabeth I on, a desire to narrow the theological inclusiveness of Anglicanism led to the emergence of church parties, each of which has tried to move the church to its own interpretation of what true Christianity is. The defining question remains whether the Elizabethan Settlement diverged too far from late patristic and medieval Catholicism, failed to go far enough toward continental Protestantism and early Christianity, or struck precisely the right balance.

The high church party has placed a "high" estimate upon the ministry, sacraments, and external forms of worship. Asserting that Anglicanism is a true representative of Catholic Christianity, its supporters declare that it has maintained the apostolic succession, sacramental system, and creeds of ancient and early medieval Christianity. While accepting the term "Protestant" for itself well into the nineteenth century, the high church party has traditionally had little sympathy with Methodism or with the Protestantism that emerged from Puritanism in England — the Baptists, Congregationalists, Presbyterians, and Quakers.

While firmly believing that they continue in the teachings of the early church fathers, the evangelical or low church party, has emphasized the Protestant element in Anglicanism. Stressing the primacy not only of Scripture over the church but also of the primitive over the medieval church, it places a comparatively "low" value upon the episcopate, priesthood, and sacraments, and makes less use of symbolic acts in worship. Preaching rooted in Scripture is important to evangelicals; their reading of church history indicates that the greatest periods of Christian growth have occurred when preaching has been strongest. The Puritans, for example, were initially members of the Church of England who held the low church view that Anglicanism had insufficiently purified itself of medieval "accretions."

The central church party (a term used more commonly in England than in the United States) has continued the tradition of the Elizabethan Settlement. Claiming that Anglicanism incorporates the best from both traditions, it typically stands (to quote a frequently used definition that may go back to Hooker) in the posture of "Catholic for every truth of God, Protestant for every error of man." Since Anglicanism is more homogeneous than it appears, the majority of Anglicans undoubtedly fall into this category. (Additional parties within Anglicanism will be discussed in the appropriate places.)

Though such parties may be the least edifying part of Anglicanism and have often given the church the appearance of a warring household, the church's vitality has seemed to spring precisely from their mutually enriching contributions. Although tensions persist, they are usually contained within a broader loyalty. Anglicanism claims to be a body that is both truly Catholic and fully Protestant, both loyal to the past in creed and polity yet gladly open to reform and change in conformance with Scripture and modern thought:

> A Church Protestant but still Catholic, reformed but carefully preserving its continuity with the past, purged of error, but treasuring jealously all that was good in antiquity, admitting the duty of private judgement, but yet respecting authority, a Church seeking to reproduce and adapt to modern conditions the life of the early Church in its best and purest days.[5]

Such descriptions inevitably point to the ideal and not the actual. Critics sometimes perceive Anglicanism as a diluted tradition that stands for less rather than more. But if Anglicanism has a genius, it lies in this attempted synthesis of Scripture, tradition, and reason. For the last one hundred years it has claimed that the Catholic tradition alone can lead to narrowness, bigotry, and fear of new information; that the evangelical tradition alone can reduce the Christian church to a static organization and cause the loss of the living tradition from which the gospel emerged; and that the humanist tradition alone can lead to a secular faith that views Christianity as an ethical system only. Thus in place of the former high church and low church arguments about whether Anglicanism is a form of Protestantism or Catholicism, the recent self-understanding of Anglicanism has tended to stress the church's distinctiveness and comprehensiveness. In ecumenical discussions other churches have recognized that the Anglican tradition represents a family of Christians distinct from Protestantism, Roman Catholicism, or Eastern Orthodoxy.

Anglicanism can be viewed as a political compromise or creative synthesis. It can and has been classified as an autonomous Catholic tradition ("Reformed Catholic," in the phrase of Perkins and others); as a Protestant tradition; as a church that is neither Protestant nor Catholic but rather a kind of *tertium quid;* or as a church that is both Protestant and Catholic and that represents a unique combination of biblical, patristic, medieval, and renaissance emphases. In the sixteenth century and today, it would be possible to find Anglicans who would espouse any of those interpretations. The majority undoubtedly hold that it fuses the best aspects of Catholicism and Protestantism. Like purple — they would say — it requires both red and blue, but blends them so as to form a third color.

Whatever its merits and demerits, it is difficult to see the Anglican interpretation of Christianity as a mere act of state. Some Christians today, as at the time of the Reformation, believe that it is the model for the comprehensive church that must exist if Christianity (with all of its wings) is ever to unite. But if the Church of England does provide a pattern of comprehensiveness for a unified Christianity, then Christians who embrace the model will have to accept both usage and abusage. For as this history will make clear, one of the prices of being an Anglican is the acceptance of some untidiness. Some Anglicans believe, in fact, that the great strength of the English Reformation is precisely that it has never quite been completed. "The Reformation *Settlement?*" a noted Episcopal scholar is reported once to have declared. "I value the Reformation as the great *un*settlement."

2

THE EPISCOPAL CHURCH IN COLONIAL AND EARLY NATIONAL AMERICA

THE RISE AND FALL OF THE ESTABLISHED CHURCH OF VIRGINIA

On Sunday, February 24, 1811, at the president's house of the College of William and Mary in Williamsburg, Virginia, a young Virginian named William Meade was examined for ordination into the ministry of the Episcopal Church. Meade's father had been an aide-de-camp to George Washington. Because his mother had thought William and Mary irreligious in an era of rationalistic religion, or Deism, Meade was a graduate of the College of New Jersey, now known as Princeton University. Meade's examiner was James Madison, cousin of President James Madison, first bishop of Virginia, eighth president of William and Mary. Helping Bishop Madison in the examination was John Bracken, rector of Bruton Parish and professor at the college.

Meade passed the brief examination. Breakfast followed. When young Meade pointed out that one of the bishop's neighbors was devoting that Sunday morning to restocking his ice house, the less censorious Madison replied that such work on the Lord's Day is permissible. As the conversation continued, Meade heard that a literary society at that Episcopal college had recently debated two questions. First, does God actually exist? Second, has Christianity been helpful or harmful to the world? He was shocked to learn that the students had affirmed one question by only a single vote.

After breakfast, the three men left in the bishop's carriage for Bruton Parish Church. It was 1675 feet from the gate of the president's house to the church. In that short distance dismay again crept into Meade's mind. Duke of Gloucester Street abounded with groups of William and Mary students. With guns on their shoulders and dogs at their heels, they were using that crisp Sunday morning to go hunting. Wending its way through students and dogs, the carriage arrived at Bruton Parish Church — once the place of worship for the royal governors of Virginia and the leaders of the American Revolution. Meade would later describe the church as being in a "wretched condition." The congregation inside numbered about eighteen, including two William and Mary professors — both, by Meade's account, adherents of Deism, the rationalistic religion of the time. Most of the other worshipers were either relatives or acquaintances of Meade.

At the appointed time in the service, Madison solemnly ordained Meade. A service of holy communion followed, during which the newly ordained Meade, dressed only in homespun, preached his own ordination sermon. When one of Madison's slaves returned with the carriage earlier than ordered, the William and Mary students left the service and drove the carriage away. It was the winter of 1811; it was also the winter of the Anglican tradition in Virginia.

The Church of England was the first denomination to come permanently to the original thirteen colonies. Though Anglican clergy accompanying English expeditions held services in the sixteenth century on the coasts of California and North Carolina, the settlement of Jamestown in 1607 by the London Company (after 1609, the Virginia Company) marked the permanent beginnings of the Church of England in America. Commercial purposes were primary for the Virginia colony, but the charter also expressed a concern for the evangelization of the Native Americans. The influence of the Puritans was pervasive in the first decades of the colony, although their clergy followed the liturgical and ceremonial directives of the Church of England. Although most colonial Anglicans came to ignore or oppose the conversion of Native and African Americans, Jamestown produced the most famous Native American convert to Anglicanism, Pocahontas. The colony required morning and evening prayer daily, two sermons each Sunday, and the administration of the holy communion every three months. During the difficult early years of Jamestown, the Prayer Book office for the burial of the dead was used frequently.

Whether one views the precise date of establishment as 1601, 1607, 1619, or 1624, Anglicanism — the faith of the Church of England — was established from the start in the colony of Virginia. "Establishment" meant that Virginia's General Assembly legislated for the church, supported it through taxes, and protected it against dissent. This government support bulwarked the Church of England in Virginia during most of the colonial period. Growing slowly but steadily, it especially flourished in the years between 1680 and 1740. But in time, as is usually the case in church history, state support almost crushed the spiritual life of a Christian church.

From 1607 on, the established church slowly grew — first in James-town, and then in ever-widening settlements along Virginia's rivers, the boulevards of the time. Whenever settlers moved too far from existing courthouses and churches, the assembly established the boundaries of new counties and new parishes. The number of parishes in colonial Vir-ginia steadily increased from forty-eight in 1671, to fifty-three in 1726, to one hundred seven in 1784. Most were smaller in size than the colonial counties.

A typical parish contained three or four churches. Virtually all had a church farm (or "glebe"). The intention of the Virginia parish system (still in evidence along the banks of such rivers as the Rappahannock) was to place a church not more than six miles — easy riding distance — from every home in the colony. Although they had more formal names, many of these Anglican churches bore unintentionally humorous names taken from rivers, settlements, and other geographical landmarks: Pohick Church, Beaver Dam Church, Difficult Church, Cattail Church, Turkey Run Church, Rattlesnake Church, even Cheesecake Church (the latter a corruption of a Native American name).

Although the General Assembly of Virginia passed the laws gov-erning its established church, groups called vestries composed of twelve laymen — always white, always male, and usually wealthy — ran the indi-vidual parishes. Their powers were immense, ranging from levying taxes to hiring and firing the clergy to handling the welfare system that was the responsibility of the church prior to the separation of church and state in Virginia. Very early these vestries became self-perpetuating, closed cor-porations. In other colonies, vestries were elected either by all members of the Church of England or by the freeholders of a parish. But in Virginia, from approximately the mid-seventeenth century on, if a member died or resigned, the remaining members elected his replacement. Thus Virginia's colonial vestries effectively kept parish control in the hands of a select few.

The vestry system clearly offered great advantages for the established church. It assured the services and the loyalty, for example, of the leading landowners — families with names such as Randolph, Carter, Byrd, Page, Nelson, and Washington. The vestries tended to hire clergy on one-year contracts, which reduced the number of unworthy clergy in Virginia's pulpits. In day-to-day matters, the system seems to have worked efficiently.

But in the long run, the vestry system made the established church in Virginia conspicuously the church of the aristocracy. In the minds of the common people (who comprised more than ninety percent of Virginia's population), it also allied the church with the English government's policy of taxation without representation. In addition, clerical supervision of parish morality suffered; generally protected by one-year contracts only, parsons were hesitant to speak out against the sins of their leading parishioners. Clergy such as Morgan Godwyn of Potomac Parish, who broke with the status quo by insisting that parishioners should allow clergy to catechize and baptize their slaves, were forced out of parishes. Finally, since the vestries asked parish residents only to pay an annual tax bill enforceable by the sheriff, the system left the Anglican laity with no knowledge of how to support a church voluntarily. By the eve of the Revolutionary War, the vestry system had begun to work silently but surely to assist the collapse of the established church.

In the first century of the church's existence in Virginia clergy from Great Britain predominated. As graduates of William and Mary entered the ministry in the eighteenth century, the number of native Virginians who served parishes steadily increased. Of the clergy who served Virginia parishes from 1723 until the Revolution, one analysis indicates that forty-five went to William and Mary, thirty-nine to Oxford, twenty to Cambridge, seventeen to Aberdeen, thirteen to Edinburgh, eleven to Trinity College, Dublin, ten to Glasgow, four to unspecified Scottish universities, two to St. Andrews, two to Roman Catholic seminaries, one to Yale, and one to the University of Halle in Germany. The university backgrounds, if any, of nine clergy are unknown.[6]

Later writers often referred to the colonial Virginia clergy with scorn. In 1857, William Meade, who became the third bishop of Virginia, dismissed the colonial clergy as "for the most part...the refuse or more indifferent of the English, Irish, and Scottish Episcopal Churches, who could not find promotion at home."[7] Meade's assessment has often been quoted, but he was an evangelical who judged the world by the rigorous standards of that movement. The great mass of records of the established church seem to portray Virginia's colonial clergy as better men than that. A recent estimate that no more than ten percent of the Virginia parsons misbehaved seems roughly accurate. As far as scholars can tell, the Anglican clergy of colonial Virginia seem to have been no better and no worse than their brethren in England at the time.

The established church of Virginia held the loyalty of the vast majority of Virginians prior to the American Revolution. Why had such an apparently strong tradition almost collapsed by the time of William Meade's ordination in 1811? Scholars cite five reasons for its fall.

First, the established church fell because of the problems (already discussed) of the vestry system. Second, the rise of anti-English feeling in Virginia during and after the American Revolution boomeranged on the Church of England in Virginia.

Third, the parish clergy of Virginia seem to have sunk steadily in public estimation from the 1740s on. The parsons not only got involved in a famous lawsuit demanding higher salaries — but they also lost it. More than that, in the minds of the common people of the colony, the Anglican clergy apparently came to be indistinguishable from the planter aristocracy. Many of the planter aristocracy wore periwigs, played cards, drank heavily, raced horses, and attended cockfights — and so apparently did numerous parish clergy of the established church. This kind of parson made the ascetic evangelicals who emerged in the Baptist, the Presbyterian, and the Methodist ministries look attractive indeed to the average Virginian.

Fourth, other Protestant denominations moved aggressively into Virginia in the decades prior to the Revolution. Dissent was nothing new to the colony, but aggressive and vociferous dissent was. In the 1740s and 1750s, the Baptists, the Presbyterians, and later the Methodists came into Virginia and presented an appealingly fresh interpretation of Christianity. The Baptists and the Presbyterians also offered a representative form of church government, with no self-perpetuating aristocratic vestries. In addition, the Methodist and the Baptist clergy, who were generally men of the people, proclaimed an emotional, extemporaneous gospel. Although Virginia allowed religious toleration from 1699 on, the terms of toleration favored the established church. When the Anglican-dominated political establishment imprisoned some of these dissenting preachers on technicalities, defections to the Baptists and the Presbyterians occurred throughout Virginia. In some areas, dissenters came to outnumber Anglicans — all of which had political consequences.

Finally, Thomas Paine's religion of natural reason and moral precepts, Deism, which will be described below, began to infiltrate the male aristocracy of Virginia both before and after the Revolution. Deism seems to have influenced women less than men. As husbands ceased attending church, the phenomenon of the "believing wife" began to appear in Virginia parishes. As a rule, women and children significantly outnumbered men in the pews of Anglican and Episcopal services (and those of many other denominations) in the decades just before and after the Revolution. Episcopal women of Virginia continued to go to church, but many of the colony's men did not. With its very pillars now weakened, the established church began first to sag and then to collapse.

And thus the story moves through the Revolutionary War to the last act. During the Revolution, most of the Anglicans of Virginia were patriots. The newest research indicates that seventy to eighty percent of the clergy of the established church of Virginia supported the American side. Tory sympathies, therefore, played little role in the church's post-Revolutionary collapse. Nor did disestablishment — removal of state support — cause the fall. In 1784, the General Assembly disestablished the Episcopal Church and placed it on the same level as all other denominations in the Commonwealth. Yet every southern colony disestablished the Church of England, and none collapsed like the church of Virginia.

What was special in Virginia was that the clamor for laws against the Episcopal Church continued for two decades following the Revolution. From 1784 to 1802, the Presbyterians and especially the Baptists of Virginia flooded the General Assembly with petitions and lobbyists urging that the Commonwealth confiscate the property of those Episcopal parishes that dated from the colonial period. These groups argued that a general taxation on all Virginians during the colonial period had purchased, built, and maintained the Episcopal churches and glebe farms. Now that the majority of Virginians were no longer Episcopalians, the argument continued, the church's buildings and land should revert to the public domain, so that Anglicanism would not retain an unfair advantage over other denominations.

In the years after 1786, the General Assembly gradually yielded to the petitions and lobbyists, and in 1802 it passed the Glebe Act. This act directed that groups in each county, called the Overseers of the Poor, seize all farms that Episcopal parishes had purchased prior to 1777 upon the death or resignation of the parish's present rector. The affected property involved all but a handful of the Episcopal Church's glebes. The act also directed the overseers to sell the glebes and use the proceeds for the public benefit. The Glebe Act further allowed Virginians to view all Episcopal churches erected prior to 1777 (again, the overwhelming majority of Virginia's Episcopal churches) as public property whenever any Episcopal parish could not maintain regular services in them.

Why were the glebes important? During the colonial period, virtually every parish in Virginia had a glebe house and a glebe farm of two hundred or more acres. The rector of the parish lived on the glebe and either rented its land out, farmed it himself, or ran a school on part of the land. In this way the rectors supplemented their salaries. Hence even when the General Assembly terminated their salaries at the start of the Revolution, Episcopal clergy still had their glebes, and the parishes still had a means of attracting and supporting clergy. But with the passage of the Glebe Act in 1802, all of this ended.

The Episcopal Church tried to fight the Glebe Act. Some of the most prominent lawyers in Virginia supported the church's right to keep its colonial property. The test case came in 1802 in Chesterfield County, where the vestry of Manchester Parish challenged the right of the county's Overseers of the Poor to seize their vacant glebe. In the chancery court, George Wythe (under whom Bishop Madison had earlier studied law at William and Mary) ruled in favor of the state.

The vestry then appealed their case to Virginia's highest court, the five-member court of appeals. Even when Justice William Fleming, an Episcopalian and a resident of the county of question, disqualified himself, the Episcopal Church still expected the court of appeals to invalidate the Glebe Act. Three of the court's remaining four members were Episcopalians of conservative legal views. Its president, for example, was the eighty-one-year-old Edmund Pendleton, who had proved an uncompromising champion of the property rights of the Episcopal Church during his years in the General Assembly.

Then the story took a strange turn. In October of 1803, just before he was to deliver the ruling of the four-member court, Judge Pendleton died in his lodgings in Richmond's Swan Tavern. In his room at the tavern searchers found, ready for delivery, the three-to-one decree of the court declaring the Glebe Act unconstitutional. But Pendleton's death rendered that decision null and void.

Appointed to Pendleton's seat on the court of appeals was St. George Tucker, a notable resident of Williamsburg and childhood friend of Bishop Madison. After hearing the arguments, Tucker voted for the constitutionality of the Glebe Act. The court of appeals — with Justice Fleming still disqualifying himself — divided two to two. Under Virginia law, the tie upheld the lower court.

Disheartened and already disorganized, the Episcopal Church in Virginia failed to continue the litigation. From the Chesapeake to the Alleghenies, the Episcopal glebes now became the property of the state. Historians have difficulty exaggerating the consequences of the seizure of the glebes for the Episcopal Church. Because of anti-English animus, the rise of Deism, the departure of the Methodists from its ranks in 1784, the loss of other members to the Baptists and Presbyterians, and a heavy postwar emigration of Episcopal families to Kentucky, Tennessee, and Ohio, the former established church of Virginia had been steadily declining since the start of the Revolution. Following the Glebe Act, it utterly collapsed.

25

The collapse took only a brief time. Shortly after the passage of the Glebe Act, the Overseers of the Poor in each county began to confiscate the glebes of those parishes that had either failed to survive the Revolutionary War or that currently lacked ministers. Approximately sixty-seven parishes fell into this category. As other parishes one by one lost their rectors to death or resignation after 1802, the overseers seized additional glebes. Consequently, having lost their only assured support for a rector and lacking experience in supporting a church through voluntary contributions, many vestries gave up the struggle and dissolved. At that point their parish churches, now viewed as public property, were left to the plunder of neighboring landowners or turned over to any denomination that could supply a minister and congregation. In parish after parish throughout Virginia, the Episcopal Church died out.

The devastation was immense. Of the seven colonial churches in Isle of Wight and Southampton counties, six disappeared. Of the three colonial churches in Portsmouth Parish, two fell into ruin. In Hungars Church on the Eastern Shore, when Episcopalians were unable to continue services following the Glebe Act, fishermen seized the organ and melted it into sinkers. In Essex County, along the Rappahannock River, vandals completely destroyed the parish church, turning even its tombstones into grindstones. Near the Tidewater town of Smithfield, the bricks and pews of the church on Burwell's Bay were used to construct a kitchen and a stable. In Prince Edward County, the Baptists and Methodists argued for years over the rights to the parish church. In Christ Church, Middlesex County, the pews crumbled, the roof fell in, and a large sycamore tree sprang up between the walls.

The effect of the Glebe Act is amply displayed by the fact that out of approximately two hundred fifty churches belonging to the established Church of Virginia at the beginning of the Revolutionary War, fewer than thirty-five (or only about thirteen percent) remain in use today as Episcopal churches. Throughout the newly independent Commonwealth there were spoons and bullets made out of pewter communion sets, chalices taken from deserted parish churches and used on family tables, baptismal fonts employed as flower bowls and horse troughs, and colonial churches crumbling into ruin. Virginia lore contains many such stories from this period, and most seem to be not apocryphal but true. If St. Paul visited Virginia, Bishop Madison told one of his diocesan conventions, he would consider its Episcopal churches "as dedicated, or rather devoted, to the demon of ruin."[8] The former established church had fallen in a post-Revolutionary atmosphere of anti-Episcopalianism

Temporarily abandoned when Anglicanism collapsed after the Revolutionary
War, St. Luke's Church (1682? 1632?) in Isle of Wight County, Virginia,
may be the oldest standing Episcopal church

and anti-establishmentarianism that is almost impossible to comprehend
in the United States of today.

As the Episcopal Church of Virginia declined, a parallel decline occurred in James Madison's activities as its bishop. Although the national
Episcopal Church held General Conventions every three years, Madison
attended none after 1795. After 1801, he was unable to provide the General Convention with the required lists of active clergy in his diocese. His
congregation at Jamestown stopped meeting after 1802. Though he published annual calls in the *Virginia Gazette,* he was able to assemble only
two conventions of Virginia Episcopalians between 1800 and 1811. In
the decade from 1801 to 1810, he ordained only one deacon. By 1811,
a committee of the General Convention had reported that the venerable
Episcopal tradition appeared likely to die out in Virginia. Although rumors spread throughout the Commonwealth that Madison had become a
skeptic and a Deist, the evidence indicates that he remained an orthodox
Christian for the time and had grown skeptical only of the future of the
church in which he had been baptized and ordained.

As college president, teacher, counselor, administrator, scientist, pastor, parent, and bishop, Madison had been doing the work of several men for decades. It is also now clear that he was dying of dropsy from approximately 1807 on. This knowledge makes all the more poignant a letter the bishop wrote on October 7, 1807. Declaring that he had previously labored for others but that he must now think of himself and of his family, James Madison — bishop of Virginia, president and professor of the College of William and Mary, and rector of James City Parish — applied to his Deistic friend President Thomas Jefferson for the post of Port Collector of Norfolk.

ANGLICANISM IN
PRE-REVOLUTIONARY AMERICA

Anglicanism in Colonial New England

The Church of England was the first denomination to come permanently to the original thirteen colonies. By 1700 the church was second only to Congregationalism (the descendants of the English Puritans) in number of churches in the colonies. By that year more than one hundred Anglican churches were scattered from Massachusetts to South Carolina, with eighty percent concentrated around the Chesapeake Bay.

In New England, where all colonies established the Congregational churches except tolerant Rhode Island (where Baptists and later Quakers were in the majority), the Church of England was viewed as an interloper. The covenanted communities of Puritan New England had come to America to escape royal absolutism and juryless tribunals. They wished to establish what they believed was a Christianity true to the apostolic record. To their descendants Anglicanism stood for repugnant and unbiblical forms of worship, church government, and spiritual life. To the Puritans the Anglican reformation was incomplete, and the history of the past one hundred years had indicated clearly to them that the Church of England would always oppress any movement that attempted to complete it.

Thus for many years even settlers in Massachusetts or its district of Maine, in New Hampshire, or in Connecticut who preferred the Church of England (their numbers included several clergy) were nevertheless obliged to attend the Congregational church; all who openly followed Anglican usages or attempted to introduce them were packed off to England or departed voluntarily for more congenial colonies. Fifty years after the landing of the Pilgrims, New England still lacked an Anglican parish. Not until the reign of William and Mary and the passage of the English

28

Toleration Act of 1689 did religious toleration come to Anglican residents of Massachusetts. Even then, Anglicans lived in the unfamiliar role of dissenters, and an entrenched majority opposed their every effort at expansion. Until 1727, for example, members of the Church of England in Massachusetts were required to pay taxes to support the churches and clergy of the Congregationalist Standing Order.

Anglican parishes were organized and Anglican churches erected in New England beginning in 1689, when four hundred people attended the first service at King's Chapel. The most impressive church in Boston at the time and the first church in New England to have a pipe organ, King's Chapel was also the first of a number of notable churches in New England to carry very Anglican and hence very un-Puritan names. Employing biblical language, Puritans applied such names as "the First Church of Christ" or "the Second Church of Christ" to their churches.

Anglican sources for church names were more traditional and imperial. In time New England had Anglican churches named King's Church (Providence, R.I., 1722), Queen's Chapel (Portsmouth, N.H., 1732), St. Paul's Church (Newburyport, Mass., 1711), St. Michael's Church (Marblehead, Mass., 1714), Christ Church (Boston, 1723 — later to gain fame through Paul Revere's ride as "Old North Church"), St. James Church (New London, Conn., 1725), and many others. The majority of the clergy who served these early Anglican parishes in New England were natives of old England. In the late 1720s and early 1730s, for example, a frequent preacher at Trinity Church (1704) in Newport, Rhode Island, was the British philosopher George Berkeley, then in America attempting to found an Anglican college in Bermuda.

As the dates of construction of the churches show, the history of Anglicanism in New England belongs almost entirely to the eighteenth century. In that same century, the *New England Courant*, a newspaper started by a brother of Benjamin Franklin, developed into a center of Anglican thought. In New England (as elsewhere), neither the number of Anglican clergy nor the number of churches give a precise picture of size. The shortage of clergy sometimes required congregations to use layreaders. In addition, where Anglicans were few in number, congregations often met in homes, schoolhouses, or courthouses rather than churches.

By 1750, New England had approximately forty-four Anglican congregations — nineteen in Connecticut, seventeen in Massachusetts (which then included Maine), seven in Rhode Island (where Anglicanism became an appealing alternative to sectarian arguments), and one in New Hampshire. The church grew more rapidly, especially in Connecticut, in the years between 1750 and the Revolution. That Anglicans began to hold public office in numbers well out of proportion to their percentage of the New England population is an indication of their increasing influence.

Anglicanism in the Middle Colonies

In New York, a former Dutch colony where the diversity of nationalities and languages rivaled that of Pennsylvania, Anglicanism became the established church in 1693. Its establishment — whose terms were somewhat unclear — was limited to the City of New York, and to Queens, Richmond, and Westchester counties.

In the first decades after establishment, the Church of England erected churches in the City of New York, Staten Island, Westchester, Eastchester, New Rochelle, and Queens. Trinity Parish, initially by law the "sole and only" parish in New York City, became the colony's preeminent parish and in time the wealthiest parish of any denomination in the United States. Having received from the government a tract of farmland in lower Manhattan, the parish retained most of the land and used its income for expenses, benefactions, and endowment. One such benefaction was King's College (now Columbia University), chartered in lower Manhattan in 1754 with the proviso that its president and chapel services be Anglican. The parish's first church, Trinity Church (1697, enlarged 1735, later replaced) was for many years the dominant building in colonial New York skyline. Surrounded now by skyscrapers, the one colonial church that survives today in Manhattan, St. Paul's Chapel (1766) on lower Broadway, is among the many churches that Trinity Parish either erected or subsidized.

Families of position and influence supported the Church of England in the colony of New York. In addition, all governors from the late seventeenth century through the Revolution were Anglicans. Yet at times members of other denominations outnumbered Anglicans in the colony by a ratio of seventeen to one. Nevertheless, the established church of New York served as a launching stage for the spread of Anglicanism into Connecticut, New Jersey, and the developing areas up the Hudson River.

Anglicans operated in a free market in the religiously heterogeneous middle colonies below New York. In the religiously diverse colony of New Jersey, the history of the Church of England was almost entirely limited to the eighteenth century, with only the parish in Perth Amboy dating from the seventeenth century. Originally proprietorial, the colony came under the control of the crown after 1702. Its legislature, dominated by Quakers and other dissenters, was successful in resisting all attempts to establish Anglicanism.

30

A "court church" tied to the English government, the Church of England grew steadily but slowly in New Jersey until the Revolution. A report in the 1720s indicated that some six hundred colonists out of a population of fifteen to twenty thousand attended Anglican services; only three Anglican congregations — Perth Amboy, Burlington, and Elizabeth Town — had a regular ministry. No single parish was typical, but an example of Anglican weakness is seen in Elizabeth Town, where in the 1730s only two hundred fifty residents attended St. John's Church and fourteen hundred attended churches of other denominations.

By 1776 the church in New Jersey encompassed only eleven clergy and over twenty congregations. St. Mary's Church (1703), in the Delaware River and courthouse town of Burlington, became a center of Anglican influence. St. Mary's was the first parish organized in New Jersey under the auspices of the Society for the Propagation of the Gospel in Foreign Parts (SPG) (which will be discussed below).

In Pennsylvania (of which Delaware was a part until 1704), the Church of England remained small but became increasingly influential. A Quaker who had suffered in England for his beliefs, William Penn established his proprietary colony as a "holy experiment" where persecuted religious groups could live together peacefully and worship freely. Some Anglicans were attracted to it by its inexpensive land and by the opportunities presented by Philadelphia, which grew to become the second largest city in the British empire. Nevertheless, Anglicans had far less reason to immigrate to Pennsylvania than the Quakers, Moravians, Mennonites, Reformed, Brethren, Schwenkfelders, Roman Catholics, Presbyterians, and others who saw the colony as literally the answer to their prayers.

As one interpretation of Christianity among many in a tolerant colony, the Church of England never rose to more than a small minority of Pennsylvania's population. But as the eighteenth century unfolded and more and more wealthy Quakers in the Philadelphia area — including even the heirs of William Penn and proprietors of the colony — converted to Anglicanism, the church's influence grew. The bulk of Anglican membership in Pennsylvania and Delaware, however, seems to have been middle class. According to the 1749 report of an SPG missionary, the "Quakers and High Dutch who are very numerous" were wealthier and of higher social class than the Anglicans in Philadelphia.[9]

The oldest and most prestigious Anglican church in the colony was Christ Church, Philadelphia (1695), established when Philadelphia was in its infancy. Within twenty years other churches were established in villages relatively close to Philadelphia: Oxford (1698), Perkiomen (1700), Great

In Philadelphia's St. Peter's Church (1761), the pulpit and holy table stand
at opposite ends. The stained-glass windows are later additions.

Valley (1700), the Welsh community of Radnor (1700), Concord (1702),
Marcus Hook (1702), Chester (1702), Whitemarsh (1702), Bristol (1712),
and Kelton (1715).

By 1750 Pennsylvania had approximately fifteen Anglican churches.
Delaware — where Anglican work began in the 1670s and where Anglican planters lived in the two southern counties — had about twelve
more. In both colonies the Church of England maintained cordial relations with and supplied clergy for the Swedish Lutherans who remained
from the seventeenth-century colony of New Sweden along the banks
of the Delaware River. This relationship prepared the way for the seven
"Old Swedes" churches of Pennsylvania, Delaware, and New Jersey to
become Episcopalian in time. Anglicans provided the major influence in
the founding of the College of Philadelphia (chartered 1749, now the
University of Pennsylvania). On the eve of the Revolution in 1775,
Pennsylvania had some nineteen clergy serving twenty-two Anglican
churches.

32

Southern Anglicanism Outside of Virginia

Colonial travelers noted that Anglican churches grew in number the closer one came to the Chesapeake Bay. As an English colony granted to a Roman Catholic proprietor by an Anglican monarch, Maryland legally had to tolerate the Church of England from the start. Although the colony (as writers have occasionally failed to note) contained a Protestant majority from its earliest period, dissenters and the irreligious gradually came to outnumber Anglicans and Roman Catholics. In 1649 its proprietor — Cecilius Calvert, the second Lord Baltimore — and its Protestant-dominated legislature officially gave religious toleration to all trinitarian Christians — something the colony (which was a business venture as well as a haven) had essentially done from the start.

Not until mid-century did an Anglican priest arrive in Maryland. By the 1670s only three Anglican clergy were at work among the more than twenty thousand settlers. When Maryland temporarily became a royal colony in 1691, Governor Francis Nicholson noticeably expanded the number of Anglican churches and clergy. In 1700 fifteen clergy holding parishes came to Annapolis to meet with the first personal representative, or commissary, sent to the colony by the bishop of London. (The duties of these agents of the bishop will be discussed below.)

After 1702, when the Church of England became established in Maryland, the number of Anglicans steadily increased. What would later occur with some of the Penn family in Pennsylvania also occurred with the Calverts: they conformed to the Church of England. By so doing, the Lords Baltimore again received their charter for the colony. By 1767 the colony had forty-four parishes. The parishes paid their clergy so well (up to ten times better than the Anglican parishes of North Carolina, for example) that priests who wished parishes in Maryland had to place their names on a waiting list.

Just below Virginia, in the "Lost Colony" of 1587–1590 on Roanoke Island, North Carolina witnessed the first recorded Anglican baptism in the American colonies (of a Native American named Manteo). It also provided the setting for the birth and baptism of the first child of English parentage (a girl named Virginia Dare) in the New World. When the colony was reestablished in the seventeenth century, Quakerism, Presbyterianism, and irreligion were strong, with a flourishing community of Moravians around Salem. Clergy often disparage populations that are uninterested in organized religion, and the missionaries sent by the Church of England to North Carolina were no exception. "A lawless and barbarous people, in general," an SPG missionary described the residents of eastern North Carolina in 1710.[10]

A series of acts during the first two decades of the eighteenth century established the Church of England in North Carolina, but the established church's progress was marked by confusion and disorder. Parishes existed largely on paper, church taxes generally went uncollected or were contested, and the established church experienced the disadvantages of state support without the compensations. Of the thirty-two Anglican parishes provided for in legislation by 1765, only five had priests or churches. So limited were the ministrations of the Church of England that when the royal governor died in Brunswick in 1765, a civil magistrate had to read the Prayer Book burial service at the funeral, for no Anglican clergyman lived within one hundred miles.

Why was Anglicanism so weak in North Carolina? Although other causes contributed, the principal answer seems to involve its laity. The colony simply lacked the substantial body of influential laypeople who were financially capable of and religiously committed to supporting an established church. To the north and south, Anglicanism in Virginia and South Carolina had that necessary base of committed lay support; North Carolina did not.

The leadership of Governor William Tryon, an energetic promoter of Anglicanism, caused the number of churches and clergy to increase notably in the decade preceding the Revolution. By 1770, eighteen clergy were at work. But the growth came too late for the church to put down lasting roots, and it was also paralleled by growth among dissenting denominations. As a result, the Anglican tradition in North Carolina virtually died out after the Revolution, and the Episcopal Church remained unorganized until 1817. The colonial law that Anglican clergy controlled all education, however, remained sufficiently effective after the Revolution that daily chapel services at the University of North Carolina were conducted from the Book of Common Prayer from its opening in 1795 until well into the nineteenth century.

Richest of the southern colonies because of its rice and indigo crops, South Carolina was a colony where Anglicanism and other denominations existed in roughly equal numbers during much of the colonial period. Founded as an English proprietary colony in 1670, the colony established the Church of England in acts passed in 1704 and 1706. Although non-Anglicans eventually outnumbered Anglicans, the established church remained dominant not only because of government assistance but also because of strong and effective lay support and a disarming policy of moderation toward non-Anglicans. Thus Anglicanism in South Carolina avoided most of the problems that handicapped its sister establishments to the immediate north and south.

A low country (or Tidewater) church in South Carolina, with cosmopolitan Charleston as its center, the Church of England especially attracted the plantation gentry, the professional class, urban merchants, and skilled craftsmen. Most of the Huguenots who emigrated from France to the colony after the revocation of the Edict of Nantes in 1685 and grew to be influential in business and politics became Anglicans. The vestry system was the foundation of local government; churchwardens supervised even elections to the legislature. To the finely appointed churches of St. Philip's (1722) and St. Michael's (completed 1761) came the elite of Charleston on Sundays.

While the established church did draw some of its membership in the low country from the "poorer sort," it generally left the backcountry — the vast, unregulated, unrefined area of the colony above the fall line, consisting of often illiterate subsistence farmers — to the Presbyterians and Baptists. The principal Anglican missionary who ministered in that area on the outskirts of civilization was uncomplimentary about his prospective congregations, calling "the Generality very loose, dissolute, Idle People — Without either Religion or Goodness."[11]

The moderate, lay-controlled established church of South Carolina operated much like that of Virginia. Vestries were subject to annual elections, but as in Virginia they controlled parish appointments and in time refused to give the clergy more than year-to-year contracts. Gaming, dancing, drinking, and alcohol had the same appeal to the plantation gentry as they did in Virginia. Because of the Huguenot immigrations, however, far more Anglican clergy in South Carolina than in the Old Dominion — sixteen percent, according to one survey — were of stricter, Calvinist backgrounds.

Substantially different was the situation in Georgia, the last established and least prosperous of the colonies. Chartered in 1732 by the philanthropic James Oglethorpe and his associates as a haven for English debtors, the colony came under the jurisdiction of the crown in 1754. Although the Church of England officially became established in 1758, its powers existed more on paper than in reality. Dissenters vastly outnumbered Anglicans, irreligion was rampant, and Anglican clergy were few. Like North Carolina, the young colony lacked the stable gentry on which Anglicanism depended in the south. Although its legislature divided the colony into eight parishes, Georgia had clergy only in

Exterior of Old St. David's Church, completed 1773, with later additions, Cheraw, South Carolina.

Savannah and Augusta by 1773. At the most, the colony had five Anglican churches.

Summary

Although Anglicanism was established in Virginia early in the previous century, the story of the Church of England in colonial America is an eighteenth-century story. From approximately 1700 on, when England's government and merchant class realized that their overseas colonies were the beginning of an empire, the goal of Anglicanism was to monopolize Christianity in England's American colonies and to replace such earlier expressions of it as Puritanism or Quakerism. Despite diverse national backgrounds, Anglican authorities hoped Americans in all colonies would live together in peace and worship according to the Book of Common Prayer. Although this Anglican campaign for an Anglican America under crown and Prayer Book extended from Massachusetts to Georgia and received extensive subsidies from the SPG, it did not succeed. America remained pluralistic in religious expression.

In colonial New England Anglicanism became a liturgical, imperial alternative to Puritanism, often at odds with the political establishment. In the middle colonies it existed as one of many competing churches — a situation similar to what the Episcopal Church encountered throughout the new nation after the Revolution. In most of the south it became a privileged, moderate church controlled by its laity. Although establishment in the south gave the Church of England a greater opportunity to influence society, it was obliged at the same time to accommodate itself more to the mores and politics of that society. Its flavor in the south was decidedly low church, just as in New England and in parts of the middle colonies it took a high church stance.

Throughout the colonies Anglicanism was characterized by lay rule, even though the SPG was an exponent of clerical authority. The Anglican laity of the colonies had far more authority and played a substantially greater role in their churches than their contemporaries did in England. In Anglicanism, as in all other mainline expressions of Christianity in America except Roman Catholicism, lay control ultimately replaced clerical authority.

By the start of the Revolution, the Church of England was the second largest denomination in America (behind Congregationalism), with over four hundred regularly meeting congregations and perhaps three hundred clergy. Of all the major churches in the colonies — the Congregationalists, Presbyterians, Quakers, Baptists, Dutch Reformed, Roman Catholics,

Lutherans, and Moravians — the Anglicans were the most widespread. Other denominations possessed strength in a few colonies, but were absent or underrepresented elsewhere.

Anglicanism's constituency in the colonies came disproportionately from the wealthy or relatively well-to-do, but its congregations also included large numbers of the poor, the illiterate, and residents of moderate means. The church's hold on classes below the middle was fragile, however, for it found it difficult to understand and to meet the religious needs of the poor and less literate. Those twin difficulties would fetter the church throughout its post-Revolutionary history.

THEOLOGY

From New England to Georgia, the Anglican churches and colleges in the colonies produced few writers who could be called theologians. Although Thomas Bray's *Catechetical Lectures . . . Giving an Account of the Covenant of Grace* and his *Short Discourse Upon the Doctrine of our Baptismal Covenant* were published in the years that Bray was commissary of Maryland and were widely used by Anglican parish libraries and SPG clergy in America, they were written in England. In Massachusetts, John Checkley, a publisher-bookseller and lay member of Boston's King's Chapel, wrote influential pamphlets and tracts advocating the doctrine and government of the Church of England. Opposed to the Puritan belief that God alone possessed freedom in matters of salvation or damnation, Checkley emphasized that men and women possessed the free will to accept or reject God's offer of grace.

In arguing for free will as a central teaching of Anglicanism, Checkley joined with other Anglican writers of the eighteenth century in England and its colonies. In the two previous centuries, a minority of Anglicans would have argued otherwise. By the eighteenth century, however, a moderate Arminianism (or an emphasis on the freedom of humans to accept or reject God's grace) had replaced the Calvinist emphasis on predestination of the earliest Anglicans in Virginia. Thus the leading theological thinker produced by colonial Anglicanism — Connecticut rector and King's College president Samuel Johnson — remained charitable toward his ancestral Congregationalism. But he emphatically drew the line at the Congregationalist teaching that God in almighty wisdom and justice had either elected all humans to heaven or reprobated them to hell wholly without relation to their faith or works.

Typical, too, was the criticism of Calvinist clergy given by an SPG missionary in Pennsylvania: "Instead of instructing the people to 'serve the Lord with *gladness*' and to have 'joy in the Holy Ghost,'" the missionary declared, "these miserable teachers advance a gloomy and dreadful religion which has . . . made many [in their congregations] fitter objects for a *Hospital than a Church*."[12] Thus in contrast to the hard marrow of predestinarian Congregationalist, Presbyterian, Baptist, and Reformed theology, colonial Anglicans came to stand for free will. "Free will, reasonableness, practical godliness and spirituality, the special value of good conduct . . . an emphasis on moral behavior . . . an historic ministry . . . the sacraments" — these were some of the components of Anglican theology in the colonies.

As the eighteenth century went on, the theology of most Christian churches came to be affected by the many-sided trans-European movement called in English "the Enlightenment" or "the Age of Reason." A period of essentially optimistic confidence that human reason and science could enlighten what dogma and superstition had obscured, it lasted from approximately 1650 to 1800. In colonial America, Anglicans of the high church persuasion as well as those in the incipient evangelical movement resisted this influence. Especially from the middle colonies south, however, many other Anglicans came to be influenced by what one scholar has labeled the "moderate Enlightenment."[13]

Within the Church of England the moderate Enlightenment infused Anglicanism with a desire for reasonableness, a concern for simplicity, an opposition to emotionalism, and an emphasis on morality. It viewed the teachings of the Bible, the historic Christian creeds, the Book of Common Prayer, and the Thirty-Nine Articles through the prism of rationality, order, balance, and moderation. It disdained irrationality, overly precise formulations of dogma, and "unseemly" zeal in religious matters. Varying from person to person and from colony to colony, the moderate Enlightenment influenced the religious views of Anglican clergy and laity throughout the eighteenth century. Anglicans in eighteenth-century America, as one writer has declared, "considered themselves modern, rational, moderate, enlightened — in a word, English."[14]

Although these moderates believed in human reason as a means of discovering religious truth, they also believed that reason needed to be supplemented by the divine revelation recorded in Scripture. But by the later colonial period, the equation had simplified for some Anglicans. Following the lead of the left wing of the Enlightenment (of which Benjamin Franklin represents a prime American example), large numbers of Anglican gentry came to believe that reason and science provided all-sufficient guides for believing in God and behaving morally; any special revelation that occurred through Scripture, they decided, was superfluous or in need of radical pruning. They were intent on returning humanity to a primitive natural religion consisting of belief in the existence of God and a simple morality. Called the "Deists," and divided into wings ranging from supernaturalist Christian to rationalist anti-Christian, their effect on the church has been described above.

Transplanted to late twentieth-century America with their views intact, most Deists of the eighteenth century would be considered optimistic, religious people; virtually all who remained nominal Anglicans were more certain of the existence of God than many orthodox Christians who sit in church pews today. Nothing could be further from the truth than Theodore Roosevelt's description of the anti-Christian Deist Thomas Paine as a "filthy little atheist." But in the eighteenth century the movement undercut organized religion, for its suspicion of special revelation and supernaturalism made Scripture, liturgy, sacraments, clergy, and churches unnecessary. As Jon Butler has observed, Deism "masqueraded as religion but was thoroughly irreligious."[15] The number of Deists within the ranks of the laity represented one reason that the Anglican tradition in the south, despite its support of the patriot cause, almost failed to survive the Revolution.

THE ROLE OF THE LAITY

Histories of the Church of England often focus on kings and clergy. From the start, however, the power in colonial Anglicanism belonged not to the clergy but to the laity, especially in the southern colonies.

Yet historians know remarkably little about the role of the laity in the colonial churches, although the research of the future into surviving letters and diaries should add to the knowledge. The few contemporaneous materials that currently allow a scrutiny of the work of laypeople in the Anglican churches — the records of the vestries, for example — are often fragmentary or terse. For lack of direct evidence, most of the contributions of Anglican laymen during the colonial period, and virtually all of the contributions of Anglican laywomen, have remained unknown to historians.

But such a list would undoubtedly be long. It would include clerks and vestry members from Maine to Georgia. It would include ordinary people who rarely missed a Sunday; an example would be the "Mr. and Mrs. Hitchcock" who were always named last, but still almost always named, on the socially graded list of recipients of holy communion in the 1730s in

St. Philip's Church, Charleston.[16] It would include the "believing mothers" or "believing wives" who read the Scriptures in the family circle, assured that their children attended church, and supervised the catechizing of their children.

From the public records the contribution of one group of laity — the colonial governors — is clear. In the absence of bishops, royal governors assumed many of the administrative duties traditionally performed by the episcopate. Although a governor could not lay on hands, he could provide the central vision and leadership required for the Church of England to be effective in his colony. As the instructions from Queen Anne to a colonial governor of New York in 1703 indicate, the governor's ecclesiastical responsibilities were large:

> You shall take especiall care that God Almighty be devoutly and duly served throughout youre Government, the Book of Common prayer as by Law established, read each Sunday and Holy-day, and the blessed Sacrament administered according to the rites of the Church of England, you shall be carefull that the Churches already built there be well and orderly kept, and that more be built as the Colony shall by God's blessing be improved, and that besides a complete maintenance to be assigned to the Minister . . . , a convenient house be built . . . and a competent proportion of Land assigned him for a Glebe . . .
>
> You are not to prefer any Minister to any Ecclesiasticall Benefice in that Our Province without a certificate from . . . the bishop of London . . . and if any person preferred already to benefice appear to you to give scandall . . . you are to use the best means for the removal of him, and to supply the vacancy. . . .
>
> You are to take care that Drunkenness and debauchery Swearing and blasphemy be discountenanced. . . . [17]

Most of the colonial governors handled the ecclesiastical side of their duties routinely. Some neglected the church; others were so zealous in its cause that they were counterproductive to its growth. A few governors, however, involved themselves with distinction in Anglican affairs in their colony.

Exemplars of such political leadership in the church's affairs include Sir Thomas Dale, the Calvinist deputy governor of the Jamestown colony. In his *Lawes Divine, Morall and Martiall,* Dale attempted to plan and create a Christian society in Virginia. Under royal governor William Tryon, the established church of North Carolina built churches, attracted clergy, and showed the first signs of health in its existence. In Virginia, Maryland, and South Carolina, the mercurial but effective Sir Francis Nicholson raised salaries, recruited clergy, helped to establish the College of William and Mary as the first Anglican college in the colonies, and encouraged missions to Native and African Americans. Other governors could be added to this list.

Laymen who held other offices in the colonies also aided the church. Deserving of special mention is Caleb Heathcote, a public official in New York and lord of the "Manor of Scarsdale," who made five missionary journeys into Connecticut to plant the Church of England. Devoted to the church, well read in its literature, cunning when necessary to advance its interests, Heathcote also encouraged attendance at the new Anglican parishes in Westchester County by threatening to direct the militia companies to drill on Sunday if the day was dishonored.

Other laypeople who were specially influential on the church's behalf include collector of customs Edward Randolph and lay writers Thomas Lechford and John Checkley — all of Massachusetts. A thorn in the bosom of the Congregational establishment, Checkley went to England in later life for ordination. In Rhode Island, collector of customs Nathaniel Kay gave endowments of land to three parishes. Typical of the colonial Anglican women whose quiet and steady support provided a bulwark against dissent and irreligion were two South Carolina mothers. Eliza Lucas Pinckney assured that her children not only attended church but also memorized the opening prayer and read the sermon text each Sunday in their own Bibles. Mrs. Thomas Broughton, wife of a member of the governor's council, reminded her son of the "eternity acoming" and urged him to reread his catechism, to remember the vows made for him in baptism, and to partake of the Lord's Supper.[18] Diaries and letters indicate that the wives of planters and merchants were often widely read in theology; Frances Tasker Carter of the great estate of Nomini Hall in Virginia impressed the family's Princeton-trained tutor with a "very extensive Knowledge" of theological matters.[19]

THE ROLE OF THE CLERGY

As for the clergy who served the colonial Anglican parishes of America, they included natives of England, Ireland, Scotland, Wales, and such continental countries as Germany, France, and Spain. Some lacked college training and simply read for orders. Many others had attended or had taken degrees at Oxford, Cambridge, Aberdeen, St. Andrews, Harvard, Yale, William and Mary, and other colleges. These colonial clergy were third and fourth sons of English squires, brothers of archbishops, men designated in the category of *"puer pauper"* while students at Cambridge or Oxford, native-born Americans, former curates in the Church of England, former pastors in the French Reformed or German Lutheran churches, former monks in Roman Catholic orders, ex-Quakers, ex-Presbyterians, ex-Congregationalists, and men who themselves later left Anglicanism. Some believed that only members of the Church of England were true Christians; most were to varying degrees more ecumenically inclined.

Most of the rectors had glebes or rectories. Many either tutored in homes or operated schools in which they taught not only the Anglican interpretation of Christian doctrine but also reading and writing. In the southern colonies many lived like planters. Yet although their holy orders admitted them to the anterooms of power and to the dining rooms of wealth, the majority of the southern rectors remained no more than second class gentry. In the north, the Anglican clergy tended to be members of the broad middle class.[20] The salaries of some missionaries were so small and the complaints of poverty to the SPG so many that some must have been shabbily genteel at best, even when allowances are made for misrepresentation. Their length of service in a single parish ranged from a few unsatisfactory Sundays to fifty two years.

What can be said of the character of these clergy? Although earlier scholarship focused on some of the more outrageous examples of misbehavior, more recent investigations have served as a corrective. What was true in Virginia appears to have been true of the other colonies: most Anglican clergy seem to have been competent in their performance of duties and sober in their lifestyles.

To be sure, the eighteenth century was a worldly age, and to greater or lesser extents many Anglican clergy reflected the worldliness of their time. In addition, when a parson exhibited behavior that would immediately alert a twentieth-century reader to probable mental illness — declaring himself an atheist from the pulpit, soliciting women for sex, running up large bills in taverns and refusing to pay them, and running down the main street of his town nude (all of which one rector in Tidewater Virginia did) — contemporaries instead evaluated the parson as immoral. A recent survey of South Carolina clergy confirms what recent studies of the Virginia clergy have displayed: ninety percent of the clergy seem to have performed creditably, ten percent did not. More Anglican clergy than history has recorded might have qualified for the touching recommendation given to the SPG in 1710 by the vestry of a North Carolina parish:

in all respects [he has been] . . . a messenger of the mild Jesus, exemplary in his life and blameless in his Conversation . . . we shall ever bless that providence that placed him among us and sho'd be very unjust to his Character if we did not give him the Testimony of a pious . . . pastor whose sweetness of temper, diligence in his Calling and Soundness of Doctrine has so much Conduced to promote the great end of his Mission . . . for tho' the Sacrament of the Lord's Supper was never before his arrival administered in this precinct, yet we have had more Communicants than most of Our Neighboring parishes of Virginia who have had the advantage of a settled ministry for many years.[21]

Notable colonial clergy included James Blair of Virginia, a Scot who arrived in Virginia at age twenty-nine and died at age eighty-seven after having held virtually every leading office in the colony. Founder and president for life of the College of William and Mary, rector of Jamestown and Bruton parishes, first commissary to Virginia, member and president of the governor's council, acting governor of Virginia for one year, ambitious and imperative both for the church and for himself, he dominated the religious scene in colonial Virginia.

Several commissaries in other colonies also made more than an ordinary contribution. As commissary to South Carolina for almost twenty years and as minister and rector of St. Philip's Church, Charleston, for over thirty years, Alexander Garden shaped the Anglicanism of South Carolina more than any other figure. One of the first native-born Americans to rise to a prominent place in the Anglican clergy, New York's William Vesey, a graduate of Harvard, guided the established church of New York in its difficult early years. Vesey served as commissary to New York for over three decades and as rector of Trinity Parish for almost five.

Ironically, the commissary who had the greatest influence on the church, Thomas Bray, spent no more than a few months in the colonies as Maryland's first commissary. Gifted with a remarkable combination of vision and administrative ability, Bray was concerned not only for the unchurched but also for persons on the margins of society. During his brief stay he saw that the Anglican churches of America needed aid and direction from the mother church. Upon his return to England, he established two "voluntary" societies. The first, the Society for Promoting Christian Knowledge (SPCK, founded 1698), which also worked in England and Wales, sent Bibles, tracts, pamphlets, and entire libraries of Christian literature to Anglican parishes. At a time when libraries were few in the American colonies, the SPCK established parish libraries from New England to Georgia.

The sister society, the Society for the Propagation of the Gospel in Foreign Parts (SPG, founded 1701), had the purpose of planting and nurturing Anglicanism among the settlers in the English colonies. To the SPG is owed much of the credit for the expansion of Anglicanism outside Virginia and Maryland. A high church organization of relatively strict devotional and moral standards, the "Venerable Society" recruited, culled with relative care, and dispatched more than three hundred missionaries to the American colonies from 1701 until 1783, spending in today's equivalent millions of dollars on their salaries and on the erection of Anglican churches. Its clergy were instructed to live simply, to send written reports to London regularly, and to avoid the worldly amusements to which some of their English brethren were addicted. New England received more than eighty missionaries, New York and South Carolina more than fifty each, both Pennsylvania and New Jersey more than forty each, and North Carolina over thirty. Only Virginia and Maryland did not require substantial aid from the society.

The purpose of the SPG was not only to plant and nurture Anglicanism in the new world, but also to "convince and reclaim" dissenters, catechize children, and convert heathens and unbelievers. Though most of the society's work in the colonies was in English, its records display a desire to evangelize such groups as the Welsh, Dutch, French, Germans, Swedes, and Native Americans. Led by missionaries such as former schoolmaster George Keith, an intense ex-Presbyterian and ex-Quaker whose quest for "the doctrine of the primitive church" caused him finally to convert to the Church of England at the age of sixty-two, Anglicanism gained converts in the middle colonies. Sharp in temper, domineering and argumentative, a person who in his Quaker phase had once barnstormed New England and challenged Puritan divines to public debate, Keith was one of those missionaries who merited Thomas Jefferson's description of the SPG clergy as "Anglican Jesuits."[22]

Under aggressive SPG leadership, the Church of England also made great gains in the eighteenth century in Congregationalist New England, especially in the Puritan citadels of Massachusetts and Connecticut. The conversion to Anglicanism on the "black Tuesday" of September 13, 1722, of seven Congregationalist ministers — Timothy Cutler, president (or "rector") of Congregationalist Yale College, Daniel Brown, Yale's sole faculty member (or "tutor"), former Yale tutor Samuel Johnson, and four Yale-trained Congregationalist ministers in neighboring towns — was symbolic. Although three of the defectors subsequently recanted, three others went to England for ordination. The conversions legitimated and hence opened the doors for Anglicanism in Connecticut. The immediate effect of the "Connecticut apostacie," one historian has noted, was similar to what would have occurred if the Yale football team had converted to communism in the 1920s.[23]

Some SPG clergy had remarkable careers. Gideon Bostwick, rector at Great Barrington for twenty-three years, claimed to have baptized 2,274 children in Massachusetts and in adjacent New York. John Talbot, the "Apostle of New Jersey," traveled on missionary journeys with George Keith, served St. Mary's Church in Burlington from age fifty-nine until his death at eighty-two, and may or may not have been secretly consecrated a bishop during a trip to England.

In South Carolina the devoted Francis Le Jau, a Huguenot educated at Trinity College in Dublin and the first SPG missionary to St. James' Parish, Goose Creek, evangelized poor whites, African Americans, and Native Americans, and protested the treatment accorded to slaves. The psychologically complex Charles Woodmason, an Anglican planter, was ordained in mid-life with the intention of eradicating dissenters from the South Carolina backcountry. After six years as the rector of vast St. Mark's Parish, he claimed to have baptized two thousand persons, married two hundred, and preached five hundred sermons. His baptisms of children sometimes included baptisms of one or both parents, whom he occasionally married as well.

The most famous of the SPG missionaries to America was John Wesley, the founder of Methodism. Then a bachelor high churchman of considerable rubrical and antiquarian ardor, Wesley served as a missionary in Georgia from 1735 to 1737. Indifference on the part of colonists and Native Americans to his ministry, controversy with local authorities over his high church demands, and a mishandled romance caused him to leave the colony earlier than expected. His brother Charles, who accompanied him, served as secretary to Governor James Oglethorpe, but returned to England under similar circumstances a year earlier.

THE GREAT AWAKENING

The ship that carried John Wesley back to England passed that carrying his successor, George Whitefield, to Georgia. In England, following his Aldersgate Experience, Wesley founded the Methodist societies and sparked the Evangelical Revival. In America, the passionately evangelical Whitefield — "the Grand Itinerant" — made seven preaching tours of the colonies and spread the parallel revival known as the Great Awakening.

The Anglican churches of the colonies gained little from the Great Awakening, though the movement permanently changed the course of American Protestantism by introducing revivalism. As the prototype of the nondenominational revivalists of nineteenth- and twentieth-century America, Whitefield probably deserves even more credit for founding the revival tradition in America than the celebrated Congregationalist minister Jonathan Edwards. But the colonial Church of England presented an almost unified opposition to revivalism and saw the Awakening not in terms of religious renewal but rather as the latest attempt of the forces of dissent to destroy Anglicanism. Thus like Wesley in England, Whitefield found most Anglican churches closed to him; though he never officially separated himself from Anglicanism, he was principally influential among the Presbyterians, Congregationalists, and other Calvinist denominations, and is buried in a Presbyterian church. With the notable exceptions of Samuel Magaw of Delaware and Pennsylvania, William Percy of South Carolina, the brooding Devereux Jarratt of Virginia, and a handful of others, Anglican clergy resisted — often bitterly — the conversion-centered, experiential religion of the Great Awakening.

Although Anglican laypeople proved more open to the message of the Awakening than their clergy, those who accepted its emotionalism and teachings tended to leave for denominations such as the Methodists and Baptists. Denominations influenced by the Great Awakening became concerned with evangelism and expanded the role of laywomen, laymen, and African Americans. The Methodist societies, for example, ceased being an evangelical college of piety within the Episcopal Church and formed a separate denomination in 1784, after which their great growth began. Though an antirevivalist backlash caused some rural poor to convert to Anglicanism in New England, elsewhere in America the Church of England tended to lose the lower social and economic classes and to become the church of the educated and wealthier Americans.

The legacy of the Awakening remained in the evangelical party, a conversion-centered and pietistic form of low church Anglicanism that revived classical Reformation teachings about sin and judgment. Though loyal to the Book of Common Prayer, evangelicals emphasized preaching aimed at conversion, classes for religious study, and lay participation. Toward dancing, card-playing, and other amusements of the world, they were as stern as the Methodists and Baptists. The evangelical party experienced its greatest strength in America in the early decades of the nineteenth century.

THE QUEST FOR
AN AMERICAN BISHOP

The lack of a bishop proved a major handicap for colonial Anglicans, although many of the laity in the Anglican churches relished the freedom from prelacy that resulted. After 1688, the colonies received agents of the Bishop of London called commissaries, who usually also headed the most important parish in a colony. These vicars of London had the functions of enforcing church doctrine and forms, presiding over the few conventions of clergy that were held, attempting to impose discipline upon clergy, and keeping the bishop informed. Though large on paper, their powers were diminished by resistance from vestries, clergy, and royal governors.

What the commissaries could not do was precisely what the American churches most needed: ordain. Thus Americans who sought ordination had to take an expensive and dangerous three-thousand-mile trip across the Atlantic, from which a safe return could in no way be assured. Of the fifty-one candidates who had traveled from New England to England seeking Anglican ordination during a period of forty years, for example, Samuel Johnson reported that ten either perished at sea or died at the hands of pirates or from illness.

SPG agitation in the 1760s and 1770s for American bishops who could ordain, confirm, and oversee may properly be seen as one of the contributing causes of the American war for independence. Among Congregationalists, Presbyterians, southern Anglican clergy, and Anglican laity in the north and especially in the south, the new aggressiveness of Anglicanism aroused old memories of repressive laws in England against dissenters and of lordly prelates who were officers of state. "What does the bishop of London have to do with us?" asked the parishioners of St. Philip's Church in Charleston in 1710.

A colonial print displays a group of Puritans and Quakers on a wharf preventing an Anglican bishop from landing in New England. The ship contains not only the bishop but also his crook-shaped staff (or crosier), his mitre (or crown), and his episcopal carriage. Holding copies of books such as *Calvin's Works* and shouting "No Lords, spiritual or temporal, in New England," the New Englanders have driven the bishop up a mast. In the foreground of the drawing, a grinning monkey prepares to throw a rock at the interloper.[24] The print displays the attitudes of most non-Anglican New Englanders, but it also reflects the views of many Anglicans, especially in the southern colonies, who treasured their freedom from episcopal control.

ANGLICANISM AND THE REVOLUTION

Although writers have long tied Anglicanism to loyalism, recent scholarship has shown that some forty-five percent of Anglican clergy from
Georgia to Massachusetts supported the American side actively or passively
in the American Revolution; most came from South Carolina and Virginia, where the majority of the members of the established church were
patriots. The figures were even greater for the Anglican laity, where a solid
majority favored the patriot cause. Benjamin Franklin (a fellow-traveler
of Anglicanism in both Boston and Philadelphia, but not a communicant), George Washington, George Mason, John Jay, James Madison
(second cousin of Bishop Madison and perhaps the most theologically
knowledgeable president the United States has had), James Monroe, John
Marshall, John Randolph, Patrick Henry, and more than half of the sign-
ers of the Declaration of Independence were Anglicans, as were many of
the generals who led the American side. Worshipers at Christ Church,
Philadelphia, included Franklin, Betsy Ross, Robert Morris, and Francis
Hopkinson.

The Anglicanism of many of these patriots and founding fathers, of
course, was Deism in an Anglican mode. But in the eighteenth century,
as today, laypeople were not examined as to whether their private theological views agreed with official doctrines taught in their denomination.
Among educated Anglicans in the later decades of the eighteenth century, a certain amount of Deism was common, just as a certain amount
of teetotalism was later common among American Protestants. If George
Washington apparently went to church on about one out of every four
Sundays except when he was president, and if he apparently never received
the sacrament of holy communion in his adult life, that was unexceptional
behavior for many male Anglican gentry during the Deistic era.[25] Thus
some enumerations of the religion of American presidents have counted
Thomas Jefferson — whose private theology was complex but probably
best described as Unitarian — as an Episcopalian, for he served on the
vestry of St. Anne's Parish in Virginia and not only attended Episcopal
services regularly but also contributed to the Episcopal Church until his
death.

The loyalist clergy (some of whom may actually have favored an American victory) believed they had to remain true to the solemn oaths they had
sworn to God upon ordination. These oaths bound them to remain loyal
to the king and to perform public worship without change from the Book
of Common Prayer (which included prayers for the king, royal family, and

parliament). They had been ordained in England, and they would remain true to it. Their suffering and courage during the Revolutionary period were great. The strength of the patriotic clergy lay in their realization that oaths, liturgies, and governments are subordinate to the commission of Christ and that Anglicanism (as American history has amply borne out) can exist without formal connection to any government.

ANGLICANISM IN
POST-REVOLUTIONARY AMERICA

Saddled with the politics of imperialism, the Church of England was disestablished in New York and in all southern colonies during or immediately after the Revolution. The losses to Anglicanism increased when its Methodist societies broke away to became a separate denomination in 1784. Having had little communication with each other prior to the Revolutionary War, the newly independent Anglican churches faced the enormous tasks of organizing themselves in each state and of seeking a national unity.

The first problem was a name. When a state of war continued to exist between the colonies and England, and when Americans were riding a wave of nationalism, the continued use of the title "Church of England" was unwise. Although used throughout this book, the term "Anglican" was little used until the nineteenth century. But the word "Episcopal" (from *episkopos,* generally translated as "overseer" and used in classical Greek to designate inspectors, temple supervisors, or municipal officials) was an old title. It dated from the struggles with the Puritans in seventeenth-century England and described persons who believed that fidelity to the apostolic church involved government by bishops and a ministry of three distinct orders. ("Bishop" itself is an Anglo-Saxon corruption of the Greek *episkopos.*) In New England and elsewhere during the colonial period, the Church of England had occasionally been referred to as "the Episcopal Church."

The first use of the title "Protestant Episcopal" occurred at a convention of clergy and laity in Maryland in 1780. In the usage of the time, the name meant that the church differed from Roman Catholic episcopalians because it was Protestant and from other Protestant churches because it was episcopal in government; the title was not intended to deny that the church was Catholic, for both in England and in New England "Catholic" was frequently used as synonymous with "Church of England."

Gradually the new name "Protestant Episcopal" spread to other states.

The General Convention of 1789, which met in Philadelphia, adopted "A General Constitution of the Protestant Episcopal Church in the United States of America" — the name by which the denomination was officially known until 1967, when the General Convention made the word "Protestant" optional. From the start both Episcopalians and members of other American churches have used the shorter "Episcopal Church" as another name for the denomination.

American Episcopalians used the name "Anglican," especially after the middle of the nineteenth century, to describe the world-wide communion of churches holding to the faith and order of the Church of England. Thus they would speak, as this book occasionally will, of Lutheranism, Calvinism, Roman Catholicism, Anglicanism, and other distinct families of Christians.

The scattered Episcopal churches took the first steps toward forming a national organization even before the Revolution was over. In 1782, the Reverend William White, rector of Christ Church, Philadelphia, and former chaplain of the Continental Congress, wrote *The Case of the Episcopal Churches in the United States Considered*. White's *Case* proposed several principles that eventually provided the basis of the Episcopal Church: first, that the church desired and acknowledged the three historic orders of deacons, priests, and bishops; and second, that the church was to be democratically operated, with both clergy and laity participating in all church councils.

In 1783, conventions of the churches in Maryland and Pennsylvania affirmed these principles. They added another that White had implied — that the worship of this church was to conform as much as possible to the worship of the Church of England. In 1784, additional meetings of Episcopalians representing various states occurred in New Jersey and New York City.

Episcopacy — the governing of the churches by bishops — proved the greatest stumbling block to unity. The church had no bishops, and most of the state churches believed that the forming of a national church structure should precede the consecration of any bishops that might be selected. In addition, some of the southern states, where laity had long controlled ecclesiastical affairs, felt no need for a potentially domineering bishop. White was keenly aware of the opposition to episcopal authority. "There cannot be produced an instance of laymen in America, unless in the very infancy of the settlements," he wrote, "soliciting the introduction of a bishop."[26]

51

The Consecration of a Bishop

But the problem was that clergy still had to be ordained, and in Anglicanism they are ordained only by bishops. After the Revolution the English bishops could no longer ordain American subjects. In the *Case,* White — who can best be described as a non-evangelical low churchman of the eighteenth-century type — had proposed a temporary system of presbyterian ordination. Until bishops could be consecrated, he suggested, three priests could lay hands upon ordinands, just as they had in early Christianity. This proposal shocked the high church Episcopalians of Connecticut.

Convinced that an Episcopal Church without episcopacy was a contradiction in terms, ten of Connecticut's clergy met secretly at the village of Woodbury in 1783 to remedy the situation. For their bishop they elected Samuel Seabury, a former SPG missionary in New York who had published several pamphlets supporting the British cause during the Revolution. The doctrine of apostolic succession required that Seabury receive consecration from a minimum of three bishops of the Church of England. But when Seabury traveled to England to seek consecration, the English bishops had a legal problem. They believed that they lacked the power to consecrate a person who could not take the required oath of loyalty to the monarchy. In addition, they feared creating a wandering bishop with no visible means of support.

Disappointed, Seabury went to Scotland, where he was consecrated by three nonjuring bishops (the successors of those high-Tory English clergy who refused to forswear their oath of loyalty to James II when William and Mary assumed the throne in 1689). Returning to the United States in the late spring of 1785, the new bishop began to organize the Episcopal Church of Connecticut. Beginning in August 1785, he ordained the first twenty-six Episcopal clergy of the new nation, most of whom came from other states. His early ordinands served parishes from Vermont to North Carolina and embraced the heir to the Fairfax claim in Virginia, the master of the grammar school adjacent to the College of William and Mary, and four former Methodist lay preachers, including the well-known Joseph Pilmore. In 1785 one Episcopalian hailed the ordinations of the "Right Reverend Father in God Dr. Samuel Seabury Bishop of Connecticut" in poetry:

From Harvards [*sic*] walls and Providence behold
The sons of science flocking to thy fold,
New York and Yale their learned offspring send,

52

And Pennsylvania greets thee as her friend,
While ruin'd temples rising from decay
Shall beam with Glory on thy Gospel day
Columbia's freemen shall united call
The[e] Father of our Church Episcopal.[27]

Yet for the other Episcopal churches in the United States, the situation was far more complex than this poem indicated. For several years unity with the Connecticut church seemed unlikely, since it refused to accept the principle of lay participation in councils. In addition, the loyalist Seabury (who was still on half pay from England for services rendered during the war) not only was disliked by most American clergy but had also now incurred the disfavor of the English bishops because of his Scottish consecration. The Episcopal churches in other states wanted national unity, but they also had to appease the English bishops, from whom they hoped to receive consecration of their bishops. If Seabury's consecration had solved the problems not only of Connecticut's churches but also of candidates for ordination, his presence in Connecticut had created more problems than solutions for other Episcopalians.

*The Organization of the
Episcopal Church*

In 1785 lay and clerical delegates from seven of the nine states south of Connecticut (the Episcopal churches of North Carolina and Georgia were too weak to send delegates) met in Philadelphia in the first General Convention. There they established a constitution, drafted an American version of the Book of Common Prayer, and devised a plan to obtain English consecration for American bishops. Meeting in Philadelphia and Wilmington in 1786, the second General Convention adopted measures that allowed White and Samuel Provoost, rector of Trinity Parish in New York City, to go to England for consecration later in the year. In the meantime, Parliament had passed an act permitting the English bishops to consecrate American bishops without requiring the loyalty oath.

Although these conventions were important, the 1789 General Convention, which met in Philadelphia in two sessions, was critical. Still at odds with the southern churches over the questions of lay participation and the validity of Seabury's episcopal orders, the churches in Connecticut (joined by those in Massachusetts) sent no delegates to the first session. This session, which lasted from late July to August 8, declared Seabury's consecration valid and removed the requirement that compelled

53

all state churches to send lay representatives to the General Convention. It also created a House of Bishops over which the senior bishop in date of consecration (called the presiding bishop) would preside. This upper house would have veto power over the House of Clerical and Lay Deputies.

Appeased, delegates from Connecticut and Massachusetts joined the second session, which began in late September and ended in mid-October. That session completed the constitution and established a system of canon law. It also adopted in final form an American Book of Common Prayer which, though revised in 1892, 1928, and 1979, has formed the pattern of worship for the Episcopal Church since that time. When the General Convention adjourned on October 16, 1789, the fragmented state churches (later called "dioceses") had finally united.

What would a political scientist say about the constitutional structure of the Episcopal Church that emerged from these conventions and was added to and revised over the years? Although several interpretations are possible, the church's government can probably best be described as *unitary*. In a unitary form of government, a central government holds legal supremacy over all other exercisers of government. It can keep and exercise much of that power itself — and so be highly centralized. Or it can distribute those powers to the forms of government that are subordinate to it — and so be decentralized.

That seems to be the form of government envisioned by William White for the General Convention. Upon analysis, the Episcopal Church appears not to be a *confederacy*, in which an association of governments (or dioceses) agree to delegate certain powers to a central agency (or General Convention) but retain the right to nullify that agency's acts and even to secede. Its form of government also does not seem to be *federal*. A federated government divides power between a central government (the General Convention) and two or more associated governments (the dioceses); separation of powers is crucial. The 1789 constitution of the church neither federated nor confederated existing sovereign churches into a new body. In the one action that may have carried the appearance of federation, Bishop Seabury and his clergy accepted the constitution at the second session of the 1789 General Convention. But the bishop and his New Englanders were accepting a constitution that included no division of powers and no protection of diocesan rights.

Thus the most exhaustive study of the polity (or government) of the Episcopal Church by a political scientist has held that it is unitary but highly decentralized:

In this decentralization, it takes on *confederal,* more nearly than even *federal* characteristics. This, however, does not make the church structurally confederal. There is no essential division of power between the General Convention and the dioceses. In fact, there is no limit at all upon the Convention's governing powers, unless it be the ancient canons and the necessity for conformity with the Catholic Faith; but these are interpreted finally by General Convention alone. Thus, the government is *unitary.*[28]

As it has worked out, the General Convention, despite its legal sovereignty, has delegated so much of its power to the dioceses and parishes that it has taken on the appearance of a confederation. The church's method of financing, the system of church courts it developed, its method of representation and voting in the two houses of the General Convention, its procedure for ordinations, its lack of a strong central executive until the 1920s or 1930s — all of these delegations of power and more reflect the republican times in which its constitution was formulated. Reflecting those times, White's *Case* specifically stated that the best government is the least government.

The constitution, canons, and Book of Common Prayer of 1789 laid the basis on which the Episcopal Church operates today. Three clerical orders still exist: bishops, presbyters or priests (the latter word is a derivation from the former), and deacons. Individual bishops ordain priests and deacons, sometimes joined in the laying on of hands by presbyters; three bishops are necessary to consecrate a bishop.[29]

When the archbishop of Canterbury and the bishops of London and Rochester consecrated James Madison as the first bishop of Virginia in 1790, the Episcopal Church fulfilled its pledge to the English bishops to defer consecrating any bishops in the United States until it secured three in the English succession. Since 1792, when Seabury, White, Provoost, and Madison consecrated Thomas J. Claggett as first bishop of Maryland, the church has consecrated its own bishops. Bishops of other Anglican churches, of the Polish National Catholic Church, and (in 1971, at the consecration of the bishop of Rio Grande) of the Roman Catholic Church have also joined in laying on hands at the consecration ceremonies of Episcopal bishops.

Like the American Constitution, which was drawn up at the same time, the constitution of the Episcopal Church displays the republican political ideals of the United States. It was wise for the Episcopal Church to adopt this form of government, since the evidence is clear that the churches that grew in the United States in the fifty years after the Revolution were precisely those who exhibited "democratization."[30] Episcopal

55

clergy continued to use the traditional hierarchical and unrepublican titles that emerged from the Middle Ages — "Reverend" for parish clergy, "Very Reverend" for deans, "Right Reverend" for bishops, and (in a change made in the twentieth century) "Most Reverend" for the presiding bishop. Members of more egalitarian American denominations have not only compared such titles to the honorifics employed for officers in the Brotherhood and Protective Order of the Elks and the Royal Society of Good Fellows, but have also asked if they do not reflect wishful thinking and suppressed desires more than reality.

But like the Book of Common Prayer and clerical garb, the titles reflect the Episcopal Church's English past. As one church historian has pointed out, the church clearly displayed its American character in 1789 by removing most medieval and hierarchial trappings from the episcopal office and making bishops subject to the laity within their dioceses. "American bishops," writes Frederick V. Mills, Sr., "were in every way more democratic than their English counterparts."[31]

Consisting of an upper House of Bishops with all bishops as members and a lower House of Deputies with an equal number of clerical and lay delegates, the General Convention of today meets every three years and in special sessions. Laity receive not only voice but also vote in the lower house; along with the clerical deputies who vote equally with them in the House of Deputies, they also must be elected by their dioceses.

Either house can originate proposals. To become legislation, proposals must pass both houses, which meet concurrently but separately. The Convention has the power to amend the canons and to alter the constitution after the dioceses have approved the proposed alteration. Although each diocese has its own constitution and ecclesiastical laws, no diocese may pass a canon that contravenes the legislation of the General Convention. Dioceses are grouped together in provinces, which have little power.

Representative conventions or councils also govern (with the bishop) each diocese, which is composed of a number of parishes. Meeting annually, they consist of the bishop, all other clergy, and at least one lay delegate — ordinarily elected — from each parish or mission. Each bishop has a council of advice, or "standing committee," composed equally of laypeople and clergy. Dioceses elect their own bishops, but bishops-elect cannot be consecrated without the approval of a majority of the diocesan standing committees and a majority of diocesan bishops. In some celebrated cases, such approval has been withheld.

Government on the parish level devolves upon the rector and the vestry, elected by communicants. Every congregation in the Episcopal Church is required "to recognize and accede to the constitution, canons, doctrine, discipline, and worship of the church, and to agree to submit to and obey such directions as may be from time to time received from the bishop in charge and council of advice."

Through 1900, General Conventions generally met in eastern cities – most frequently in Philadelphia and New York City. During the twentieth century, General Conventions have convened in cities from Boston to Honolulu, and have met in Philadelphia and New York only once. While the early conventions sometimes lasted as little as four days (although the General Convention of 1874 lasted one month), those in the twentieth century have tended to last two weeks. Between General Conventions, the House of Bishops usually meets at least once for consultation. Though less so in the years since World War II, the composition of the House of Deputies has been tilted toward the upper classes. An analysis of the 1910 General Convention showed that eighty-six percent of the lay deputies were lawyers, bankers, manufacturers, or business executives, while only one was a farmer and none were skilled or unskilled workers. At the same convention the clerical deputies consisted of eighty percent rectors, fifteen percent cathedral deans, educators, or archdeacons, and less than five percent missionary clergy.

The achievement of the conventions of the 1780s was considerable. A very American system of church government was created. A church identified with England had survived the war for independence from England. Delegates from scattered state churches had fashioned a national church that combined the ministry and liturgy of the English established church with the constitutional forms of American republicanism. Bishops claiming the apostolic succession were elected by ballot. After 1789, it seemed clear that "the most monarchical and magisterial Protestant church in Europe" was not going to "disappear over the horizon in the new American republic."[32]

Although Samuel Seabury and other bishops and presbyters are important, no writer can exaggerate William White's role in the organization of the Episcopal Church. Tactful, dignified, conciliatory, conscientious, and republican, he was at the center of Episcopal activity in America from 1779 on. His *Case* largely shaped the form of the church. Unanimously elected president of the first General Convention, he wrote the appeal to the archbishops and bishops of the Church of England for episcopal succession. Second only to William Smith of Pennsylvania, he adapted the Book of Common Prayer for use in a newly independent America.

Bishop William White (1748–1836) in his eighty-eighth year. After the original by Albert Newsam, a deaf and dumb child whose education Bishop White sponsored and who became a celebrated lithographer.

During the four decades he served as presiding bishop, he wrote most of the pastoral letters of the House of Bishops. The history of White's life is largely the history of his church during the same period. Not only historically but also spiritually, he was the father of the Episcopal Church.

Nevertheless, in the first decades after the General Convention of 1789, the future appeared dark to many Episcopalians. Disestablishment had taken the revenues of the church in the colonies where it had been established; evangelical denominations had drawn away its poorer members; Deism had disaffected its male gentry; and death had taken many who remained faithful. In a nation of four million, the Episcopal Church had perhaps ten thousand adherents. The new nation was overwhelmingly rural, but the church's remaining strength lay in urban areas. Although the church's leadership now centered on the episcopate, New Jersey lacked a bishop until 1815, North Carolina had no bishop until 1823, Georgia was in want of one until 1841, and Massachusetts possessed one only for six of the twenty-two years between 1789 and 1811. Attendance at General Conventions was so sparse that the House of Bishops held its meetings in a small bedroom in 1808. Convinced that the Anglican tradition would die out with the old colonial families, Samuel Provoost, first bishop of New York, became so discouraged that he resigned his office.

And so the story returns to where it started — to the president's house of the College of William and Mary and to a dilapidated Bruton Parish Church in Williamsburg, Virginia, on February 14, 1811. In the bishop's own city, at the regular time of worship on a Sunday, only eighteen persons could be gathered to witness an ordination. The students of William and Mary, formerly the chief supply of vestry and clergy for the Church of England in Virginia, passed the old church by. The ordination of young William Meade was the last ordination performed by Bishop Madison, and probably no one who witnessed that simple service realized its significance. With its land sold, its churches abandoned or deserted, its few remaining laity and clergy in despair, and many observers regarding it as extinct, the Episcopal Church in Virginia — as well as in the nation — needed revivalists in the truest sense of the word. In William Meade and others of his generation, it got them. And because of these new leaders and a combination of other circumstances, the former established church began to rise again.

But that's another story.

3

THE GROWTH OF THE
EPISCOPAL CHURCH

Largely because of the legacy of the war for independence from England, the former Church of England in the United States grew slowly in the twenty years after 1789. When the General Convention printed the first list of Episcopal clergy in 1792, the enumeration came out as follows:

Massachusetts	no list received
New Hampshire	no list received
Rhode Island	2
Connecticut	22
New York	19
New Jersey	9
Pennsylvania	14
Delaware	3
Maryland	34
Virginia	61
South Carolina	15

Even these numbers may have been inflated, since some of the names were those of superannuated priests ordained during the colonial period. The General Convention apparently lacked contacts in the states of Georgia and North Carolina, where the Anglican tradition had almost died out. Unorganized until 1817, the Diocese of North Carolina did not secure a bishop until 1823. Georgia, which had only one active Episcopal parish in 1790, remained unorganized as a diocese until 1823 and lacked a bishop until 1841. Maine had no Episcopal clergy from 1809 to 1817.

The turn of the nineteenth century saw bishops in seven states. Episcopal work had been organized in five additional states. Everywhere else in the United States, however, the Episcopal Church was either unorganized or in danger of extinction. To be sure, the social and economic class and level of influence of the small number of Episcopalians were generally high. "Born in affluence," a eulogist declared of a communicant of St. Mary's Church in Burlington, New Jersey,

> the best blood in New Jersey, on both sides, mingled in her veins; always abounding in what the world calls wealth; her father, the President of the Congress of the United States; herself admitted, as freely as any ever was to that house of all houses, the mansion of General Washington, a cherished inmate of his family; her husband, to whom she was most happily married, General Washington's Attorney General. . . . [33]

But fewer than one in four hundred citizens of the new nation were Episcopal communicants. Fears of "prelacy" hampered the work of the bishops, and many members of other denominations hoped that the aristocratic and now orphaned Anglican tradition would die out in the United States.

THE REVIVAL OF THE EPISCOPAL CHURCH

Assessments vary about whether the first twenty years of the church's united existence represent a period of suspended animation or of quiet revival. But the years around 1811 are generally considered a turning point in the church's history. After 1811 the church revived in the wake of, and sometimes in reaction to, the so-called Second Great Awakening — the series of religious revivals and awakenings that swept back and forth across the new nation for several generations in the nineteenth century. In 1811, John Henry Hobart was consecrated as assistant bishop of New York and Alexander Viets Griswold as bishop of the Eastern Diocese. The year also witnessed the ordination of two future leaders in the denomination, William Meade and Jackson Kemper. During the next year, William Holland Wilmer began his work in Virginia, where in 1815 he published the first edition of *The Episcopal Manual.*

Vigorous, contentious, and efficient, John Henry Hobart was in charge of his 45,000-square-mile diocese from the time of his consecration as assistant bishop, since the elderly bishop of New York, Benjamin Moore, was partially paralyzed. A high churchman in the tradition of Lancelot Andrewes, William Laud, and other divines who flourished during the reigns of Charles I and II, Hobart believed the episcopate, the priesthood, the sacraments, and the visible church to be the appointed channels for God's grace. Although not a ceremonialist like the later ritualists (discussed in chapter 4), he stressed the importance of apostolic succession and emphasized the distinctiveness and superiority of the Episcopal Church — "*the* church" — over other denominations. Married to the daughter of an SPG high churchman who was a leading advocate of a colonial episcopate, Hobart continued that tradition in the early nineteenth century.

Hobart's watchword was "evangelical faith and apostolic order." Under his aggressive nineteen-year leadership, the Episcopal Church in New York expanded from 25 clergy, 40 churches, and 2,300 communicants to 133 clergy, 165 congregations, and 6,700 communicants. His influence extended far beyond the confines of his diocese and life, which ended prematurely in 1830. His legacy was continued during the nineteenth century in the church party variously called "Hobartian churchmen," "old-fashioned high churchmen," and "evangelical high churchmen."

Alexander Viets Griswold and William Meade were both evangelicals. A man of plainer cloth than most of his contemporaries in the episcopate, Griswold increased the number of parishes in his Eastern Diocese (a temporary one that brought together all of the New England dioceses except Connecticut) fivefold by the time of his death in 1843. Like Hobart, he confirmed over one thousand persons on an early tour of his diocese.

Ordained during the period when the General Convention feared for the future of the Episcopal Church of Virginia, the ascetic, single-minded Meade quickly attracted fellow evangelicals to Virginia. In 1814 Richard Channing Moore, an evangelical who was then preaching to crowded congregations in New York City, was consecrated as bishop of Virginia. Using such evangelical methods as circuit riding, preaching that aimed at conversion, and strict discipline, Moore and his clergy revived the Anglican tradition in Virginia. By 1835, Virginia was the fourth-largest diocese in the Episcopal Church in communicant membership. Elected assistant bishop of Virginia in 1829, Meade succeeded Moore as bishop in 1841.

KEMPER AND DOMESTIC MISSIONS

Jackson Kemper's ministry is tied up with the organization called the Domestic and Foreign Missionary Society, which in turn is tied up with the story of Episcopal expansion in areas west of the Alleghenies and north of the Ohio River. As early as 1792, the General Convention considered a proposal to send Episcopal missionaries to the frontiers of the United

Maryland rector John P. K. Henshaw (1792–1852), later Bishop of Rhode Island, is depicted in the garb favored by early evangelical clergy.

States. From 1796 on, the individual dioceses formed missionary societies. Though the General Convention had asked them to send missionaries west, the societies, with very few exceptions, limited their work to the boundaries of their own states.

Thus when Episcopal clergy went into western areas prior to 1835, they went either as freelancers or in response to a call from a group of lay-people. The General Convention would consecrate bishops for developing areas of the United States only when the Episcopalians who lived there voluntarily formed dioceses and elected a bishop. Not until 1821 — a year in which Indiana, Illinois, Tennessee, Mississippi, Louisiana, Missouri, Michigan, and Arkansas combined had more than half a million residents but only two Episcopal clergy — did the General Convention form the Domestic and Foreign Missionary Society. The voluntary character of this society — members paid annual dues to renew their membership — and its discouraging lack of results soon forced the church to find another strategy.

In 1835, using the New Testament for its model, the General Convention decided that missions should not be a subsidiary committee but rather a responsibility of the entire church. A tacit agreement gave the responsibility for foreign missions to the evangelicals and assigned missions in the new areas of America to the high church party. This agreement was almost immediately regretted by the evangelicals, who subsequently formed their own domestic missionary society. "What a mistake! What a blunder," a young leader of the evangelical party reportedly declared when he learned of the decision.[34]

Changing missions into a church-wide responsibility was the first innovation of 1835. A second was the General Convention's decision to create missionary districts in those new areas of America and to send missionary bishops to them even before any Episcopal work had been started. The model for the new plan was that of the New Testament apostle.

A forty-five-year-old graduate of Columbia and a high churchman, Kemper was the first missionary bishop sent west. That the nineteenth century was more than one-third over before he was sent illustrates the first of four reasons the Episcopal Church lagged behind other denominations in western membership. When Kemper and other bishops made the first tours of their missionary districts, they found that the Baptists, Methodists, and Presbyterians (the Roman Catholics were still a relatively minor presence in the west) had already established churches. These early arrivals had swallowed up the churchgoing population among the settlers, including many of Episcopal background.

Dioceses of unmanageable size represented the second reason. Even when the General Convention divided the west and new south into missionary districts, it generally made them too large for any one bishop to supervise efficiently. Kemper had responsibility for the areas that are now Indiana, Wisconsin, Minnesota, Iowa, Missouri, Kansas, and Nebraska. The missionary district of Joseph C. Talbot (consecrated in 1860 as missionary bishop of the Northwest) covered one million square miles; Talbot described himself as "the bishop of all outdoors." Salt Lake City was the seat of Bishop Daniel S. Tuttle (consecrated 1867), but he carried the title of "Bishop of Montana, with Jurisdiction in Idaho and Utah."

All of this undercut the church's growth on the frontier, for Americans in the nineteenth century traveled by foot, horse, stage, or train. "I have never realized, as on this visit, the value and importance of a missionary episcopate," the first bishop of Kansas wrote after an initial tour of his infant diocese in 1865:

> A congregation, upon the frontier, few in number and of limited pecuniary resources, far away from the centers of Church sympathy and influence, not informed as to the method of procuring ministerial supplies, not acquainted with the clergy, and not knowing to whom to apply for assistance, is dependent, in a degree utterly beyond the comprehension of persons . . . [from] old and populous Dioceses, upon the supervision and aid of the Episcopate.[35]

Yet the policy of the Episcopal Church forced its missionary bishops to spend more time traveling than they did preaching, encouraging scattered and often dispirited clergy and congregations, or establishing new Episcopal churches.

A third hindrance for the missionary bishops stemmed from a lack of financial support. Missionaries required salaries; congregations required buildings. But the Episcopal Church could fund its missionaries only to the extent that its parishes were willing to contribute to their support. And its parishes had relatively little interest in what was happening in the churches of the new south and west. As late as 1862, fewer than half of the parishes of the Episcopal Church contributed to the Domestic and Foreign Missionary Society. The average contribution for missions per Episcopal communicant approximated one dollar a year. Thus in 1876 the church could find only $4,000 to spend on missionary work in Kansas, a state in which approximately 400,000 people lived. That amount was one-seventh of what the Presbyterians spent in Kansas during the same year, one-eighth of what the Congregationalists spent, and one-fifteenth of the Methodist expenditure. From the start of his episcopate, the tireless Kemper lamented what he could not accomplish simply because of lack of funds.

Finally, a shortage of missionaries continually handicapped Episcopal missionary work. After the first tour of his district, Kemper reported that he could immediately employ one hundred clergy; seven years later, he had been able to secure only thirty-one. By 1840 the Baptists had almost as many clergy at work in Missouri as the Episcopal Church had in all states and territories west of the Alleghenies combined.

The shortage of clergy stemmed from more than lack of funding. Most Episcopal clergy came from reasonably comfortable backgrounds; the frontier mission field held relatively little appeal. Missionaries who went west could anticipate low salaries, isolation, danger, substantially lowered lifestyles, and unremitting work. One writer suggested that Americans should compare the czar's practice of exiling political offenders to Siberia with the sending of cultivated people to North Dakota;[36] in such an atmosphere, the Episcopal missions in that state did not seem a beckoning land. In memorable but rather archaic wording, Bishop Alexander Garrett of North Texas said that he needed clergy who could "ride like a cow-boy, pray like a saint, preach like an apostle, and having food and raiment be therewith content."[37]

The denominations that had the most success in evangelizing the new south and west — the Baptists and Methodists — had such ministers. Episcopal seminaries undoubtedly produced men who could fit Bishop Garrett's description, but these seminarians tended to have so many other excellent qualities that they were snatched up by established urban parishes before the end of their senior year. The overriding problem — one that is difficult to comprehend from the perspective of the late twentieth century, when the number of Episcopalians who wish to be ordained far exceeds the number of positions (although not necessarily remote missionary positions) available for them — was that the Episcopal Church lacked an adequate supply of clergy even to staff adequately the congregations that already existed. From the colonial period on, Episcopal congregations had outnumbered Episcopal clergy.

That the church faced other obstacles not of its own making in the new areas cannot be denied. Though Episcopal missionaries attempted to appeal to all settlers, the churches they established generally attracted the more prosperous and educated people. In the deep south, for example, the Episcopal Church largely became the church of the wealthier planters, despite the earlier work of clergy such as Devereux Jarratt and Charles

Woodmason with poor whites. Throughout the new territories and states the result was that people of lower economic and educational levels felt out of place. Protestants accustomed to emotional sermons and to extemporaneous worship often found Anglicanism too formal and too worldly. On New Testament grounds, Baptist farmer-preachers, Methodist circuit riders, and Disciples of Christ elders criticized the social behavior and manner of living of Episcopalians.

Yet what some persons considered handicaps, others saw as attractions. In the nineteenth century, Americans were moving west at the precise time that the revolt from Calvinist orthodoxy was accelerating. The intellectuality, sensibility, and Arminian (or free will) theology of the Episcopal Church inevitably appealed to many settlers of Congregationalist, Presbyterian, or Reformed backgrounds who had broken with the Calvinist doctrine of predestination. Many of the greatest Episcopal leaders in the nineteenth century were reared in Calvinist denominations.

The dignity and beauty of Episcopal worship and the church's episcopal polity and claims of antiquity also attracted many Americans, especially in an era of romanticism, when writers such as Sir Walter Scott evoked the mystique of the Middle Ages. In frontier areas social respectability could also prove an advantage, for Episcopal churches provided a sense of civilization and a means of escaping the crudities of daily life. When an Episcopal church was established, many western towns believed they had "arrived."

To a lesser degree, the church also benefited during the period of western settlement from the reaction against emotionalism in the Methodist and other denominations, from the decline of Quakerism, and from the resistance to German-language services in Lutheranism. In areas of the south and west where they found no churches of their own, Roman Catholics often opted for the Episcopal Church. Christians seeking to escape narrower backgrounds also responded to the Episcopal Church's toleration of alcohol, dancing, Masonic membership, and many shades of theological opinion. Even the observance by Episcopalians of Yuletide traditions and Christmas services — rare among Protestant denominations of English origin until after the Civil War — served as an attraction.

To form a congregation in new areas, Episcopal missionaries combed the countryside for people who had been brought up as Episcopalians or who were thought to be friendly to the Episcopal Church. Often they would preach in a new community and begin a congregation with those who responded favorably. Occasionally Episcopalians in new settlements would take the initiative and ask for a clergyman. Until churches were built, the missionaries used homes, courthouses, schools, stores, and the churches of other denominations as places for Episcopal services.

To found and establish parishes, missionaries distributed Bibles, Episcopal tracts, devotional works, and Books of Common Prayer. Some missionaries established parish libraries and reading rooms. Primary schools, secondary schools, and Sunday schools, which initially taught children not only religious education but also reading and writing, proved an important means of nurturing youth in Episcopal teaching. Most bishops also established hospitals. The majority of the colleges and theological seminaries started by the bishops in the new areas ultimately failed, but Kenyon College (founded by Bishop Philander Chase in Gambier, Ohio) and its theological seminary, Bexley Hall, stood as examples of what most western bishops hoped to do.

Methods of evangelization used by Episcopal missionaries included itinerancy, in which one missionary served a number of preaching stations and parishes. In North Dakota, Bishop William D. Walker fitted a sixty-foot Pullman railroad car as a traveling chapel with eighty seats and took services to remote settlements. Placards in the railroad stations of small villages would announce the date and time of Walker's arrival, and the number of residents who attended when the "Cathedral Car" arrived was sometimes double the size of the village.

In rural areas of the south, "associations," in which a number of clergy converged on a town and held several services a day for several days in a row, built up parishes. In the later years of the nineteenth century, "parish missions" in city churches featured a noted Episcopal preacher who held intensive public meetings for up to two weeks. Widely publicized in frontier areas, visitations by bishops provided a major opportunity not only for encouragement of a congregation but also for evangelization of the unchurched. Often all of the residents of a frontier town would turn out to see and to hear "the bishop."

Relatively few settlers of the new south and the west seem to have come from Anglican backgrounds. But since the majority of settlers for much of the nineteenth century came from British or German stock, the Episcopal Church should not have found the west and new south alien ground. Historically, it could claim to be the mother church of all British Protestants; liturgically, it was similar to Lutheranism. That it failed to become a major presence in most parts of the deep south and the west stemmed largely, as missionary bishop after missionary bishop lamented, from its slowness to seize opportunities.

The effects have been long-lasting. On the eve of World War II, the ratio of communicants to population in the Diocese of Virginia was one to thirty-four; in the post-Revolutionary state of Alabama, it was one to two hundred forty-three. In 1990, approximately 120,000 baptized Episcopalians lived in Massachusetts. To reach the same number in the west, one must combine all of the baptized Episcopalians in the states of Iowa, Missouri, Kansas, Oklahoma, Arkansas, and Mississippi. In the far west, Episcopal membership is higher in ratio to population, for the church's missionary organization was largely in place by the time those states began to receive significant numbers of settlers. But the Episcopal Church is nevertheless often invisible. "Out in the West," an Episcopal priest noted in 1991, "you are lucky to find an Episcopal Church every fifth town."[38]

Simple theology, emotional religion, clergy who spoke the language of the people, and a regularly present church staff — these were the ingredients of success in the west and new south. The Episcopal Church unquestionably could have established a stronger presence in the new areas of the United States. That its missions policy kept it from doing so saddened and angered Episcopal missionaries well into the twentieth century. In 1887 the noted rector and preacher Phillips Brooks lamented to a missionary leader that the Episcopal Church

is fast on the way to becom[ing] a small, fantastic sect, aping foreign ways, and getting more and more out of sympathy with the great life of the country.... Look at the West and see what our Church means there. Where are the dioceses that you strove to build a quarter of a century ago? Well, well, the work will be done by somebody, even if our Church refuses to do it. But what a chance we had![39]

Yet twentieth-century readers would be wise not to be overly critical of the Episcopal Church's failure in the new south and west. The Congregationalists and the Presbyterians — the two denominations closest to Episcopalians in social and economic level — also found these new territories and states uncongenial. Like the Episcopalians, they opposed revivalism and emotionalism in worship. Like the Episcopalians, they also preferred the non-itinerant, college-educated pastor who presented the Christian message quietly and logically Sunday after Sunday. To be sure, the Presbyterians had more success than the Episcopalians in the new areas of the United States, but the Congregationalists lagged far behind. Although it is as clear to historians today as it was to Jackson Kemper one hundred fifty years ago that the Episcopal Church missed a major opportunity in the frontier areas, it is equally clear that it faced some inherent difficulties.

Denominational statistics belong in the category of the inexact sciences, but the most widely accepted figures place the Episcopal Church next to last among the mainline churches (ahead only of the Congregationalists) in the growth of congregations in the period between the Revolution and the Civil War. The precise number of parishes that survived the Revolution is unknown. Although the reports of bishops or dioceses to the early General Conventions are frequently incomplete or unclear, the lists of clergy submitted to the 1792 General Convention indicate that the number of active Episcopal parishes approximated one hundred eighty. By 1820 the diocesan reports mention approximately four hundred congregations. Especially in the case of the 1792 reports, readers should be forewarned that some of these congregations contained only a handful of worshipers and that others existed only on paper.

The figures become more and more precise as the nineteenth century advances. On the eve of the Civil War — at a time when perhaps thirty-four percent of Americans maintained a regular relationship with a church or synagogue — the General Convention of 1859 reported 2,120 parishes. By 1886 the General Convention reported 71 bishops, 3,689 other clergy, 344 candidates for ordination, 1,203 lay readers, 4,338 church and chapel buildings, 2,072 mission stations, and more than 422,000 communicants. Although church membership was steadily rising in the United States, more than half of the population still remained outside of the churches.[40]

THE THEOLOGY
OF WILLIAM H. WILMER

In the field of theology, the Episcopal Church has produced at least five theologians in its four hundred years of history whose achievements merit discussion in a history. William H. Wilmer has a claim to being its first theologian following independence from the Church of England. Although a distinctly minor figure today, he was viewed as a significant thinker and leader by many of his nineteenth-century contemporaries.

A native of Maryland, educated at Washington College and ordained in 1808, Wilmer came to Virginia from Maryland in 1812 to assist in the resuscitation of the Episcopal Church. Subsequently he was one of the founders and original faculty members of the Protestant Episcopal Theological Seminary in Alexandria, Virginia. For much of the nineteenth century, his *The Episcopal Manual: or an Attempt to Explain and Vindicate the Doctrine, Discipline and Worship of the Protestant Episcopal Church...* (published in 1815 and in subsequent editions) provided a basis for the

Episcopal evangelical understanding of Christianity. Using as its sources Holy Scripture, the Thirty-Nine Articles, the Book of Common Prayer, the catechisms and writings of certain sixteenth-century Anglican theologians, and the Books of Homilies of the Church of England, it professed "to take a middle course" between the Protestant denominations to the left of the Episcopal Church and the "zeal . . . for externals" of high church Episcopalians.

The moderation of Wilmer's evangelicalism is displayed when he comes to the subjects of John Calvin (a figure whom some evangelicals revered) and episcopacy (an office that some evangelicals viewed as non-essential). In *The Episcopal Manual* Wilmer finds the Geneva reformer a "genuine scripturalist" who "deserves . . . veneration as an able asserter of the doctrines of grace." But he also judges that Calvin "ran to excess upon the subject of the divine decrees and . . . seemed to destroy the free agency of man and . . . the foundations of virtue."[41] Where some of Wilmer's fellow evangelicals believed that bishops were originally identical to presbyters, Wilmer finds "three orders of ministers in the primitive church, Apostles afterwards called Bishops, Presbyters and Deacons."[42]

In chapters ranging from "Original Sin" to "the Lord's Supper," with sections on such subjects as "Family and Public Devotion," Wilmer enunciates the doctrines he and others taught throughout most of the nineteenth century at Virginia Theological Seminary. A compilation, a catechetical handbook, a devotional manual, and a focused exposition of the evangelical interpretation of Anglicanism, *The Episcopal Manual,* however thin, has a claim to the title of the first theology of the Episcopal Church. "It will not soon be superseded in general estimation by any similar publication," an editor declared in his preface to its 1841 edition, fifteen years after Wilmer's death. Although the *Manual* knows nothing of the difficulties to Christian belief that emerged later in the nineteenth century and seems slender and unremarkable to twentieth-century readers, the evaluation an observer gave to Wilmer's sermons also applied to it at the time of its publication: "well matured evangelical thought."[43]

MISSIONS TO NATIVE AMERICANS

As in other denominations, the history of the Episcopal Church's work with Native Americans is a record of the efforts of a small number of committed and idealistic individuals. Although the Church of England was the only established church in the southern colonies, the few clergy (such as Francis Le Jau of South Carolina) who attempted to evangelize

Native Americans confronted a variety of obstacles. The language barrier, the occasional wars, the strangeness of each other's customs, the boredom caused by Anglican catechetical methods — all combined to hinder the work of Anglican missionaries. Above all, the Native Americans saw nothing in the lifestyles of the settlers that attracted them to Christianity. As parish clergy of the established church whose primary responsibility was to white residents, the clergy lacked the time and freedom to work with Native Americans. The principal attempt to Christianize Native Americans in the south — the Indian school founded at the College of William and Mary — was unsuccessful and closed during the Revolution.

In the north, the fear of Native American allegiance to the French and the impulse to "convert the heathen" combined to encourage the SPG to evangelize tribes of the Iroquois nations, especially the Mohawk. The SPG provided missionaries, chapels, and Mohawk versions of several books of the Bible and the Book of Common Prayer. Following the Revolutionary War, the Episcopal Church continued this work in New York under Bishop Hobart — a popular figure among Native Americans — by establishing a mission to the Oneidas. Under the leadership of Eleazar Williams, a missionary of mixed Native American and white parentage, many Native Americans moved from New York to Green Bay, Wisconsin, in the 1820s, where the church founded another mission.

While the Green Bay mission prospered, the apostolic James L. Breck established an additional Episcopal mission to the Chippewas in Minnesota in the 1850s. Consecrated first bishop of Minnesota on the eve of the Civil War, Henry B. Whipple immediately interested himself in the condition of the twenty thousand Native Americans who lived in his diocese. Well-connected and influential in the reform of the United States government's policy toward the Native Americans, Whipple was chair of the government commission that met with the Sioux after the massacre of General George A. Custer's military force. He wrote the preface to Helen Hunt Jackson's *A Century of Dishonor* (1881), a classic account of unjust policies toward Native Americans. To be more useful on the reservations he carried simple medicines and learned to pull teeth. One of his first ordinations was that of Samuel D. Hinman, who began a lifelong and unsung mission to the Sioux and translated the Book of Common Prayer into Dakota.

The great surge of Episcopal missionary work to Native Americans began in the 1870s. In response to pleas from Whipple and William Welsh (an Episcopalian from Philadelphia who headed the congressional Board of Indian Commissioners), the church formed the Indian Commission under its board of missions. The commission chose William Hobart Hare

The "Oneida Indian Band" in front of the Church of the Holy Apostles in Oneida, Wisconsin, ca. 1923.

(grandson of John Henry Hobart) to be the bishop of Niobrara, a missionary district that encompassed the western half, and subsequently all, of present-day South Dakota.

Although whites lived in the area, Hare's primary responsibility was to Christianize the Native Americans of the Great Plains. "The Apostle to the Sioux" built upon the work of Hinman and became the leading figure in the church's work among Native Americans. After more than thirty years of camping on the plains and crossing South Dakota by wagon, Hare had confirmed over seven thousand Native Americans. By 1909, the year of his death, ten thousand of the estimated twenty thousand Native Americans of South Dakota were baptized members of the Episcopal Church. To this day, the Diocese of South Dakota claims a sizable Native American membership.[44]

The first Native American to become a bishop, Harold S. Jones, was the suffragan (assistant) bishop of South Dakota from 1971 to 1976. As of 1992 three other Native Americans have been elected to the episcopate. William C. Wantland, a Seminole, was consecrated bishop of Eau Claire in

1980. Steven T. Plummer, who had earlier been the church's first Navajo priest, became bishop of the new diocese of the Navajoland in 1990. In 1991 Steven Charleston, a Choctaw, was consecrated bishop of Alaska.

Work among Native Americans attracted many Episcopal women. Usually serving as nurses or as teachers and principals in Native American schools, women worked among the Shoshoni and Arapaho in Wyoming, the Chippewa and Sioux in Minnesota, the Cheyenne in Oklahoma, and tribes in other states and territories. Episcopal women's missionary societies — either associated with one parish or emerging from several neighboring parishes — added financial support. After visiting the Santee Indian mission in Nebraska in 1869, a prominent layman complained that the all-male board of missions in New York City "so far had not given a dollar, that the work had been done entirely by Auxiliary societies of women."[45] When the Woman's Auxiliary to the Board of Missions was founded in 1871, most of these societies joined it.

The last great expansion in missionary work came among Native American Eskimos and white settlers in Alaska after the turn of the century. Its central figure was Peter Trimble Rowe, first bishop of Alaska. A man of immense stamina who covered vast distances by boat, dog sled, and eventually airplane, Rowe established missions, schools, and hospitals across Alaska. Assisted by the courageous archdeacon Hudson Stuck, he served as the church's northernmost bishop for forty-seven years. By the time Rowe died in 1942, he had aroused the interest of Episcopalians across the nation in the church's work in Alaska. More recently, the church has created a mission and a bishopric among the Navajos of New Mexico, Arizona, and Utah.

Among the many obstacles confronting Episcopal missions to Native Americans were the staggering number of dialects, the shortage of missionaries, the scattered settlements, and the migrations forced upon Native Americans by the U.S. government. The church not only established many schools to educate Native American youth, but also trained Native Americans to become clergy among their own people. Today clergy rolls in the Diocese of South Dakota continue to include such names as Two Bulls, Broken Leg, Two Hawk, and Bear's Heart.

FOREIGN MISSIONS

The first Episcopal missionary sent overseas by the Domestic and Foreign Missionary Society went to Greece in 1828. Because of the agreement between the two church parties to divide the responsibility for missions,

Hudson Stuck (1863–1920), the devoted Archdeacon of Alaska, on the trail.

most of the early missionaries and staff for the overseas missions were evangelicals. Before the Civil War, the society had established missions in Turkey, Liberia, China, and Japan, all of which received American bishops. Among the colleges established by the church were St. John's College, Shanghai, and St. Paul's College, Tokyo.

By the turn of the century, missions had been founded in Haiti, Mexico, Puerto Rico, and the Philippines. The black nationalist leader James T. Holly served as the first bishop of the Haitian church. The first bishop to take up residence in Manila was the influential Charles Henry Brent, later to become a leader in the international movement for church unity.

Women in the church supported foreign missions by financial contributions, by distributing supplies and educational materials, and, finally, by serving as missionaries themselves. Working both individually and in communities (see the discussion of sisterhoods in chapter 6), women gained recognition of their work by the missionary bishops, if not by the larger church. "I should regard a sisterhood as one of the most valuable additions to the work that can possibly be made," said Bishop Joseph Schereschewsky of his work in China in the late 1800s.[46] In a list of the one hundred ninety Episcopal missionaries serving China from 1835 to 1907, ninety-five (or fifty per cent) are women. Thirty-two of the ninety-five listed were wives of missionaries, appropriately included for their valuable (if often unpaid) contributions to the mission effort; five women on the list were physicians. The contribution of women to the foreign missions of the church deserves more study than it has received. Current research suggests that Episcopal women serving overseas were often the first in the church to encourage the training and education of native women. Partially as a result of that emphasis, many of the missionary women and the native women they trained stated in 1924 that they participated more fully in church government than did their women counterparts in the Episcopal Church in the United States.[47]

Today, the Episcopal Church is represented throughout Central and South America and the Caribbean; it has also extended its missionary work to Taiwan. Several of the missions have developed into independent national churches — a development encouraged by the General Convention. The church operates theological seminaries in Mexico City and the Philippines, and supports colleges in Liberia and the Philippines. From the nineteenth century on, the Episcopal Church has established self-supporting parishes for American residents and travelers in the major cities of Europe, with a bishop in place since 1971. In 1990 the total number of baptized Episcopalians reported by overseas dioceses exceeded 200,000.

THE WOMAN'S AUXILIARY

Women "require to be under the direction of wise *men*," wrote the English bishop of Salisbury in 1871 in response to an inquiry concerning how women could best work in the church.[48] The inquiry came from a committee of the Episcopal Church's board of missions charged to submit a plan for "engrafting upon the present missionary agencies of the Church, the organized, as well as the individual work of women."[49] Although the committee eventually proposed a women's organization that would have the power to engage in its own projects, to control funds, and to appoint some of its members to the mission committees of the church, the all-male board of missions followed more nearly the advice of the bishop of Salisbury.

After receiving authority from the 1871 General Convention, the board appointed Mary Abbot Emery as national secretary and commissioned her to set up a woman's auxiliary under the supervision of the board of missions. Although women oversaw the auxiliary's day-to-day operations, they had no voice on the board of missions and therefore exercised neither full financial nor administrative control over their group.

The auxiliary (the first nationwide women's organization in the Episcopal Church) provided financial and other support for the missionary work of the church. It also attempted to recruit Episcopal women for the mission fields. Mary Emery and three of her sisters shaped the infant organization. Mary served as its first national secretary, resigning upon her marriage to the Secretary of Domestic Missions, A. T. Twing, but continuing to contribute vitally as a volunteer. Succeeding Mary in 1876, Julia Chester Emery held the position of national secretary for forty years. Susan Lavinia Emery served on the national missions staff as editor of a children's publication on missions. Through World War I, Margaret Theresa Emery coordinated the "box work" — so called because of the boxes used to ship clothing, medical supplies, books, and other items requested by missionaries. The national secretaryship held by Mary and Julia Emery represented the highest position then open to women in the Episcopal Church.

The major task confronted by Mary Emery — one that she accomplished in just two years — was to unite the scattered Episcopal women's groups into an effective national organization. Prior to 1872, many different women's groups (including missionary and tract societies) had existed in various parishes. Under the leadership of the Emerys, the auxiliary not only grew in importance after 1872 but also provided a needed boost to the church's funding of its missions. As the auxiliary's financial punch increased, however, so did tensions with the male board of missions. The tensions occurred particularly over what were known in missions circles as "specials" (funds contributed by local auxiliaries and designated by them for special missionary bishops). "I know that 'specials' are a little out of favor," an Episcopal woman wrote to Bishop Rowe along with her contribution, "but being a spinster of seventy-nine I claim the right to do as I please after having paid toll to the Board."[50]

Increasingly concerned with control over their collected funds, the woman's auxiliary established the United Thank Offering in 1889. A voluntary gift presented at the triennial conventions of the church, the offering was intended to supplement rather than to replace the auxiliary's financial support of the board of missions. In exchange for the freedom given by the board of missions to use the United Thank Offering as they wished, in 1901 the auxiliary agreed to pledge $100,000 annually to the regular budget of the board.

After the pivotal year of 1901, Episcopal women began to respond dramatically to this new offering. From $21,000 in 1892, the United Thank Offering grew to $243,000 in 1910 and then to $669,000 in 1922.

By 1904 — and in most succeeding years — the woman's auxiliary used the entire sum to train and pay women workers in the church. By 1934, the United Thank Offering funded over fifty percent of women mission workers in the church. By its hundredth anniversary year of 1989, it had raised $75 million for the mission and outreach of the church.

Thus the auxiliary both provided the means and accomplished the ends of bringing women into the ranks of the Episcopal Church's full-time, paid staff. To be sure, the church did not treat these women workers equally. Women staff members generally received meager pay. They could not become ordained members of the clergy, and they could not enter the central administrative apparatus of the Episcopal Church. Even when they were finally granted seats on the board of missions in 1934, they were allocated only four of the thirty-two places — a subordinate arrangement that persisted for decades. But the auxiliary's financial support enabled new possibilities of service for Episcopal churchwomen.

AFRICAN AMERICAN EPISCOPALIANS

Since slavery was centered in the south, where the Church of England was the established church during the colonial period, Anglicanism had a head start in the evangelization of African Americans. The first incorporation of African slaves into the Church of England in America apparently occurred at Jamestown in 1623, when a couple named Isabelle and Anthony and their son, William, were baptized. Feeling little religious responsibility toward their slaves, however, Anglican planters throughout the seventeenth century resisted the efforts of clergy such as Morgan Godwyn of Virginia to evangelize African Americans.

The opposition was based not only upon a belief in the inferiority of black-skinned people but also upon the fear that baptism meant eventual manumission — a fear so prevalent that four colonial legislatures in the south passed official acts disclaiming it. For many slaveowners it was easier to believe that slaves were too barbarous and shallow a part of creation to become Christians. Since Christianity in all centuries has displayed the ability to infuse humble people with a sense of individual potential — to "empower" them, in the idiom of the late twentieth century — it was not surprising that slaveowners also noted (and complained) that slaves who had become Christian often became "uppity."

From its founding in 1701 until the American Revolution, the SPG devoted part of its ministry to the religious instruction of slaves. Elias Neau, a layman employed as a catechist by the SPG, operated a school for slaves in his home in New York City from 1704 until the early 1720s. In the south, as the eighteenth century progressed, the number of planters who allowed their slaves to be baptized increased. Most slaves, however, still remained outside of Christianity at the time of the Revolution.

In the American colonies, as in England, Anglicanism upheld the structures of society and taught respect for authority; that had been one of the crucial differences in England between Anglicanism and the republican ideas of Puritanism. The doctrine of absolute slave obedience that became the dominant ethic for southern slaveowners (and that influenced later race relations in the United States) owes some of its popularity to southern Anglican clergy. In colonial Maryland, Thomas Bacon expressed precisely that view; the sermons he delivered on the responsibilities of slaveowners and slaves were reprinted a century later for use in antebellum Episcopal missions to slaves. In colonial South Carolina, Francis Le Jau found it expedient to require slaves to swear prior to baptism "that you do not ask for the holy baptism out of any design to free your self from the Duty and Obedience you owe to your Master while you live."[51] That Anglicanism upheld the rights of the slaveowners instead of the rights of the slaves was not surprising. As Moses Finley has noted, most religious systems from ancient to modern times have supported slavery.[52]

The surge of work with African Americans came after 1800 during what historians have called the Second Great Awakening. In the antebellum south, Episcopal evangelicals developed an active, paternalistic ministry to slaves. Institutions employed in missionary work among southern African Americans included Sunday schools, catechetical schools, and plantation chapels. Household servants of Episcopal families often attended white churches, sitting in slave galleries or in special sections in the back or sides. In town churches, Episcopal parishes occasionally formed African American congregations led by white clergy and supervised by white laity. Whether in urban or rural Episcopal churches, preaching remained "a wholly white phenomenon. Blacks listened."[53]

The total number of African American Episcopalians in the antebellum south approximated only 35,000. Missionary work was most successful in South Carolina, where an estimated fourteen thousand African Americans were Episcopalians at the time of the Civil War. In the north, beginning in 1794 with St. Thomas African Episcopal Church, Philadelphia, a small number of Episcopal churches were formed among free African Americans. The pastor of St. Thomas, Absalom Jones, was the first of some twenty-five African Americans ordained to the Episcopal ministry by northern bishops or the bishop of Liberia by 1865.

Relatively few African Americans became Episcopalians in the nineteenth century. They joined Baptist and Methodist churches in far greater numbers. Despite its head start over other denominations, the Episcopal Church failed to evangelize African Americans for many reasons. The church was slow in establishing a presence in the Cotton Belt, for example, where the majority of African Americans eventually lived. The British model of ordaining only educated men and worshiping according to a formal, written liturgy kept the Episcopal Church from adapting to the religious needs and emotional expressions of the slaves. Finally, a church identified with the gentry lacked a natural link with the lower classes. In more recent years, African Americans have tended to become Episcopalians as they have moved into the professional classes. The first two African American justices of the Supreme Court, for example, both attended Episcopal churches.

Slavery and the Civil War

Unlike other denominations, the Episcopal Church did not formally divide over the issue of slavery. Abhorring schism above all else, and realizing that resolutions on slavery would inevitably bring disputes, the church avoided an official stand on human bondage. Anglican habits of compromise were partially responsible for this neutrality, as was economic self-interest for some Episcopalians. In keeping with their emphasis on personal religion, many evangelical and high church Episcopalians also felt that slavery was a purely political issue and therefore outside the sacred concerns of the church. In addition, those Episcopalians who knew southern planters from college or from summer resorts seem to have been repelled by the characterization of slaveowners given in abolitionist publications.

As individuals, however, a number of Episcopal laity and clergy became involved in the controversies over slavery. In the south, Episcopalians who published defenses of slavery included George Washington Freeman, bishop of Arkansas, and Thomas Roderick Dew, president of the College of William and Mary. Three northern clergy — Samuel Seabury (grandson of the bishop), N. S. Wheaton, and Bishop John Henry Hopkins of Vermont — published similar defenses based on biblical literalism and political conservatism.

In the north, Episcopal laymen William Jay and John Jay (son and grandson of Revolutionary statesman John Jay) were active abolitionists. Alexander Crummell, an African American priest from New York City who was serving as a missionary to Liberia, published a tract supporting

Although the House of Bishops met amicably in Richmond in 1859, the southern dioceses subsequently followed their states into secession.

abolition, as did three white Episcopal clergy — Evan Johnson, John P. Lundy, and Thomas Atkins. The noted Boston rector Phillips Brooks strongly opposed the publication of Hopkins's defense of slavery. Another Boston rector, E. M. P. Wells, served as a vice president of the American Anti-Slavery Society. Northern Episcopalians who accepted the lawfulness of slavery but opposed its extension included Bishop William R. Whittingham of Maryland, Bishop Alonzo Potter of Pennsylvania, and Free-Soil leaders William H. Seward and Salmon P. Chase.

In both the north and the south, Episcopalians supported the American Colonization Society and its goal of returning free blacks to Africa. Many in the laity were among the founders of the society; as a presbyter, Bishop Meade of Virginia served as its first national agent, though he later became discouraged by its record of achievements. Beginning in 1835, the denomination sent missionaries to the society's colony of Liberia. In 1850 the General Convention elected John Payne, a white graduate of mission-centered Virginia Theological Seminary, as the first bishop for Africa. Although the venture in colonization was not a success, some Episcopal congregations were still sending funds to it at the time of the outbreak of the Civil War.

Given the Anglican tradition of independent national churches, the formation by the eleven southern dioceses of an independent Protestant Episcopal Church in the Confederate States of America was inevitable. The new church's constitution, canon law, and prayer book were patterned closely upon those of the parent church. Jefferson Davis and Robert E. Lee were among its leading laymen; two other graduates of West Point — Bishop Leonidas Polk of Louisiana (who owned several hundred slaves) and William N. Pendleton, a Virginia rector who became Lee's chief of artillery — served in the Confederate army as generals. The Confederate church consecrated Richard Hooker Wilmer as bishop of Alabama in 1862, a consecration the northern dioceses ratified following Lee's surrender. The first pastoral letter issued by the Confederate bishops declared that the south's slaves were "a sacred trust."

The war between the north and the south not only disrupted parish life but also destroyed many Episcopal church buildings. During the northern occupation the Confederate clergy's canonical obligation to pray for the president of the Confederacy (rather than for the president of the United States) caused the arrest of some Episcopal clergy. In Alabama, northern military authorities temporarily suspended all Episcopal clergy and services in 1865 when Bishop Wilmer directed his clergy — who were still technically in the Confederate church, even though the Confederacy had surrendered five months earlier — to omit the prayer for the President of the United States from all services of worship. When Wilmer appealed the military order directly to President Andrew Johnson, Episcopal churches were reopened.

But Episcopalians emerged from the Civil War less divided than might have been expected. Because so many of the southern and northern bishops were friends, because the northern church refused to accept the schism as permanent and still began the roll call with Alabama at its General Conventions of 1862 and 1865, and because the presiding bishop of the northern church was the southern sympathizer John Henry Hopkins, reconciliation occurred with remarkable smoothness. By 1866 all of the southern dioceses had returned to the Protestant Episcopal Church in the United States of America. The achievement was significant. The Methodists and the Presbyterians — who also divided into northern and southern churches over the question of slavery — did not reunite until the twentieth century, and the northern and southern wings of the Baptists continue as separate bodies today.

African American Episcopalians
After the Civil War

Following the Civil War, many African Americans in the south left the slave galleries and decorous services of the Episcopal Church for the more spontaneous worship of the Baptists and Methodists. At the

A West Pointer, Bishop Leonidas Polk (1806–1864) took leave from the
Diocese of Louisiana in 1861, "buckled the sword over the gown,"
and died as a Confederate general.

General Convention of 1868, the southern dioceses reported major losses of African American communicants, with South Carolina reporting the departure of over ninety percent. "Of the four millions of African Americans upon our soil," a report to the General Convention declared in 1877, "the mass is untouched by our Church."[54]

Southern African Americans who remained in the Episcopal Church soon discovered they lacked the status and freedom they would have received in denominations founded and controlled by African Americans. Although the Baptist, the African Methodist Episcopal, and the African Methodist Episcopal Zion churches had African American clergy and bishops, in the Episcopal Church white pastors generally led African American congregations. Because of lay opposition, most southern dioceses also refused to grant full membership to African American congregations. From 1875 to 1889, for example, the Diocese of South Carolina was racked over the request of St. Mark's Church, Charleston (a self-supporting African American congregation with a white rector), to be admitted to the diocese.

The ultimate solution of South Carolina, like that of most southern dioceses, was to impose a color line. All African American congregations were segregated into a separate diocesan organization under the direction and authority of the bishop, assisted by an African American archdeacon. Many southern bishops and clergy initially supported full rights for African American congregations. The General Convention, however, took no action, preferring to leave racial matters to the individual dioceses. Not until the 1950s did every diocese of the Episcopal Church grant African Americans equal voting representation.

The work the Episcopal Church accomplished for its remaining African American members in the south revolved around societies like the Freedman's Commission and the American Church Institute, which promoted African American welfare in education. Schools for African Americans founded under Episcopal auspices after the Civil War include St. Augustine's College (1867), Raleigh, North Carolina; St. Paul's College (1889), Lawrenceville, Virginia; Voorhees College (1922), Denmark, South Carolina; and a number of secondary and vocational schools. Significantly, the work among freed slaves fell largely to women in the church. Women teachers and principals generally staffed the schools, becoming the first large group of women paid wages by the Episcopal Church.

The request for ordination of an African American layman in Virginia prompted the incorporation of the Bishop Payne Divinity School in Petersburg, Virginia, in 1884. A branch of Virginia Theological Seminary, it was named for the first missionary bishop sent to Africa by the Episcopal Church. Its faculty was originally composed entirely of whites.

The years between 1874 and 1940 also saw repeatedly unsuccessful attempts in the General Convention to create missionary districts in the United States for African Americans, headed by African American bishops. The proposal was blocked primarily by northern dioceses, on the grounds that it would make segregation a permanent feature of national Episcopal church life.

In 1910, however, the church followed a different approach when the General Convention established the office of suffragan bishop. The convention directed dioceses to use the new title for assistant bishops who, as the canon it passed declared, "in all respects act as the assistant of the Bishop of the Diocese and under his direction."[55] The new office carried relatively little authority.[56] Suffragan bishops lacked a vote in General Conventions until the 1940s. And unless a later diocesan convention elected them to the office of diocesan bishop, they remained suffragan bishops until retirement, death, or resignation.

In part this new canon of 1910 responded to the desires of dioceses in the west and northeast for bishops who could supervise expanding missionary work. It mentioned neither race nor color. Yet it opened the way for African Americans to become bishops, for few dioceses at the time would have elected an African American who might become a diocesan. Suffragan bishops had no right of succession, and it was also clearly understood that no African American suffragan would be given episcopal supervision of white congregations.

Edward Thomas Demby became the first African American bishop in the United States when he was consecrated suffragan bishop of Arkansas in 1918; later in the same year, a graduate of St. Augustine's College, Henry B. Delany, was consecrated suffragan bishop of North Carolina. Both were viewed as "suffragan bishops for colored work" and given the mission of ministering to current African American Episcopalians and attracting more. The first African American bishop to have jurisdiction over white congregations, John M. Burgess, was consecrated suffragan bishop of Massachusetts in 1962. Eight years later Burgess became the first African American diocesan bishop when he became bishop of Massachusetts. By 1989, when the Episcopal Church elected its first woman bishop (who is also African American), almost thirty African Americans had served in the episcopate. By 1991 they had headed such highly visible jurisdictions as Washington (D.C.), Long Island, and Southern Ohio.

The situation for African American Episcopalians in the north and

A native of Michigan, Bishop John M. Burgess of Massachusetts (1909–   ) was the first African American to hold jurisdiction over white congregations.

west differed significantly from that of African American clergy and laity in the southern dioceses. Prior to the Civil War, large congregations of African American Episcopalians had existed in such cities as Philadelphia, New York City, and New Haven. From Bishop White's ordination of Absalom Jones in 1795 through 1865, northern bishops had ordained almost twenty African American clergy, and Bishop Payne of Liberia had ordained seven more. Most prominent of the African American priests was the scholarly Alexander Crummell, a free African American raised in

Manhattan's St. Philip's Parish and educated at Cambridge University. One of the best-educated African Americans of his time, Crummell served as an Episcopal missionary to Liberia, as rector of St. Luke's Church in Washington, D.C., and as organizer and president of the American Negro Academy.

After the Civil War influential congregations of African American Episcopalians emerged in Newark, Buffalo, Detroit, Chicago, St. Louis, and other cities. Most were founded by African American clergy, though some were led by white rectors. In northern and western dioceses, lack of equal accommodations at meetings and lack of representation in positions of leadership were the principal problems African Americans encountered; their churches and clergy were not denied diocesan membership or voting rights. Although a number of the northern bishops such as William Scarlett of Missouri were outspoken integrationists, these marks of a color line generally were not removed until the 1950s and 1960s. In 1921 a small number of African Americans left the Episcopal Church in New York City when George Alexander McGuire, a West Indian priest influenced by the militant message of racial pride taught by Marcus Garvey, established the African Orthodox Church as the unofficial church of Garvey's Universal Negro Improvement Association.

Since some African Americans were communicants of predominantly white churches outside the south, membership figures for African American Episcopalians during the decades after emancipation can only be approximate. As of 1922, George F. Bragg's *History of the Afro-American Group of the Episcopal Church* lists 288 exclusively African American congregations in 58 dioceses with two bishops, 176 clergy, and about 32,000 communicants. Total Episcopal membership in the same year approximated 1.1 million, with some 6,000 clergy. With approximately 1,700 communicants, St. Philip's Church, in the Harlem area of Manhattan, was the largest African American congregation in 1922.

IMMIGRANTS AND
THE EPISCOPAL CHURCH

The Episcopal Church benefited relatively little from the massive immigration that began in the 1830s and continued through World War I. The obstacles were many, though some were of the church's own making. The natural tendency of the immigrant groups toward clannishness, for example, and their lack of prior knowledge of Anglicanism or the American principle of voluntary membership, tended to discourage immigrants from considering the Episcopal Church, as did the Anglo-American background of the majority of Episcopal clergy and laity. The atmosphere of cushions, carpets, and rented pews, the requirement for English literacy built into Prayer Book worship, and the emphasis in so many Episcopal churches on non-eucharistic services of Morning Prayer with sermon also served as deterrents for many.

From English immigrants — the so-called invisible immigration to the United States — the church inevitably gained its greatest numbers. The percentage of Anglicans among the English and Anglo-Irish immigrants is unknown. But a large number clearly remained loyal to the established church of their homeland. New Episcopal churches sprang up wherever the English settled in the nineteenth century — in the mill towns of New England, in the mining districts of Illinois, in the farming communities of the Plains states, and in the orange groves of landboom Florida. To assist these Anglican emigrants, the Episcopal Church established the Anglo-American Church Emigrant's Aid Society in 1855. As early as 1875, blacks from the British colonies in the West Indies had formed an Episcopal parish in Florida.

For a time, the Episcopal Church also found promising ground among Swedish Americans. Beginning in 1845, a group of Swedish American clergy led by Gustaf Unonius, a graduate of Nashotah House Theological Seminary in Wisconsin, argued that the Episcopal Church better represented the high church Lutheranism of Sweden than did the pietistic Augustana Synod, the principal Swedish church in America. Calling themselves the "National Church of Sweden" and using its liturgy, they established more than a dozen Episcopal parishes among Swedish immigrants along the east coast and in the midwest. In 1866 Bishop Henry J. Whitehouse of Chicago secured an agreement with the Lutheran bishops of Sweden (which they later revoked when the Augustana Synod protested) that clergy in Sweden would recommend to parishioners who planned to emigrate to America that they join Episcopal congregations when no Lutheran churches existed in their area. More Swedish-Americans probably became Episcopalians through the normal process of assimilation than through evangelism, but the Swedish congregations provided a colorful interlude in Episcopal history.

With several other immigrant groups the Episcopal Church encountered some success. Though attempts to evangelize German immigrants failed in many places, German Lutherans felt a kinship with the Episcopal liturgy and tended to be open to the Episcopal Church when Lutheran services were not available. From 1874 on, when the Book of Common Prayer became available in German, the Church German Society attempted to train German-speaking Episcopal clergy. Its work centered in chapels established by parishes in eastern cities. Typical was the work among Germans done by Grace Church on the lower east side of New York City. Episcopal parishes abandoned separate work with Germans when the American-born generations assimilated into regular parish structures and demanded services in English.

Initially, Italian immigrants seemed to present a special opportunity for evangelism by the Episcopal Church. Some Italians — especially males — arrived in the United States already disaffected with Roman Catholicism because of its opposition to the united Italian kingdom that had incorporated the former papal states. Others stopped attending church when they experienced the Irish domination of American Roman Catholicism, which could extend even to Irish priests staffing Italian parishes.

Using an Italian translation of the Book of Common Prayer and tracts in Italian such as one entitled *Return to the Faith of Your Forefathers*, dioceses from Connecticut to Chicago established missions to unchurched Italians. Often staffed by former Roman Catholic priests of Italian birth, the Episcopal churches in Italian neighborhoods bore such names as La Chiesa dell' Annunziata or La Chiesa della L'Emmanuello. In Hackensack, New Jersey, and in Youngstown, Ohio, groups of Italians left the Roman Catholic for the Episcopal Church and organized churches with such distinctive Italian names as the Church of St. Anthony of Padua and St. Rocco's Church. By the 1920s the church's department of missions and church extension could report twenty-two missions to Italians. More than half were in New York.

The Episcopal Church also attracted some Jewish immigrants and their children. Some converts from Judaism — like Henry Judah Mikell of Atlanta, Isaac Lea Nicholson of Milwaukee, and the scholarly Samuel Isaac Joseph Schereschewsky of China — became bishops. The church had some success with the Hungarians in Indiana and New Jersey, with the Czechs (many of whom were estranged from Roman Catholicism), and with the Chinese and Japanese. Some Cubans who worked in the tobacco fields and new industries of Florida also became Episcopalians in the nineteenth century. Blacks from the British West Indies affiliated with Episcopal churches in the south and northeast. Among the Poles, for whom nationalism and Roman Catholicism were intertwined, the church was able to establish only a few missions. Episcopalians attempted virtually no missionary work among the Roman Catholic Irish, for whom religion, nationalism, and dislike of things English were combined. Individual

Lithuanian-born Samuel Isaac Joseph Schereschewsky (1831–1906),
Missionary Bishop of China, carried rabbinical habits into his translating
of the Bible and Prayer Book into Mandarin.

Irish-American Roman Catholic laity and clergy such as the able frontier
missionary and author John McNamara became Episcopalians.

Although the Episcopal Church sponsored some missions to immigrants of Eastern Orthodox background, Anglo-Catholic influence
increasingly caused the church to seek fellowship and intercommunion
rather than converts from these ancient churches. In the Diocese of Fond
du Lac, an attempt in the 1870s to form an Old Catholic movement
among Belgian immigrants who had become disaffected with Roman
Catholicism created far more problems than it did new parishes.

The vast immigration to the United States of the later nineteenth
and early twentieth centuries caused the rapid growth of Roman Catholicism, Lutheranism, and Judaism in America. It radically changed the
composition of many American cities and states. As World War I chaplains
discovered when large numbers of soldiers reported no religious affilia-
tion, many of these immigrants were open to evangelization. But for a
variety of reasons — lack of representatives to meet ships, delayed trans-
lations of the Book of Common Prayer into foreign languages, failure to

establish a "foreign-born division" in its Domestic and Foreign Missionary Society until the extraordinarily late date of 1920 (only a few years before large-scale emigration to the United States ended), and an overall lack of interest in evangelization — the Episcopal Church was again slow to seize its missionary opportunities.

Yet Episcopal parishes inevitably became the church homes of many new Americans. Most of the immigrants came to the northern cities, and the cities were precisely the places where the Episcopal Church possessed strength in the nineteenth century. Thus in the 1890s, one confirmation class in an Episcopal church in New York City reportedly included "one Jew, one Baptist, two French Protestants, three Unitarians, three Congregationalists, seven Methodists, nineteen Romanists, twenty-eight Presbyterians and fifty-two Lutherans" in addition to young people or adults born Episcopalian.[57] In the 1940s, a census of an Episcopal parish in Connecticut revealed more than thirty national strains.

The impact of immigration, missionary effort, and intermarriage is seen in the 1991 *Episcopal Clerical Directory,* which lists clergy with names such as Orsini, Jensen, O'Rourke, De Chambeau, Likowski, Kontos, Van Sant, Orozco, Noisy Hawk, Giovangelo, Berdahl, Desroisers, Sugeno, O'Brien, and Valdes-Perez. In the more than two hundred years since the General Convention of 1789 consisted of a bishop named White, clerical deputies named Beach, Moore, Frazer, Ogden, Waddel, Spieren, Magaw, Blackwell, Pilmore, Bend, Couden, Sykes, Claggett, Ferguson, Bisset, and Smith, and lay deputies named Rogers, Cox, Coxe, Jones, Ogden, Hopkinson, Powel, Clarkson, Sykes, Duff, Reading, Carmichael, Frisby, Andrews, Burrows, and Brisbane, the former Church of England had developed considerably in the United States.

4

CHURCH LIFE AND
WORSHIP

There is something so familiar and festive about Sunday worship in a typical Episcopal church that observers may forget that Episcopalians did not always worship in this manner. The choir in fresh white surplices, the clergy in colorful hoods, the procession to the chancel led by a crucifer, the hymn sung by strong voices, the church building with its elaborate ornamentation, vaulted arches, and distant altar with cross and candles — this model of Episcopal worship is well known to many Americans. Yet the model dates only to the later nineteenth century and probably would have shocked Episcopalians of the seventeenth and eighteenth centuries.

Of all American Christians, Episcopalians may be the most involved in the structure, language, music, colors, and millinery of worship. Traditionally, they are also among the most interested in the architecture and interior arrangements of churches. Since their first service in the American colonies, they have worshiped according to a common service book. But their church buildings and the worship that occurs within them have evolved.

To see the change that has occurred, a reader needs only to compare Christ Church, Boston (Old North Church), the frame church from which Paul Revere reportedly received his signal, with the Episcopal Cathedral of Saints Peter and Paul in Washington, D.C., commonly known as the Washington National Cathedral. The two buildings exemplify distinct approaches not only to worship and architecture but also to the function of a church building. The Episcopal Church generally followed the first model for over two centuries, changed to the second model after approximately the 1870s, and since the 1950s has been gradually returning to a version of the first model.

The interior of St. Paul's Church, Albany, New York, 1928.

TYPES OF CHURCHES

The key to understanding a religious building may be the worshiper's perception of it. Worshipers generally will categorize the building either as a house of God, a house of the people of God, or a shrine.

A house of God is a building (like the Jerusalem Temple or a temple of Hinduism) where worshipers believe that their God is more present than anywhere else on earth. Such structures usually have a center of worship where worshipers believe that God is specifically present and which they acknowledge through genuflection, bowing, or prostration.

Worshipers hold no such conviction about a house of the people of God. Like the meeting houses of the New England Puritans or the synagogues that emerged in Judaism as an alternative to the Jerusalem Temple, worshipers go to houses of the people of God to praise and pray, to receive religious instruction, and to transact their congregational business. If God is specially present in the building, it is because two or three are gathered there together in his name rather than because of any special indwelling divine presence in the building.

The third category of religious building, the shrine, is a building or place viewed by worshipers as possessing a special presence, but generally that of a saint or lesser god.

The New Testament does not indicate that the earliest Christians desired special buildings for worship. Early Christians worshiped in domestic and secular buildings. They viewed them as "houses of the church" that centered on Christians rather than as "houses of God" that focused on holy places.

This concept of worship and architecture changed when the Roman emperor Constantine established Christianity as the official religion of the Roman empire in the fourth century. Church history seems to indicate that a community of faith that had formerly seen itself as unattached to any place borrowed the concepts of shrines, temples, altars, sacred things, sacred places, and sacred times from the pagan religions around it. It began to erect distinctly ecclesiastical buildings and to associate the presence of God with places rather than with people. For a model it used the principal Roman hall of justice, adding to it features taken from the homes and tombs of Christians. What had been called "the house of the church" now became "the house of God."

The development reached its height in the Middle Ages, when gothic churches were constructed with remote chancels and altars, elaborate reredos, and separate rooms for the laity and clergy. The nave was for the laypeople; the chancel was reserved for clergy and holy things. Infused with a dim religious light, full of rich visual symbols, with multiple altars and Hosts in pyxes hanging over the high altar, the medieval churches represent the apex of the house of God tradition in Christianity.

CHURCHES DURING
THE REFORMATION PERIOD

The Protestant Reformation of the sixteenth century marked a partial return to the pre-Constantinian model. No Reformation group except the Anabaptists and other radical sectarians returned to the original model of the house church. On the basis of Scripture and the practice of the early church, however, such continental reformers as Ulrich Zwingli and John Calvin urged Christians to worship in houses of the people of God, or meeting houses.

In England, where more than nine thousand surviving medieval churches made new churches largely unnecessary during the sixteenth century, church buildings were generally changed only in their interiors. During the period of Calvinist influence in the reign of Edward VI, the minute books of churchwardens indicate that Anglican church walls were whitewashed (to cover the murals and depictions of the saints), windows changed from stained to plain glass, and altar crosses and rood screens taken down. Wooden tables not only replaced stone altars but were also moved into the midst of the congregation.

Whatever their strengths and weaknesses, the changes were attempts to change a house of God into a house of the people of God. The Roman Catholicism of Mary's rule generally returned altered churches to their medieval arrangements. During the long rule of Elizabeth, architectural alterations generally followed the Anglican *via media,* though a return to more medieval church interiors and vestments occurred (amidst great controversy) during the period of the Stuart kings (1603–1714). Not until the 1630s was the first church of any significance (St. Paul's, Covent Garden) built in England to conform to the different presuppositions about worship that had informed the Book of Common Prayer.

But when Christopher Wren became the chief architect of the Church of England following the Fire of London (1666), a new model of Anglican church began to appear. The few surviving Anglican churches built in the American colonies prior to the Wren era display the transplantation of the gothic style. By the end of the seventeenth century, however, churches inspired by Wren or by successors such as James Gibbs predominated.

WORSHIP IN COLONIAL ANGLICANISM

In the almost four hundred years of their existence in America, Episcopalians have experienced the first two concepts of the church building, as a house of God and as a house of the people of God. Few have experienced the third, for the Episcopal Church has only a small number of shrines, most of which are American parallels of medieval English shrines.

When colonial Americans entered Anglican churches, they entered meeting houses, or buildings viewed as houses of the people of God. No atmosphere of mystery embellished the design. Some of the Anglican churches erected during the colonial period in Maryland and Virginia, for example, could be mistaken from the exterior for courthouses or other public buildings.

Sometimes cruciform but generally rectangular in shape, colonial Anglican churches by English canon law had to be oriented (that is, when worshipers faced the holy table, they faced toward the orient, or east). The wall against which the holy table was placed was usually flat rather than semicircular. Although some of the earliest churches were constructed in the gothic style, most were built in the Georgian style current after the start of the eighteenth century. Like Independence Hall in Philadelphia and the public and domestic buildings in Colonial Williamsburg, Georgian churches were characterized by symmetry of design, gable or hipped roofs, beaded weatherboards, and Flemish bond brickwork (a pattern of alternating long and short bricks). Georgian architecture generally included raised paneling, ornamental doorways, clear glass panes in sash double-hung windows, and sometimes steeples adapted from earlier gothic architecture.

Today, Episcopal worship generally focuses on an altar or holy table. Most Anglican churches in colonial America, however, contained three liturgical centers: the baptismal font, the holy table, and the pulpit. The majority also placed the font in a special baptismal pew just inside the principal west entrance, a medieval location symbolizing that Christians enter the church through baptism. The holy table was placed against the east wall. On all but the infrequent Communion Sundays, however, the service revolved around the pulpit rather than around the font or the holy table.

The large colonial pulpits — many of which were "three-deckers" — deserve special discussion. Although pulpits are now associated with preaching, throughout the colonial period and into the nineteenth century they were the focus of the entire liturgy on most Sundays. They had one enclosed tier, or "deck," at floor level, where the lay reader, or "clerk," (generally selected because of the quality of his voice), led the singing and responses. The rector used the second, higher deck to read Scripture and to lead prayers. From the top deck, which rose ten or more feet from the floor and was surmounted by a sounding board that projected his voice, he preached his sermon. Anglican churches in colonial America also had "two-decker" pulpits — which followed the same design, but eliminated the middle tier.

Pulpits were generally more imposing in eighteenth-century Anglican churches because the Anglican worship of the time emphasized the read or spoken word. Painted tablets containing principal summaries of the Word — the Ten Commandments, the Lord's Prayer, and the Apostles' Creed — were placed by the pulpit in each church. Except on Communion Sundays, the service was conducted entirely from the pulpit. Hence the concern was to place the pulpits where everyone could see and hear the clerk and rector.

The formative architect for this model was Christopher Wren, who designed what were known as "auditory churches" for the Church of England in the seventeenth and early eighteenth century. Inspired by Wren's designs and by architectural design books, Anglican churches in the American colonies generally located pulpits where all in the congregation could hear the read and spoken word. In rectangular churches, the pulpit was placed at one of three places — at the midpoint of the north wall (the most likely location), in the center aisle some yards in front of the holy table, or in the center of the east wall above the holy table. In cruciform churches, the architects or pattern books placed the pulpit at one of the points where the transepts intersected the main church. Again, the holy table (a true table, with legs) was always against the east wall.

All of these locations sprang from a concern to keep Anglican worship from being a "dumb show" — something Anglican liturgists considered the contemporary Roman Catholic Latin mass to be. In addition to desiring Anglicans to worship in a language understood by the congregation, church designers wanted every worshiper to be able to hear the service and the sermon. In the nineteenth century, a new approach to liturgy (one that fostered an understanding of the church as a house of God) caused Episcopalians to redesign the interiors and to replace the furnishings in many colonial churches.[58] Worshipers and visitors can still see pulpits in their original eighteenth-century locations, however, in St. Peter's Church,

AN EIGHTEENTH CENTURY CHURCH

reredos

altar

altar rails

box pews throughout

the "three decker": pulpit desk reading desk clerk's desk

font near west door

All worshipers were supposed to be able to see and to hear the priest and clerk in eighteenth-century "auditory" churches.

New Kent County, Virginia (at the midpoint of the north wall), in Trinity Church, Newport, Rhode Island (in front of the holy table), in St. Peter's Church, Philadelphia (in the center of the west wall), in Aquia Church, Stafford County, Virginia (where the south transept intersects the main church), as well as in other colonial Episcopal churches scattered along the eastern seaboard.

Just as the pulpits were high in colonial Episcopal churches, so were many of the pews. Generally box-shaped, with plank seats on three or more sides (which occupants sometimes cushioned), they were high more for reasons of warmth than for reasons of privacy. Since most of the churches were unheated, worshipers often brought footwarmers with them. The backs of the churches and the galleries (if a church had them) often contained slip pews (pews arranged in straight or slightly rounded lines) or backless benches. Some Anglican churches separated men from women and children in the colonial period, but most apparently did not. Where segregation of the sexes was the custom, it tended to occur in the fronts of churches, where male officials (especially in colonies where the Church of England was the established church) might sit as a body. It also occurred in the back pews and galleries, where slaves, poor whites, and students from the parson's academy sat.

And seating was important in the colonial period. Today Episcopal churches have difficulty persuading worshipers to sit in the front pews, but in colonial America, the closer a family sat to the holy table or to the pulpit, the higher its social or economic rank. Today, too, visitors to colonial Episcopal churches may hear guides explain that the galleries once served as slave galleries. Some did — but many were private galleries built at a family's expense to serve a family and its guests much the same way as boxes serve in the theater.

In colonial America most Anglican churches held services on Sunday mornings and afternoons, on four special days (Christmas, Good Friday, Ascension Day, and King Charles the Martyr Day), and on Wednesdays and Fridays during Lent. Since Sunday schools were still unknown, the clergy catechized the children following the morning services during Lent. In cities such as New York or Philadelphia, services might begin at an earlier hour, but in rural areas they generally started at eleven in the morning in warm months; in cold months they began at noon. The hours allowed time for rural parishioners to reach the church and for the sun to warm the unheated building.

Except on the infrequent Communion Sundays, the Sunday morning service consisted of Morning Prayer, the Litany, Ante-Communion (the first part of the Communion Office, ending with the gospel), a sermon, and concluding prayers. By twentieth-century standards, the service was lengthy, lasting from seventy-five to ninety minutes and up to thirty minutes longer (or a total sometimes of two hours) when communion was administered. Although some evidence exists that the length of the service hindered conversions to Anglicanism, worshipers received a "rich dose of Scripture: a chapter from both testaments, an epistle and gospel, plus ample psalmody and canticles."[59]

The need to go through the three Prayer Book services, rather than the length of the sermon, extended the services. Except for the few evangelical clergy who were influenced by the Great Awakening and by the Methodist movement of John Wesley, most eighteenth-century Anglican clergy seem to have preached for twenty minutes or less. The sermons of the evangelicals aimed at conversion, but most of the other Anglican clergy in the American colonies seem to have preached dispassionate, reasoned discourses of a theological, philosophical, or moral nature. Sermons on the distinctive principles of Anglicanism were also common.

Unlike Episcopal services today, no procession began the colonial Anglican service. At the appointed hour the minister (a term then commonly used) simply walked to the pulpit, often speaking to the people in the pews as he passed them. As for garb, the clergy generally wore white priestly surplices, often changing during the singing of a psalm to scholarly black robes with muslin bands before entering the top deck of the pulpit to preach. If robed, the clerks wore similar long black cassocks with bands.

Like the Puritans, the colonial Anglican congregations did not sing hymns. Rather, they sang "the Psalms of David in Metre" — for psalms, unlike hymns, were held to be of divine authorship. A metrical psalm such as "Old Hundredth" (still in the Episcopal hymnal as Hymn 377) began the service. The priest and the clerk led the singing from their places in the pulpit. In some parishes the clerk would read each line before the congregation sang it, not only because churches did not furnish Prayer Books to worshipers but also because some members of the congregation could not read. If the church had an organ to accompany singing and to play voluntaries, it was located in the west gallery, where some congregations also placed singers and musical instruments.

The clergy "administered" (and that was the eighteenth-century word) the holy communion at least four times a year, and sometimes more frequently. On Communion Sundays they would leave the high pulpit at the offertory and stand by the holy table, in most cases at its north end, where they would be halfway turned toward the congregation. That position allowed the congregation to observe the breaking of the bread and other "manual acts" required during the holy communion service; it also kept the clergy from turning their backs to the people and appearing to be intercessors between God and the congregation.

Parishioners who did not plan to commune would leave the church at the end of the Ante-Communion service, while those remaining would "draw nigh" to the holy table and gather around it, sometimes using special kneeling pews built adjacent to the holy table. In most parishes only a minority of the parishioners remained to receive holy communion, though the numbers notably increased at Easter.

The overall percentage of communicants was small not so much because of anti-sacramentalism (although lay adherence to church forms could be erratic in the established churches) but because the parties in England who valued frequent celebrations of the Lord's Supper — the evangelicals and the high church party — were few in number in the American colonies. Recent scholarship, however, has shown that the worship of Anglicans and other Christians in the eighteenth century was more sacramental than earlier writers had realized. In colonial Anglicanism the evidence is clear that a parish's respect for the rector could influence the number of laity who received holy communion. There is also some indication that the percentages were higher in small and middle-sized parishes than in larger ones.

EPISCOPAL WORSHIP FROM 1789 THROUGH THE 1840S

Any Episcopalian who reached adulthood in colonial America but lived into the early decades of the nineteenth century would have experienced few unsettling changes in worship or architecture. Episcopal churches remained firmly in the house of the people of God tradition.

From 1789 through the 1820s, most new churches were constructed in a modified Georgian style called late Georgian or federal. After that decade, most were constructed in the style called classical revival. Characterized by gable roofs and columned porticos (or porches), these churches resembled the temples of ancient Greece and Rome, the major distinction being the frequent addition of a steeple over the west end. Both late Georgian and classical revival churches had straightforward lines, clear glass windows, and an overall lack of mystery. No canon of the Episcopal Church now required that the churches be oriented.

Inside, the Episcopal churches of the early national period remained auditory churches. They differed from their colonial counterparts principally by following the Lutheran and Calvinist practice of grouping the pulpit, the holy table, and the font into a small chancel area set against the flat wall. A high pulpit with sounding board continued to dominate the typical church. The pulpit had stairs leading from one level to the next, the three required tablets flanking it, and a reading desk below it. On floor level in front of the reading desk was the holy table, with a rail on three sides. To one side was the font. The intention was to have all liturgical activity grouped together at the front of the church, so that congregations might witness all parts of the service with equal convenience.

This new chancel arrangement lent itself to slip pews, since the

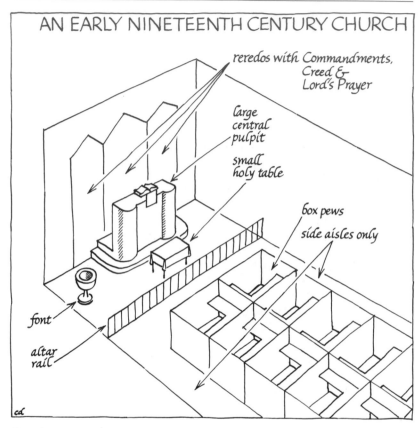

AN EARLY NINETEENTH CENTURY CHURCH

reredos with Commandments, Creed & Lord's Prayer

large central pulpit

small holy table

box pews

side aisles only

font

altar rail

Worship continued to be centered on the reading and preaching of the Word in the Episcopal churches of the early nineteenth century.

congregation now needed to look toward only one liturgical center. In addition, Americans were now heating their churches with stoves, making high box pews less necessary. For these and other reasons, most Episcopal churches built after the first few decades of the nineteenth century used slip pews, and box pews began to disappear.

During these years, Episcopal churches continued to look like the meeting houses of other Protestant denominations. Worship continued to be Word-centered and to consist of Morning Prayer, Litany, and Ante-Communion. To add time for longer sermons, many evangelical parishes omitted the Ante-Communion service except on Communion Sundays. Whether high or low, most parishes continued to celebrate holy communion infrequently.

Congregations now sang hymns as well as psalms, for the Episcopal Church adopted its first hymnbook in 1808. The church adopted hymns taken from the Lutheran, Methodist, Roman Catholic, and other traditions, but retained the most popular of the metrical psalms. Most churches now had organs, placing them in the gallery directly opposite the chancel, with unrobed quartets rather than choirs generally leading the singing. Parishes generally depended upon the voluntary services of members for music, and the standards of church music were lower in Episcopal churches than they became after the late nineteenth century. At mid-century the bishop of Ohio declared that his visitations to parishes had caused him to hear

> music which, had it been found in the Temple at Jerusalem, when the Saviour overturned the tables of the money-changers, would have been driven out of the sanctuary with the same indignation that said, 'Take these things hence: my house shall be called a house of prayer.'[60]

By the 1820s most Episcopal Churches had developed Sunday schools — something unknown to churches of the colonial period. Originally providing secular education as well as religious training, the schools reached out not only to children of the parishes but also to those in the surrounding communities. Sunday schools reinforced catechetical training and often included strict memorization requirements with public examinations. As public education in America expanded, Episcopal Sunday schools began to focus only on religious instruction.

Of the processions, crosses, robes, hangings, colors, and candles (except to provide light on dark days) which now so characterize Episcopal worship, this post-Revolutionary era still knew nothing.

> Visual symbols, even the cross, were lacking altogether, and ceremonial minimal. [Eucharistic] vestments were unknown, the use of incense in church unheard of, candles rare, and holy communion three times a year considered sufficient in most parishes.[61]

But a liturgical and architectural revolution lay ahead.

THE OXFORD MOVEMENT

The issues raised in the 1830s and 1840s by the Oxford Movement formed a central tension that has colored the Episcopal Church's worship and theology ever since. Begun in England in 1833 by Anglican priests John Keble, E. B. Pusey, and John Henry Newman, the cause was initially spread by a series of essays called *The Tracts for the Times*. That two of the three leaders were Oxford dons gave the movement its title; the alternate term "Tractarianism" came from the movement's first publications. The movement taught a high doctrine of the church, ministry, and sacraments, and emphasized three teachings as essential to Christianity.

First, the Oxford Movement emphasized apostolic succession. Asserted by the Eastern Orthodox, Roman Catholics, and many Anglicans, the doctrine of apostolic succession teaches that bishops derive their power from an unbroken succession of ordinations going back to the apostles. The bishops transmit the power of the Holy Spirit to the clergy they ordain. Only these clergy, according to the doctrine, possess true authority or can administer true sacraments in the church of Christ; all other ordained ministries — Presbyterian, Baptist, etc. — are held to be irregular or defective in the eyes of God.

This doctrine led naturally to a higher view of the clergy. It tended to restore their position (in the words of an Anglo-Catholic writer) from "mere preachers and social visitors, to their Apostolic and Catholic position as Priests, as trainers and physicians of the Spiritual life."[62] It also gave Anglicans a sense of closer identity with the Roman Catholic and Eastern Orthodox churches (who also claimed the apostolic succession) while it distanced them from Protestant denominations (who believed the doctrine a fiction and who held the only true succession to be that of fidelity to apostolic faith).

Second, the Tractarians emphasized baptismal regeneration, the teaching that the waters of baptism are not merely symbolic of admission to the Christian community but actually change the Christian from the condition of guilt and sin to a state of spiritual rebirth. This doctrine again carried with it a loftier concept of the church, the sacraments, and the clergy.

Third, the movement emphasized the Real Presence, the doctrine that the body and blood of Christ is in some way really present in the bread and wine of the eucharist and not simply signified or symbolized. From this emphasis came more frequent services of holy communion, more elaborate ceremonies, and more reverence for the consecrated bread and wine.

The sources of the Oxford Movement are to be found in the pre-Reformation heritage of Anglicanism, in the patristics-oriented high church movement of the Carolinian period, in the emphasis on personal religion of Anglican evangelicalism, and in the veneration of things medieval in the romantic revival. When the movement spread to the United

States in the early 1840s, it built upon the tradition of Hobartian high church Anglicanism.

Following the Civil War, the second phase of the movement became prominent in the United States. Called "ritualism" or "the Catholic revival" (because its adherents used late patristic, medieval, or post-Reformation Roman Catholic ritual in worship), "Puseyism" (because of the leadership of E. B. Pusey), or "Anglo-Catholicism" (because its adherents emphasized the continuity of the Church of England with the Catholicism of the patristic and medieval periods), the movement expressed its theology and worship in late patristic and medieval forms. In the eyes of many, its teachings reversed "three hundred years of moving ever farther away from medieval practices in worship" and rejected "a century and a half of rationalism that had shown little patience with either Protestant or Roman Catholic supernaturalism."[63]

Influenced in its views of architecture by the medievally minded Camden Society of Cambridge and by the Ecclesiological Societies of London and New York, the movement broke with the concept of auditory churches. It replaced Georgian and classical revival churches with deep-chanceled churches built in medieval styles. Gothic revival (which many Anglo-Catholics considered the only "proper" church style) was the movement's preferred style. It was no surprise that at least five of the greatest American architects of the nineteenth and early twentieth centuries — James S. Renwick, Richard M. Upjohn, Stanford White, Bertram Grosvenor Goodhue, and Ralph Adams Cram — were either raised as Episcopalians or converted to the Episcopal Church. Upjohn's orthodoxy was sufficiently firm that he refused an invitation to design a leading Unitarian church in Boston because he opposed that denomination's denial of the incarnation.

In keeping with its medieval vision, Anglo-Catholicism replaced plain church windows with stained-glass and flat east walls with recessed chancels. Altar-centered churches replaced pulpit-centered churches; the common chancel arrangement became one in which the pulpit was on one side, the lectern or prayer desk on the other, and the holy table centered against the wall. Episcopal churches now also began to display crosses on table-altars, on spires, and on interior and exterior ornamentations. From 1846, when Upjohn and Renwick designed two major Episcopal churches that still stand in Manhattan in the gothic revival style — Trinity Church, Wall Street, and Grace Church at Broadway and 10th Street (a low church parish of which Renwick was a member) — the goal was to construct church buildings that expressed the awe and mystery of the

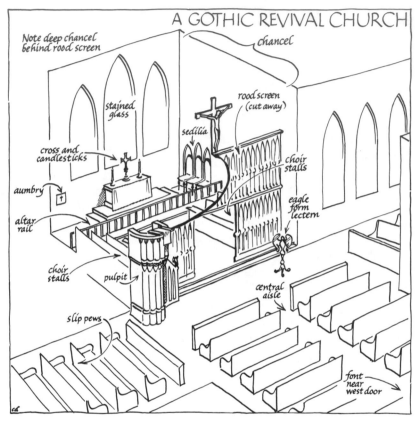

The Oxford Movement touched off a revival of medieval architecture and
sacramental worship among Episcopalians.

Christian faith. Churches that could not be rebuilt often were radically
altered inside. "By 1900," an Anglican liturgist notes, "almost every Anglican church from the Orkneys to Land's End and from Alaska to New
Zealand had undergone retrofitting in response to the Catholic Revival."[64]

In liturgy, Anglo-Catholicism emphasized the eucharist, the observance of saints' days, voluntary private confession and priestly absolution,
and prayers and requiems for the dead. In ceremonial, it tried to express the mystery and holiness of God and to make public worship more
glorious by using images, candles, colors, scents, and body language of
reverence and obeisance. When celebrating the eucharist or mass (terms
reintroduced into Anglicanism by the movement), Anglo-Catholic clergy
wore the eucharistic vestments that had developed in Christianity over

the centuries; bishops wore copes and mitres. Services began and ended with incense-laden processions and recessions of clergy accompanied by crucifers, candlebearers, and surpliced choirs. A retinue of ceremonial assistants unknown to Episcopalians of earlier generations — acolytes, thurifers, boatmen, banner bearers, taperers, crucifers, candlebearers, and masters of ceremony — emerged in many churches. Long forgotten ritual practices — requiems for the dead, votive candles, eucharistic parades, kneeling before statues — returned to Anglicanism; new ones, such as novenas to the Blessed Virgin Mary or benedictions of the Blessed Sacrament, were borrowed from post-Reformation Roman Catholic devotion. As worship became increasingly choreographed and formal and as parish churches began to copy the choral services of cathedrals, the standard of church music rose markedly and became more and more professionalized.

In addition to returning late patristic and medieval worship to Anglicanism, Anglo-Catholicism restored monastic orders for men and women. As exemplified by the career of James O. S. Huntington, founder of the monastic Order of the Holy Cross, who lived and worked in the slums of the lower east side of Manhattan and founded the influential Church Association for the Advancement of the Interests of Labor, these orders displayed a great concern for the problems of society.

The title of Ferdinand C. Ewer's *Catholicity in Its Relationship to Protestantism and Romanism* (1878) displays another characteristic of the movement: ritualism was concerned to contrast real Catholicism (which it claimed to possess) with "Romanism." It considered Protestantism so far beyond the pale that some of its adherents, like many Roman Catholic writers of the time, would not even dignify the word with a capital P. At the heart of the movement was the confidence that a Christian could be a Catholic without being a Roman Catholic.

The early manifestations of Anglo-Catholicism in America centered in the semi-monastic community formed in the 1840s by James Lloyd Breck in Wisconsin. In later years bishops and clergy such as Ewer of Manhattan and James DeKoven and Charles C. Grafton of Wisconsin, architects such as Cram of Massachusetts, dioceses such as Fond du Lac and Eau Claire in Wisconsin, and churches such as Advent in Boston and Saint Mary the Virgin in Manhattan became the movement's leading representatives in America. Like all movements, Anglo-Catholicism had low and high and liberal and conservative wings. By the early decades of the twentieth century, Episcopalians could tell the altitude of an Anglo-Catholic parish by such things as whether it used the word "eucharist" or "mass," whether its clergy were expected to remain single,

"The Fond du Lac Circus": This widely disseminated photograph taken at an Anglo-Catholic consecration in Fond du Lac in 1900 caused heated controversy among Episcopalians.

whether it prayed to the Blessed Virgin Mary, and whether it used the rosary and held such services as benediction of the Blessed Sacrament. The highest Anglo-Catholic churches might be described as "nosebleed high," just as the most Protestant of the evangelical parishes might receive the description "snake low."

Anglo-Catholic interpretations of faith and worship were not espoused in Episcopal parishes without opposition. In older dioceses, the opposition not only from evangelicals but also from traditional high churchmen of the Hobartian variety was vigorous and long lasting. As evidenced in the General Conventions of 1868, 1871, and 1874, the confrontations were frequently bitter. Critics viewed the movement as a theatrical cult whose adherents misread both church and liturgical history. Episcopalians who considered themselves Protestants objected to the use of garments and practices in Episcopal worship that they had always regarded as distinctly Roman Catholic. "Episcopalians might object to attending a place," a letter in the Chicago *Sunday Times* complained in 1878,

> where the grand old service of the Protestant Episcopal Church, that noble liturgy which was the early love of their fathers and mothers and forefathers for generations before them, is so distorted, patched, and be-

dizened with old follies and new assumptions as to be repugnant to the average Episcopalian.[65]

That a number of Anglo-Catholics later converted to Rome amid great publicity only reinforced their suspicions.

Certainly the ritualist movement fueled the combative spirit in Anglicanism. If Anglo-Catholics were valiant for what they considered the truth, evangelicals had long been so. In reaction, low church Anglicans moved in an even lower direction for a time. Bishop Meade, for example, who had been raised in post-Revolutionary Virginia to bow at the name of Jesus, found the practice so favored by the ritualists that he would consciously grip the pew in front during the recitation of the creed so as not instinctively to bow.

For many decades the image of the Episcopal Church as a circus of ecclesiastical gladiators brawling on one side with censers and monstrances and on the other side with Bibles and temperance manuals clearly kept some potential converts from it. Though the original emphases of both Anglo-Catholicism and evangelicalism called for a life of prayer, discipline, and devotion, the significant issues in later decades often revolved around candles, titles, and ecclesiastical millinery. Slavery, child labor, twelve-hour workdays, and impoverished lives were just outside the doors of Episcopal churches. But for many years questions about matters of church style and worship dominated the concerns of many Episcopalians.

The Oxford Movement and Anglo-Catholicism challenged the eighteenth- and early nineteenth-century belief that Anglicanism was simply another form of Protestantism. Positively (as some broad church and liberal evangelical Anglicans came to realize), the movement reversed the centuries-old process by which Anglicanism had been casting out its nonconformists; unlike the Puritans and the Methodists, the Anglo-Catholics remained within the church to witness to its heritage. Henceforth Anglicanism not only would be a more comprehensive church than it had been since the Elizabethan period but would also become the most comprehensive church in Christendom. "There have always been in the Church two classes of men," the bishop of Minnesota wrote at the turn of the twentieth century,

one magnifying the blessed Orders and Sacraments of the Church because they are the gifts of Christ and His channels of grace, the other magnifying the personal faith of the sinner in Jesus Christ and seeing in sacraments witness of the love of the Saviour. Both hold opposite sides of Divine truth. . . .[66]

The vested choir (ca. 1861–1863) at the Church of the Advent in Boston,
one of the early centers of Anglo-Catholicism.

Anglo-Catholicism attracted persons not only of Protestant but also of Roman Catholic and Eastern Orthodox backgrounds into the Episcopal Church. For many it made Episcopal worship rich, real, and fascinating. By 1900 the movement was strong in certain parishes and dioceses in the east and west. It was especially prevalent in the "Biretta Belt" dioceses in Wisconsin, Illinois, Indiana, and adjoining states. (The name stemmed from the practice among Episcopal clergy in those states of wearing the cap with tassel, or biretta, favored by Roman Catholic clergy.)

Anglo-Catholicism's concern for more elaborate standards of worship and many of its "innovations" — colored stoles, vested choirs, chanted psalms, altar-centered chancels, candles on the table-altar, processions and recessions, three-hour services on Good Friday, and more frequent holy communion — subsequently became widely accepted both in the Episcopal Church and in Protestant denominations. The terms "celebration," "eucharist" and "mass," the practice of daily and early celebrations, the employment of the word "priest" rather than "minister" for Episcopal clergy, the titles of "Most Reverend" and "Primus" for presiding bishops and "Father" for priests, the identifying of presiding episcopates by Roman numerals, the use of unleavened wafers and of a chalice of wine mixed with water, the devotion to the Blessed Virgin Mary, the use of the sign of the cross, the employment of chants in worship, the practice of genuflection, the concept of smaller dioceses, the cathedral system, the rebirth of religious orders — all of these practices and beliefs entered the Episcopal Church under the influence of Anglo-Catholicism.

"Ritualism will grow into favor, by degrees, until it becomes the prevailing system," the bishop of Vermont prophesied in 1867.[67] In many ways Episcopal history has fulfilled that prophecy. From the 1840s on, Episcopal parishes have moved steadily in the direction of a higher ceremonial and a fuller sacramental life. By the 1930s, even the staunchest low church parish had been strongly influenced by the Oxford and ritualist movements. From the 1870s on, the normal usage of Episcopal churches steadily became:

> An altar of stone or carved wood, vested with colored frontlet, and bearing a cross. . . . Flowers on the altar, weekly communions, careful observance of the Church's seasons, vested choirs with processions and processional crosses. . . . [68]

Even before the 1870s were over, Bishop Whittingham could say to a friend: "What was counted High once is Low now."[69]

Yet the Anglican tradition in the United States continues to display a marked tendency to keep to a middle way between Protestant and Catholic extremes. A century and a quarter since the introduction of ritualism into the Episcopal Church, Episcopalians who identify themselves as Anglo-Catholics remain a minority in the church. And when a movement emerged in the twentieth century that attempted to return to an even more apostolic emphasis in worship, vestments, and church architecture, another revolution occurred.

THE LITURGICAL MOVEMENT

Since the end of World War II, and especially since 1979, Episcopal worship has been influenced by the liturgical movement. Stemming from research into the origins of Christian worship performed by French Benedictines in the later nineteenth century, the movement reached the Church of England just before World War II and began to influence the Episcopal Church from the 1940s forward. When the General Convention officially adopted the 1979 Book of Common Prayer, the church was committed to worship that reflects the teachings of the liturgical movement.

To understand what the movement teaches, Episcopalians need only compare worship in their parish churches to worship under the 1928 Book of Common Prayer. In most parishes they will find at least the following changes. Congregations participate more fully in worship: laypeople read the lessons and the prayers, carry the bread and the wine to the clergy for consecration, and assist in the administration of the elements. The principal service of a parish is more frequently the holy communion (increasingly called "the eucharist"), and clergy face the people (instead of turning their backs on them) when celebrating it. Parishes emphasize the fullest possible communion of the congregation, including baptized children. Baptisms become important public celebrations. Over a three-year period congregations are exposed to the principal part of the Scriptures through readings and sermons on the lessons for each Sunday. Sunday schools tend to follow the liturgical year and attempt to incorporate children more fully into the worship life of the church. Whether preaching or celebrating the eucharist, the clergy wear vestments that are often less ornamental than those they formerly wore.

Some of these practices already existed in Episcopal worship; some did not. But all are now part of the worship prescribed for Episcopalians because they are found in the earliest Christian liturgies. Most Episcopalians welcomed this return to the earlier forms of Christian worship, for the

The liturgical movement has caused the building of new churches and the refitting of old ones in an effort to recreate the early Christian understanding of worship.

claim of Anglicanism since the time of Cranmer has always been that its faith and worship is true to that of the early church.

As a result, the revision that resulted in the 1979 Book of Common Prayer is the most extensive the Episcopal Church has experienced. Under the title of "Rite I," the new Prayer Book retains almost unchanged versions of Morning Prayer, Evening Prayer, and The Holy Communion (now called "The Holy Eucharist") from the old Prayer Book. Under the title of "Rite II," the new book includes the same offices in new structures that incorporate the recoveries of the liturgical movement. Rite I services employ traditional language; Rite II and all other services use contemporary language. Although a future revision conceivably could drop them, the Rite I services were purposely retained in the 1979 Prayer Book to give a sense of continuity with the worship of Anglicans in previous centuries. With the exception of a small percentage of hurt and angered Episcopalians who left the church in part because of it, the new Prayer Book has become a unifying factor. Catholic and evangelical at the same time, it has tended to make the worship of traditionally low church parishes higher by returning to early Christian norms. By reducing the antiquarian, romantic, and medieval features the ritualists tacked on to Episcopal worship, it has tended to make the worship of Anglo-Catholic parishes lower.

As with any liturgical revision, there are grounds for criticism. To go from the service of Holy Communion in the old Prayer Book to The Holy Eucharist, Rite II, of the new Prayer Book, an Episcopal professor of English declared, "is like finding that Shakespeare has been rewritten":

> The new Rite. . . . often seems pleasant enough, but [it is] thin. The emphasis on penitence is no longer there. Sins are no longer "intolerable" . . . There is no . . . emphasis on . . . "newness of life." . . . Poetic statement has been dismissed, partly with . . . a kind of heavy literalness. . . . Praise has been flattened out. . . . The service moves in a cheerful monotone. . . . The language . . . is. . . . bland, consumable. . . . It seems to be felt that we shall be nearer to God if we are not caught by language. . . .
>
> Those who . . . are upset by the changes are often accused of . . . a reactionary fondness for archaic speech. . . . But . . . we are, I believe, lamenting the loss of substance. . . . My own life would have been so much the poorer without the [Elizabethan] Book of Common Prayer that I feel a kind of horrified pity for an Anglican and Episcopalian posterity which may have to do without it.[70]

These words, of course, come from a scholar of the English language who speaks with some of the accents of the Protestant Reformation. They do not come from a liturgical historian, a biblical scholar, or an historical theologian. Yet there is much to be said for the critique; the Christian vocabulary is always in danger of devaluation.

But if Episcopal worship has suffered a loss of the bark and steel of Elizabethan language in the new Prayer Book, it has gained in many other ways. The translation of biblical words is more accurate; the content of the liturgy more faithfully represents the worship of early Christians. The effect has been to make Episcopalians feel more at home not only in other Episcopal parishes but also in Lutheran and Roman Catholic parishes that have similarly been influenced by the liturgical movement. Just as the law of prayer is the law of belief in Christianity, so the liturgical movement

114

has developed hand-in-hand with the ecumenical movement. The new approach to liturgy in the Episcopal Church has repudiated many of the elements reclaimed for worship in the nineteenth century by the ritualists. But it has only intensified the linkage of the church to two other major movements — the quest for church unity and the concern for social justice of that pivotal century.

5

SOCIAL AND INTELLECTUAL CHALLENGES TO WORLD WAR I

In the nineteenth and early twentieth centuries, the Episcopal Church had to confront a number of intellectual challenges, including evolution, higher criticism, the search for church unity, and the social gospel. Part of the Episcopal Church's response was the development of its first systematic theologians.

Higher criticism involved the scientific investigation of the sources, date, authorship, and form of biblical books. The work of the higher critics was controversial in all denominations, for some of their assertions questioned the historical accuracy and hence the theological reliability of these books.

Less controversial was lower, or textual, criticism, which attempted to recover the text of a biblical manuscript in its original form. Christians could more easily accept assertions by the lower critics that scribes over the centuries had made errors in copying than they could the suggestions of the higher critics that Eden was not on a map, that Adam's fall did not occur on an historical calendar, and that Moses did not write the Pentateuch (the first five books of the Old Testament).

Episcopalians adapted to the revolution in religious thought gradually. Like virtually all trinitarian American Christians of the time, they believed in the divine inspiration and hence the infallibility of the Bible. To admit error in any part was to call the whole of scriptural revelation into question. The patrician Bishop William Lawrence of Massachusetts, who was born in 1850, recalled in 1923 the views of the Bible he acquired growing up in the Episcopal Diocese of Massachusetts:

> The chief emphasis was upon the Old Testament, and of course both Old and New Testaments, being inspired, were true to the word and letter. The world was created in six days in the year 4004 B.C., for Genesis and the

date on the margin of the family Bible said so. Adam and Eve, the serpent, Noah and the flood . . . Jonah and the whale, Joshua and the sun . . . were facts as real as anything that happened yesterday. . . .

The brains of our elders, our parents, Sunday School teachers, and ministers were forced to great agility in meeting the problems. . . . We were led to assume that there were two worlds, the one of our every-day, matter-of-fact life, where answers to questions were straight, and the other of . . . faith. . . . [71]

Taking their stand on that world of faith, the American House of Bishops condemned the controversial *Essays and Reviews* (1860), in which writers from the Church of England accepted the methodology of the higher critics and called into question some formulations of Christian doctrine and the authorship of the Pentateuch. The majority of the bishops who supported this censure had been born in the eighteenth century or in the first decade of the nineteenth century, and they could not accept the changes ensuing from these new ideas.

But *Essays and Reviews,* like the earlier *Tracts for the Times,* heralded a new movement in Anglicanism; one of its seven authors later became archbishop of Canterbury. In response to the challenges, Anglicans concerned with a quest for truth from all sources gradually came together in England and America in the broad church movement. More an attitude of mind than a party of church practices, broad church Episcopalians like Phillips Brooks tried to assimilate the new scientific knowledge and critical approach to the scriptures into a positive, confident Christian worldview. "How well I recall the voice and flashing eye of Phillips Brooks," Lawrence recalled,

as, standing by the lectern pulpit, . . . he lifted the people to such a spiritual conception of the inspiration of the Old Testament. . . . Facts, interpretations, truths, errors, shook themselves into right perspective, and the congregation realized how the whole creation had 'groaned and travailed' until the day when the word was made flesh. . . . [72]

Although theirs was an intellectual movement rather than a party of church practice, the broad church Episcopalians were initially more congenial with the Episcopal evangelicals, who were rooted in the Reformation, than with the emerging Anglo-Catholic party, which was oriented toward the late patristic and medieval periods. Like Brooks, many ordained broad churchmen began their ministries as evangelicals. As younger Episcopalians increasingly adopted the approach of the broad church party, the evangelical party became a party of aging conservatives

Perhaps the greatest preacher of Victorian America, bachelor Phillips Brooks
is shown in 1890 holding the child of a friend. He died unexpectedly
a few years later.

and steadily faded. But their place in the Episcopal spectrum was filled by
those of the broad church tradition, who for some decades were called
"Prods" at Episcopal seminaries of higher-church orientation.

Besides Brooks, who proved a pied piper for broad church ideals, leading figures in the movement in America were William R. Huntington,
rector of Grace Church, New York; Alexander Viets Griswold Allen, professor at the Episcopal Theological School; and bishops Henry C. Potter
of New York and Thomas March Clark of Rhode Island. The Episcopal
Theological School in Cambridge, Massachusetts, which gained a reputation for relative rigor within the Episcopal seminary system, was the
movement's intellectual center. From 1874, church 'congresses' — forums

Known for seeing large questions in a large light, Bishop Thomas March Clark (1812–1903) of Rhode Island was one of the earliest broad churchmen.

across party lines that met in major cities — represented the principal means by which the movement brought major intellectual issues before the consideration of the church. "To the loyal, all things are loyal," declared Bishop Whipple of Minnesota at the first congress.

For several decades, broad church leaders were the only figures to insist that the Episcopal Church could not ignore the new intellectual currents. In 1889, however, English members of the Anglo-Catholic party produced *Lux Mundi,* a series of essays that purported to be an attempt "to put the Catholic faith into its right relation to modern intellectual and moral problems." Although many Anglicans attacked *Lux Mundi* as heretical, the book showed that even conservative parties in the church were beginning to accept the methods of higher criticism and the new scientific points of view. A leading British Anglo-Catholic, Bishop Charles Gore, spoke out for "a Catholicism which is Scriptural, liberal-spirited, and comprehensive, but always Catholic."[73]

For a time the Anglo-Catholic party in America was slower to adapt to the intellectual challenges than its counterpart in England, and the early opposition to the broad church movement in America came from Anglo-Catholics and the older evangelicals. During the first three or four decades of the twentieth century, the term "liberal" (often used as an adjective, as in "liberal Catholic" or "liberal evangelical") replaced "broad church." In the same decades theological radicals came to be called "modernists." Today "liberal" remains in the church's vocabulary, but it no longer serves as an appropriate synonym for "broad church." In the original sense of the term, all but a small number of contemporary Episcopalians are "broad church" in their theological understanding.

To a large extent, the Episcopal Church avoided public controversy in the course of debating the intellectual challenges facing it in the years between the Civil War and World War I. Several other denominations — most notably the northern Presbyterians, who underwent a series of major heresy trials — were swept by controversy. Within the Roman Catholic priesthood and seminary system, a papal encyclical and a repressive use of the Index of Forbidden Books were necessary to silence the "modernists." But in the most famous case in the Episcopal Church, Bishop Potter aroused vigorous protest in 1899 when he ordained Charles A. Briggs, the leading Old Testament scholar in the United States. An otherwise theologically conservative professor at Union Theological Seminary in New York, but a man whose personality invited contention, Briggs had left the Presbyterian Church after being tried for heresy for questioning the Mosaic authorship of the Pentateuch.

Trials of Episcopal clergy that received national publicity included the depositions from the ministry in 1891 of Howard McQueary, rector of St. Paul's Church, Canton, Ohio, and in 1906 of Algernon S. Crapsey, a highly respected Rochester priest of Anglo-Catholic background. The records of their trials indicate that both men remained strongly oriented toward the person and social teachings of Jesus Christ. At a time when many in America and elsewhere believed that science was undercutting the entire dogmatic system of the Christian faith, both McQueary and Crapsey had become convinced that Christianity must broaden the definition of some of its doctrines or lose thinking people to unbelief. They went further than the Episcopal Church of their time permitted, but neither might have been brought to trial had they not embarrassed their bishops.

Unlike most Protestant denominations, the Episcopal Church gradually assimilated the revolutionary intellectual trends with relatively little public trauma. Beginning in the 1870s with the Episcopal Theological School, which quickly became the center for the new intellectual forces among Episcopalians, the church's seminaries "fell" one by one to higher criticism. Conservative faculty and trustees suspicious of change caused some of the church's seminaries to take two more decades before they revised their curriculum to include higher criticism. Following the lead of the Lambeth Conference of Anglican bishops, the House of Bishops formally declared in 1899 that the reverently critical study of the Bible was necessary not only to maintain the Christian faith but also to protect it.

Episcopal clergy ordained in earlier years and the average Episcopalian in the pews, however, could still be distrustful of the new approach to Scripture. In the last decades of the nineteenth century, some conservative evangelicals participated in the prophetic Bible conferences that led to the later fundamentalist movement. As late as 1915, a bishop who had graduated from Virginia Theological Seminary in the 1880s attended the revivals of the fundamentalist champion Billy Sunday and sometimes opened them with prayer. "He leaned towards fundamentalism," a writer noted of the bishop, "although not insisting that others share his belief. His was a childlike faith."[74]

By World War I the majority of Episcopal clergy had accepted the scholarly methods (if not all the conclusions) of higher criticism. The transition was remarkable, in light of the existence throughout the twentieth century of a significant number of Christians in America who continued to believe that the Christian faith must be protected from biblical scholars. Yet the changes in outlook occurred with more pain than writers have sometimes portrayed: "You who are under fifty years of age have no conception of the searchings of heart, the sorrows over a lost faith, the anxiety of parents over children, the tragic experiences of those days," Bishop Lawrence declared in 1923 of the 1870s and 1880s.[75]

That Anglicanism was able to accept these changes with relative ease stemmed from its conception of comprehensiveness. It also stemmed from the fact that Anglicanism expressed its faith in terms of the historic creeds and the Book of Common Prayer rather than through an official doctrine of the literal inerrancy of Scripture. The low church emphasis on the right of private judgment and the Anglo-Catholic emphasis on the guidance of the Holy Spirit when the church interprets Scripture also contributed; what the church has interpreted, the church can also — so the argument went — reinterpret. Since Episcopalians had also never emphasized the Old Testament in the manner of many Protestant denominations, the revised understanding of such stories as the Genesis flood or the falling of the walls of Jericho caused fewer problems. Finally, the Episcopal Church's emphasis on reason and respect for sound learning, which it inherited from the English intellectual tradition, not only enabled but obliged it to adapt to the new intellectual challenges.

THEOLOGY

The nineteenth century also saw the emergence of the first systematic theologians in the Episcopal Church. One of those pioneers who lived into the twentieth century but who is almost forgotten today is Francis J. Hall. Raised in the Church of the Ascension, Chicago's pioneer Anglo-Catholic parish, Hall was the parish's first acolyte and a member of its first vested choir. After studying under the Anglo-Catholic leader James DeKoven at Racine College and completing his theological studies at the General Theological Seminary in New York and Western Theological Seminary in Chicago, Hall began to teach theology at Western in 1886. He concluded his career by teaching at General Seminary from 1913 until 1928.

An Anglo-Catholic whose thought was rooted in the patristic and medieval periods, Hall had also read widely in Reformation materials and in portions of modern theology. He was cautious about higher criticism, but utilized Darwin when presenting the doctrines of Creation and the Fall of humanity. Through compiling and synthesizing, he attempted to produce a version of the theology of Thomas Aquinas (the most influential of the medieval theologians) for the twentieth century. Like Thomas, he tried to do as much as he could with a discernment of the nature of God reached through reason. In a clear and precise style, he also attempted to state systematically and fully what the Anglican position was on Christian doctrine.

Published in ten volumes from 1907 through 1922 and described by its author as "a connected treatment of the entire range of Catholic Doctrine as it is maintained in the Episcopal Church and the Reformed

Catholic Tradition of the Anglican Communion," Hall's *Dogmatic Theology* became required reading in Episcopal seminaries of high church and Anglo-Catholic orientation. His *Theological Outlines* (in print from 1892 to 1935) also became a standard of American Anglo-Catholic theology. Well into the 1950s, some Episcopal bishops required their candidates for ordination to display a knowledge of "Daddy" Hall's theology. Followers hailed his *Dogmatic Theology* as "an Anglican *Summa Theologica*" (the title of Aquinas's principal work). It says something about changing fashions as well as the transitoriness of most theological writing that Hall often goes unmentioned in books on American theology today.

If Hall was a product of the Anglo-Catholic "Biretta Belt" of the midwest, William Porcher DuBose (who was in college when Hall was born) blended the Pauline concern of southern evangelicals with a high church concern for the sacramental church. A Huguenot descendant and a product of plantation life in South Carolina, DuBose graduated from The Citadel, where he underwent a significant religious conversion. He studied for additional years at the University of Virginia and at the short-lived theological seminary of the Diocese of South Carolina. After serving as an infantry officer in the Confederate Army, he was ordained into the Episcopal ministry. He inaugurated theological education at the University of the South in Sewanee, Tennessee, and taught there — beloved by his students — from 1871 until his death in 1918.

DuBose did not publish his first book until he was fifty-six years old, but in the following nineteen years he published six theological works. They were of such quality that a contemporary at Oxford called him "the wisest writer on the other side of the Atlantic; indeed . . . the wisest Anglican writer . . . on both sides of the Atlantic."[76]

Where Hall was immersed in the church fathers and Middle Ages, DuBose found his starting-point in the apostolic and patristic periods. Evangelically rooted in the New Testament but high church in his view of the church and the sacraments, he was less comprehensive than Hall and set up no system of theology. Rather, he was an incarnational theologian who wrestled daringly with the challenges the nineteenth century was daily presenting to orthodox Christian belief. If recent studies have suggested that he may have accepted more of the assumptions of nineteenth-century theological liberalism than previously assumed, most of his contemporaries viewed him as a creative champion of orthodoxy. "Holding firmly to the old truths," the trustees of Sewanee wrote at the time of his death, "he brought out from them new faith to meet new doubts — new truths to meet new needs."[77]

DuBose's theology underwent shifts, but he focused it on the idea that the universe was in a continual process of evolution and movement toward God. The Christian church, he wrote, was not set apart from this cosmic evolution; rather, the church reflected it and testified to the sacramental universe. Over and over again DuBose linked evolution to the Christian assertion that "the Word became flesh and dwelt among us":

> We cannot kick against the pricks; the world has begun to make the discovery, and it will not go backward in it, that the natural is God's way. The natural is the rational and divine. There is no real break between the natural and the supernatural; the one is only the higher or further other. We shall come to see that Adam and Christ are the same Man; that earth and heaven are one continuous life.
>
> Under the prevalence of the modern scientific principle of evolution we have discovered that the great primal truth of God creating is neither denied nor obscured. . . . God was in Christ *sub specie hominis*, not *Dei* [under the aspect of man, not God]. He was here to fulfill and manifest Himself in us, and us in Him.[78]

When DuBose died, one Episcopal magazine asserted that everyone "agreed . . . that he was the greatest theological scholar in the Episcopal Church."[79] The statement was a clear exaggeration, given the popularity of Hall's *Dogmatics* among Anglo-Catholics. Although DuBose has perhaps remained more important in the history of American theology than Hall, he may have had more admirers in the Church of England during his lifetime than in the Episcopal Church.

CHURCH UNITY

Tensions among church parties have characterized ecumenical relations in the Episcopal Church in the same way that conservative-liberal tensions have affected such discussions in other denominations. While some Episcopalians have looked for unity toward the Eastern Orthodox, Roman Catholic, and Old Catholic churches, others have looked first toward Protestant denominations. The Episcopal Church's relations with other denominations were generally distant and occasionally antagonistic during the colonial period. At the General Convention of 1792, Bishop James Madison of Virginia attempted to open the way for the Methodists to return to the Episcopal Church. A more dedicated and creative bishop than church history has recognized, Madison secured the passage of his proposal in the House of Bishops, but it failed in the House of Clerical and Lay Deputies.

124

In the nineteenth century, under the leadership of the evangelical party, the Episcopal Church began to cooperate with such interdenominational societies as the American Bible Society, the American Sunday School Union, the American Tract Society, and the Evangelical Alliance. The high church party, and later the Anglo-Catholic party, opposed such cooperation on the basis of the distinctiveness of Anglicanism and its claimed possession of the apostolic succession; evangelicals viewed such attitudes as petty condescension. In the west, Episcopalians of all parties generally maintained cordial relations with denominations other than the Latter-day Saints. After the 1830s the rapid growth of the Roman Catholic church and the "romanizing" influences of the Oxford and ritualist movements revived Reformation memories and ushered in a long period of hostility among many Episcopalians toward Roman Catholicism.

As for relations with Protestant denominations, the Muhlenberg Memorial, presented to the House of Bishops in 1853 by New York rector William Augustus Muhlenberg and others, urged that Episcopal bishops contribute to a wider unity. The memorial advocated that the bishops ordain qualified Protestant clergy who could accept the heart of Episcopal teachings, but at the same time allow them to continue to minister in their denominations. In Muhlenberg's words, his plan envisioned

> an ecclesiastical system broader and more comprehensive than that of the Protestant Episcopal Church, . . . identical with that Church in all its great principles, yet providing for as much freedom in opinion, discipline, and worship as is consistent with the essential faith and order of the Gospel.

Muhlenberg concluded: "Only on such a basis can we hope for a 'Religion of the Republic.' "[80]

Vigorously discussed and studied for six years, supported by most evangelicals and by Episcopalians holding moderate views, opposed by the clergy and laity of the emerging Anglo-Catholic party, denounced and advocated, the memorial ultimately failed. Its lasting creation in the Episcopal Church was the commission on church unity (now called the Standing Commission on Ecumenical Relations), which, under various names, has remained perhaps the most active ecumenical agency in any denomination in America.

More systematic was the Chicago-Lambeth Quadrilateral of 1888, which emerged out of proposals made in *The Church Idea: An Essay in Unity* eighteen years earlier by the prophetic William Reed Huntington, then rector of All Saints' Church in Worcester, Massachusetts. The quadrilateral, which is still the official ecumenical platform of the Episcopal

Church, listed four essentials to church unity: the Scriptures, the Apostles' and Nicene creeds, the two sacraments — baptism and the Supper of the Lord — held to be clearly ordained by Christ, and the historic episcopate. On that basis the Episcopal Church held unity discussions with Lutherans and Presbyterians in the years prior to World War I.

Additional ecumenical relationships with Protestantism prior to World War I included the "Open Pulpit" canon of 1907, which permitted non-Episcopal clergy and laity to speak publicly in Episcopal churches, and a cooperative relationship with the Federal Council of Churches (founded in 1908) without actual membership. Overtures in the direction of the Catholic churches included closer relations with Eastern Orthodoxy, the Old Catholic Church, the Polish National Catholic Church, and the Church of Sweden.

THE SOCIAL GOSPEL

The medieval belief that a Christian social ethic must permeate society informed the codes of the colonial Anglican establishments. From 1785 until the rise of the social gospel in the high Victorian period, the social witness of the Episcopal Church was generally limited to parish charities, to participation in such movements as prison reform, and to the support of institutions for those who were destitute, widowed, orphaned, or handicapped. The separation of church and state, the evangelical and traditional high church emphasis on "personal religion," the widespread view among Episcopal clergy in the nineteenth century that ministers should not engage in politics, the dominant individualism of American culture, and the nation's economic dogma of laissez-faire combined to discourage Episcopal social concern. When William Paret was called in 1876 to the rectorship of the influential Church of the Epiphany in Washington, D.C., and asked its vestry the extent of their work with the poor, "the answer was that the parish had no poor; every pew was let."[81]

Yet the middle- and upper-class Episcopal Church was the first denomination in America to welcome the social gospel's critique of industrial society. It was the first to urge the improvement of wages, working and living conditions, and the rights of working men and women. Few observers of American Christianity expected the Episcopal Church to be pro-labor, and Christians in other traditions were quick to see the paradox: why — asked a journal of another denomination in 1891 — was "the Church of wealth, culture, and aristocratic lineage . . . leading the way?"[82]

Scholars generally explain this paradox by pointing to the medieval heritage of Anglicanism, to the rise of Anglo-Catholicism (many of whose adherents in England had allied themselves with organized labor), to the spreading influence among Episcopalians of the Christian Socialist movement of the Church of England since its founding in 1848, and to the concentration of the membership of the Episcopal Church in cities, where social and political problems were obvious. In addition, the Episcopal Church undoubtedly pioneered the social gospel because of the leadership provided by respected bishops. That bishops from old families — and the Episcopal Church was full of them — criticized the ethics of American businesses and advocated the improvement of the working and living conditions of the poor had a way of reassuring economically comfortable Episcopalians about social reform.

As early as the 1870s, church congresses were discussing social problems. By the next decade, Episcopalians had established the earliest organizational expressions of the social gospel in America. Among the most important was the Church Association for the Advancement of the Interests of Labor, founded in 1887 with almost fifty bishops among its members. Centered in New York with small chapters scattered across the nation, CAIL studied the contemporary problems of working men and women (and children) in light of the Christian belief in the incarnation. It investigated sweatshops and tenements, offered plans of mediation in strikes, and instituted the observance of Labor Sunday (the Sunday before Labor Day) in the Episcopal Church.

Founded in 1891 and named after the Church of England organization of the same name, the Episcopal Christian Social Union focused on disseminating information about social problems through publications, lectures, and conferences. Typically, it assigned a Harvard University historian to study the violent Pullman strike of 1894 and then published his findings. For ten years at the turn of the century, it had as its traveling secretary and principal publicist William D. P. Bliss, a Knight of Labor and Socialist who filled churches, auditoriums, and clubrooms inside and outside the United States with lectures on social problems.

These and several other social gospel organizations within the Episcopal Church did much to break down the hostility that had caused labor leaders to denounce Christian churches as "organized hypocrisy" and "allies of capital." Although the General Convention moved more slowly than church organizations, its delegates began to concern themselves with questions of social justice from the 1890s on. For a time, even Henry George, author of *Progress and Poverty* and proponent of taxing the privileged classes and redistributing wealth, was sympathetic with the Episcopal

Church because of its social statements. When the church established permanent committees and departments to deal with the problems of American society, these voluntary organizations disbanded one by one. Their witness was continued after 1919 by the Church League for Industrial Democracy (later called the Episcopal League for Social Action), which counted more than one thousand members by the Depression.

Bishops active in the social gospel movement included Potter of New York, who mediated many strikes; Charles D. Williams of Michigan, a forceful and persistent critic of the ethics of the emerging automobile industry; Franklin S. Spalding and Paul Jones of Utah, both of whom were members of the Socialist party; and the eloquent and able Chauncey Bunce Brewster of Connecticut, who never permitted the Episcopalians of his large diocese to forget their obligations to the less privileged.

Priests included Bliss, who converted from the Congregationalist ministry after deciding that the Episcopal Church was the denomination that could most influence the restructuring of American life according to Christian principles; Irish-born William S. Rainsford, rector of St. George's Church in Manhattan, whose concept of the parish church as a community center spread throughout American Christianity and formed the basis of the Institutional Church Movement; Caleb S. Henry, a convert from Congregationalism who espoused the right to apply religion to politics; Philo W. Sprague of Massachusetts, author of *Socialism From Genesis to Revelation;* R. Heber Newton, a leader in the Society of Christian Socialists; Bernard Iddings Bell, who had a notable ministry among intellectuals in Chicago and New York; and Elisha Mulford, author of *The Nation* and *The Republic of God.*

Overlooked until recently has been Irwin St. John Tucker, a talented, colorful, and impatient priest who was radicalized by the Triangle Shirtwaist fire and subsequently played highly visible roles in the Socialist party while serving parishes in New York and Chicago. Before he died at the age of ninety-six, Tucker had been indicted and sentenced to Leavenworth as a Socialist under the Espionage Act of 1917. He had helped to found the Hobo College, had briefly converted to the Roman Catholic Church before returning to the Episcopal Church, had served as head of the copy desk for the Chicago *Herald-Examiner,* and had become a Republican.[83]

Lesser-known advocates of the social gospel such as Harold S. Brewster, who graduated from Amherst and the Episcopal Theological School when the movement was at its height, lost their churches in southwestern mining towns when they became card-carrying members of striking locals. One of the relatively few southern Episcopalians active in the social gospel was Edgar Gardner Murphy, who began his ministry in Texas by protesting a lynching and ended as executive secretary of the reform-minded Southern Education Board.

Episcopal laypersons — especially Richard T. Ely, professor at the University of Wisconsin and Johns Hopkins University, popular speaker at The Chatauqua Institute, and founder of the American Economics Association (which was in part an outgrowth of the social gospel movement) — played a major role in implementing the social gospel. The American novelist Winston Churchill gained wide attention with his *The Inside of the Cup* (1913), a novel (originally serialized in *Hearst's Magazine*) about the rector of an affluent Episcopal church in St. Louis who is converted to the views of the social gospel. Although Ely, James O. S. Huntington, and Bernard Iddings Bell were Anglo-Catholics and believed that the sacramental life was the primary motivating force toward a reconciliation of all classes and races, most of the leaders of the social gospel in the Episcopal Church came from its broad church wing, for in all denominations the social gospel was generally associated with theological liberalism. Some, like Rainsford, began as evangelicals.

Less well known is the important role of Episcopal women in the social gospel movement. As early as the 1850s, long before calls to action were heard from the General Convention, Episcopal Sisters of the Holy Communion served among the dispossessed. They were later joined by deaconesses and sisters from other orders. The composition of Episcopal membership also provided the church with a large pool of talented volunteer laywomen who worked among the poor. Serving as physicians, nurses, coordinators of Girls' Friendly Societies (a predecessor in Anglicanism of the Girl Scouts), settlement house workers, factory inspectors, and in many other capacities, far more Episcopal women contributed to social gospel concerns than we can know. Excluded from the pulpit and from other positions of church leadership, most of these women could not become the voices of the social gospel movement and hence are not remembered in history today.

Some Episcopal women did have voice, however, including Harriette Keyser of New York City, who edited the influential quarterly published by CAIL and served as its national secretary for thirty years. Professor Vida D. Scudder of Wellesley College, who published widely on the social responsibilities of Christians, worked in the settlement house movement and was influential in the Society of the Companions of the Holy Cross. And the first woman Cabinet member in American history, U.S. Secretary of Labor Frances Perkins, influenced many of the reforms of Franklin D.

Bishop William Scarlett (1883–1973), an advocate of the Social Gospel,
and Secretary of Labor Frances Perkins investigate the working conditions
of miners during the Depression.

Roosevelt's New Deal, including the Social Security Act of 1935 and
the Fair Labor Standards Act of 1938. These and countless other women
made significant if often unrecognized contributions to the social gospel
movement in the Episcopal Church.

An all-male organization that combines evangelism with social outreach is the Brotherhood of St. Andrew, founded in 1883 in the undercroft

of St. James' Cathedral in Chicago. Evangelism has always been its primary goal, but its ministry to men and youth has involved work with soup kitchens, youth groups, prison inmates, and the unemployed. Although the brotherhood's greatest strength occurred earlier in the century, it had approximately thirty-five hundred members in some four hundred chapters as of 1992.

During the years from the Civil War to World War I, most Episcopalians undoubtedly remained not only suspicious of social engineering but also conservative on economic and social issues. Many continued to believe that salvation was an individual process only and that the church's duty was to inspire individuals who as Christians would then improve society. Then as now, more clergy than laity believed that the Episcopal Church ought to speak on social questions. Those were the years when captains of industry held the best pews in Episcopal and Presbyterian churches and a writer could claim that even the Roman Catholic Church was "lined up with property, with the wealthy, with the state, with capitalism, with all the forces of reaction."[84] In any strike employers could generally expect most churches in the United States to take their side.

At the same time, families slept four and five to a room in tenements, street car drivers and conductors worked seventeen-hour days, and strikers and strikebreakers clashed violently in cities across America. Charges of communism and anarchism tainted most public discussion of improving working conditions. In such a context the statements that emerged from Episcopal organizations and from the General Assembly were striking. "Nothing is more difficult, nothing requires more divine grace than the constant manifestation of love to our fellows in all our daily acts; in our selling, buying, getting gain," wrote Richard T. Ely.[85]

SISTERHOODS AND DEACONESSES

Excluded from the Episcopal diaconate and priesthood by canon and from positions of leadership by custom, women served the church throughout the period prior to the Civil War through unpaid, volunteer activities. Bible and tract societies, mission auxiliaries, sewing circles, altar guilds, and Sunday schools characterized "women's work," as did the duties of a rector's or missionary's wife. "Thoughtful, grave, and seriously inclined from her earliest youth," a eulogist said in 1848 in words typical of those delivered at the funerals of wives of clergy,

... she was engaged up to the time of her marriage as a teacher in the Sunday school, and was always at her post. She wrote many letters to her relatives and school friends, ... few would be found in which there was not some reference to religion, while many of them were wholly upon that subject.... She was the instrument in God's hand of turning... feet into the path of peace.[86]

In the mid-nineteenth century a new possibility for church service opened for women when the Oxford Movement launched the founding of sisterhoods in America. The sisterhoods emerged as an alternative to "women's work," but their establishment faced numerous obstacles.

The prospect of ordered communities of women, or "women religious" (the medieval term for nuns), alarmed many Episcopalians. Whereas the Oxford Movement inspired many sisterhoods, it also fostered anti-Roman Catholic sentiments in the Episcopal Church at large. In fact, the founders of the first Episcopal sisterhood in America were not supporters of the Oxford Movement. Time and again Anne Ayres and William Augustus Muhlenberg meticulously described how their Sisterhood of the Holy Communion (established in Manhattan in 1852) differed from a Roman Catholic order. Patterned after a Lutheran community in Germany, it not only eschewed lifetime vows and religious garb but also organized the routine of its members around works of service rather than a devotional schedule.

Some Episcopal women, however, sought the structure of a more traditional order. In 1865, three former members of the Sisterhood of the Holy Communion founded the Community of St. Mary in New York, complete with daily offices, traditional habits, and vows of poverty, chastity, and obedience. Overcoming low church accusations of "Roman extravagance" and "mawkish Mariolatry," the sisterhood grew steadily in members and expanded to other cities.[87] The community's work among the poor and the sick — notably in Memphis during the yellow-fever epidemic of 1878 — quieted most critics.

Another community, the Sisterhood of the Holy Nativity — founded in 1882 in Fond du Lac, Wisconsin, by Bishop Grafton — listed "a desire to leave the world" (a most un-Protestant approach to life) as an attitude required of aspirants.[88] Every Episcopal sisterhood — there were approximately twenty-two by 1905 — faced the tension of Protestant-Catholic identity. Communities of both leanings were formed. A woman who attended Smith College and the Boston Museum School of the Fine Arts described the reaction of her Episcopal mother and rationalist father when she told them "the astonishing news" that she planned to enter the Order of St. Anne:

> It was one of the most terrible experiences of my whole life, because they were utterly shattered. My father felt that I was rejecting all that he had ever done for me. . . . My mother was heart-broken. . . . My father was totally unable to accept it, disinherited me, and never saw me again, but my mother stayed with me. However, . . . until my life profession she hoped and argued with me whenever she could to come home and come out. . . . [89]

Episcopal orphanages, hospitals, shelters, schools, retreat houses, and other institutions benefited from the work of sisterhoods. Several communities played a prominent role in defining modern nursing and nursing education in the United States. Lacking formal sanction by the church, most sisterhoods developed their own networks of financial support through the help of volunteers and benefactors. Some lay assistants received wages; the sisters worked without pay.

The work of the sisterhoods encompassed areas of ministry previously unaddressed or dominated by men. Although they helped to redefine the roles of women in the denomination, their communal life, unpaid status, and celibacy made them an alternative for relatively few. The Community of St. John the Baptist, for example, recorded only seventy professions from 1870 to 1970. The Episcopal Church clearly needed to establish a vocation for women.

Responding to churchwomen — especially the voice of Mary Emery Twing — the General Convention of 1889 officially sanctioned the office of deaconess "to assist the minister in the care of the poor and sick, the religious training of the young and others, and the work of moral reformation."[90] The canon required that deaconesses be single or widowed and that they complete two years of training. Unlike most sisters, deaconesses wore less "Catholic" clothing, did not generally live in communities, and were salaried. They could not take lifetime vows.

Supported by the woman's auxiliary, some of the newly trained deaconesses entered mission work. Others found employment as parish workers, teachers or headmistresses, or matrons of orphanages. To train them, the church established deaconess training schools in New York, Philadelphia, San Francisco, and later in other cities. The two-year training consisted of an abbreviated seminary curriculum, with the addition of such specialized courses as nursing.

The executive board of the woman's auxiliary elected at the Triennial
Convention in Denver, 1931.

Although deaconesses often left legacies of untiring Christian service in the parishes and institutions they served, confusion over their role
hindered the order from the start. "Our deaconesses have been tolerated
rather than authorized by the church," a commission report to the General Convention of 1922 states. "Neither they, nor the people generally,

134

have been quite sure what they were or what they were commissioned to do."[91] Eighteen years later a similar report to the General Convention reads: "There exists some confusion as to what a Deaconess is and what she does."[92]

One thing was clear: the office of deaconess was not the female counterpart to the office of deacon. Bishops "ordained" deacons, but, in the language of the church's commissioning service, they "set apart" deaconesses. Although deaconesses were considered to be called by God, they remained clearly subordinate to male clergy even after theological training and a profession of vows. They could minister to the sick, teach the young, and perform administrative duties, but they could neither celebrate the eucharist nor — except when a male deacon or priest was unavailable — preach or lead worship. The congregations they served were often those that were too small to support a male priest. As a result, they often became full-time, salaried doers of "women's work."

Another difference illustrated the subordinate status of deaconesses. Whereas deacons took lifetime vows and could marry, deaconesses were required to be unmarried or widowed. Any deaconess who chose to marry had to resign her office. In keeping with the views of the day, many of the delegates and bishops to the General Conventions — all of whom were male — viewed marriage not only as the ultimate vocation for women but also as one that required a woman's full attention.

Most deaconesses, on the other hand, found their vocation in their office and were committed totally to it; some even went beyond the canon and took lifetime vows. When the General Convention temporarily allowed married women to become deaconesses in the 1930s, sixty-one percent of the deaconesses polled argued that their work required a full-time dedication possible only to unmarried women. At the time few Episcopalians (or Americans) considered the possibility that women could combine marriage and career.

Although many deaconesses found fulfillment in their vocation, for most Episcopal women the office failed to provide a viable option for a church career. The ranks of deaconesses steadily declined — from over two hundred in 1934 to one hundred in 1943 to less than eighty in 1964. Not until the 1970s, when the canons afforded them equal status with men in the Episcopal Church, did women enter church vocations in significant numbers. (Women's ordination to the diaconate and the priesthood in the Episcopal Church is discussed in chapter 6.)

THE CHURCH AND EDUCATION

Primary and Secondary Schools

From the parsons' academies of the colonial period to the preparatory schools of late Victorian America, the Episcopal Church has been second among mainline denominations in America only to the Roman Catholic Church in primary and secondary education. The Episcopal Church has been especially noted for the boarding schools that emerged under its sponsorship in the late nineteenth and early twentieth centuries.

Although their origin lay in the Anglican parsons' academies of early America, Episcopal boarding schools date from the antebellum period. William Augustus Muhlenberg's Flushing Institute (1828), William R. Whittingham's College of St. James (1842), and George Shattuck, Jr.'s St. Paul's School (1855) were the most influential early models. Paralleled by Eton, Harrow, and other public schools in England, Episcopal boys' preparatory schools such as Groton and St. Mark's in Massachusetts and St. George's in Rhode Island stretched in time as far west as Hawaii. Over the decades many of these Episcopal schools developed into fashionable academies, but the original purpose of most was to nurture young boys in the Anglican faith and to direct them into lives of Christian service.

Led by headmasters such as Groton's Endicott Peabody (memorialized in Louis Auchincloss's novel, *The Rector of Justin*) and Samuel Smith Drury of St. Paul's (who typically greeted a boy brought to visit with the words "How-do-you-do-my-boy-have-you-been-baptized-and-confirmed?"), the schools concerned themselves with more than inculcating Christianity and the beginnings of a liberal education. They also taught discipline, morality, manners, dress, and what the Victorians called "manliness." The imposing Peabody and his wife said good night to every boy at Groton every night when they were in residence; wherever they were, students and alumni learned to brace for the impact when he greeted them by laying his strong hand on their shoulders.

Over the years these Episcopal schools, especially those in New England, played a major role both in preparing graduates for Ivy League colleges and in grooming the economic, political, and social leadership of America. Numerous graduates also became Episcopal vestrymen, priests, and bishops. Americans who attended Groton include President Franklin Delano Roosevelt, Secretary of State Dean Acheson, architect Ralph Adams Cram, and statesman Averill Harriman. Choate graduates include President John F. Kennedy, financier Paul Mellon, and

136

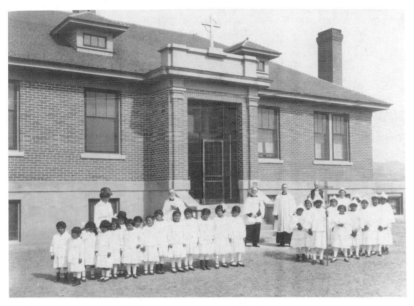

Students and clergy at the Fort Hall School, Idaho, in 1921. The Episcopal Church established similar schools among African Americans and Appalachian whites.

presidential candidate Adlai Stevenson. William Randolph Hearst, John D. Rockefeller, Jr., and Cornelius Vanderbilt, Jr., attended St. Paul's School.

Founded in the early twentieth century and often begun as finishing schools (particularly in the east), Episcopal boarding schools for girls generally emerged later than those for boys. In the 1930s most of the schools turned to college preparatory curricula. Schools for girls included Rosemary Hall and St. Margaret's in Connecticut, St. Mary's in New Jersey, St. Timothy's in Maryland, Chatham Hall in Virginia, Margaret Hall in Kentucky, St. Mary's in Tennessee, and Annie Wright in Washington.

Headmistresses rather than headmasters usually ran these schools for girls. Many considered their positions to be lifetime commitments. Instrumental in founding the National Association of Episcopal Schools, Ruth Jenkins served as headmistress of Annie Wright Seminary (now Annie Wright School) in Tacoma, Washington, for over twenty years. At Virginia's Chatham Hall, Dean Virginia Holt ran a tight ship during a tenure of more than thirty years, controlling everything from the temperature of the swimming pool to the delivery of eggs to the counseling of college-bound seniors. Like Sister Rachel Hosmer, who was headmistress of Margaret Hall for twenty-five years before being ordained an Episcopal priest in 1977, many of the women not only encouraged academic excellence but also tried to instill a sense of self-confidence and social consciousness in their students.

Over the decades critics of Episcopal boarding schools (including some graduates) deplored their social register atmosphere and the homogeneity and snobbery of their students. Critics and supporters alike viewed them as groomers of the American aristocracy. But the 1960s and early 1970s witnessed changes that included coeducation, minority recruitment, and emphasis on academic excellence.

The same decades and the 1980s saw the establishment of a large number of new Episcopal primary and secondary schools across the United States. Extending from Florida to the Pacific Northwest, and usually (but not invariably) operating as day rather than boarding schools, the institutions emerged for many reasons. Some were established during the period of intensive church growth of the 1950s. Inspired by the success of such early education programs as Head Start, others began as nursery schools in the 1960s. In the 1970s and 1980s still others grew in response to a perceived decline in public education and attempted to provide rigorous academic programs and value-oriented education. Some were founded because of the "white flight" response to integration.

Along with the older Episcopal boarding and day schools, these newer schools may represent the principal way in which Americans of other religious backgrounds first come into contact with the Episcopal Church. Approximately seventy-five percent of their students are either unchurched or come from other denominational backgrounds. In recent years secondary education has been an area of growth in the Episcopal Church.

Higher Education

Among major American denominations the Episcopal Church ranks last in establishing and maintaining church-related colleges. Why a denomination with the heritage of Oxford and Cambridge, with a high level of learning among its clergy and laity, and with an appreciation of architecture, liturgy, and music should have spawned such a weak record in higher education is one of the mysteries of American religious history.

That the America of the 1990s contained only seven Episcopal colleges undoubtedly would have surprised the educated American of the eighteenth century. Compared to other denominations, Anglicans took the lead in higher education in early America, either obtaining the charters for or actually opening the first colleges in Virginia, Pennsylvania, New York, Maryland, and South Carolina.

Planned under a different name as early as 1618 with initial construction of its first academic buildings ended by an Indian massacre in 1622, The College of William and Mary, Williamsburg, Virginia, was chartered in 1693 and opened in 1697. King's College, New York City (1754, now Columbia University) was founded by Episcopalians. Although unaffiliated with any denomination, the College of Philadelphia (now the University of Pennsylvania) was chartered in 1755 with strong Episcopal influences. St. John's College in Annapolis, Maryland, now claims a 1698 date of founding by Episcopalians, but was not chartered for college-level work until 1784.

The influence of the Episcopal Church on these pre-Revolution foundations has lessened with time. Reeling from the financial losses of the Civil War, William and Mary survived by entering the state college system of the Commonwealth of Virginia in the late nineteenth century. And although all the presidents of Columbia University continued to be Episcopalian until Dwight D. Eisenhower assumed that office following World War II, Episcopal Church yearbooks dropped the university from their list of Episcopal institutions after 1908.

From the end of the Revolution through the end of the Civil War, the Episcopal Church chartered or opened almost forty colleges. Like similar colleges established in other denominations to give ministerial candidates and other students a college education, many of these schools proved short-lived. Other institutions of higher education established during this period for the Episcopal Church survived, but are no longer connected with the denomination. This list includes Washington College (founded in 1782) in Maryland, the College of Charleston (1785) in South Carolina, and Lehigh University (1865) in Pennsylvania. Until recent years, Trinity College (founded in 1823) in Connecticut was an Episcopal college. Today only four colleges established by Episcopalians before the Civil War — Hobart College (1822) in New York; Kenyon College (1824) in Ohio; the University of the South (1857) in Tennessee; and Bard College (founded in 1860 as St. Stephen's College) in New York — remain affiliated with the Episcopal Church.

Of the twenty-six colleges that Episcopalians founded in the United States in the years following the Civil War, only three — St. Augustine's College (Raleigh, North Carolina), St. Paul's College (Lawrenceville, Virginia), and Voorhees College (Denmark, South Carolina) — remain officially tied to the church today. All were established as colleges for African Americans. Disaffiliation should not always be interpreted as a complete loss, however, for the atmosphere of some of these former church colleges remains Episcopal.

Theological Seminaries

During the colonial period, young men who wished to enter the Anglican ministry in the American colonies normally attended a college such as William and Mary, which had a faculty of theology. After studying for the ordination examinations of the Church of England, they traveled to England for the examinations. Because of shipwreck and disease, the trip was dangerous. If successful in the examinations administered by the bishop of London or a bishop substituting for him, young men were ordained deacon and priest in England. Converts from other denominations and Anglicans who had attended non-Anglican colleges read for orders under the direction of a local rector, often living in his parsonage and assisting him in the work of the parish. In the absence of theological seminaries, the apprenticeship system continued after the Revolutionary War, with American bishops ordaining qualified candidates.

In 1817 the General Convention established the General Theological Seminary in New York City as the official or "general" seminary for the entire Episcopal Church. The seminary's distance from other dioceses and its distinctively high church tone quickly prompted the creation of additional seminaries.

The theological and liturgical changes of the 1960s and 1970s render generalizations about seminaries tenuous. As in the case of denominations ranging from the Baptist to the Roman Catholic, the contemporary Episcopal Church contains factions that can broadly be called liberal, moderate, and traditionalist. The old divisions based upon the shibboleths of "churchmanship" are largely dead. Most Episcopalians probably now fall into a category that could be termed "central church."

Of the seminaries that survive today, however, Nashotah House (1842), Nashotah, Wisconsin, has traditionally represented Anglo-Catholicism and in recent years Episcopal traditionalism; the Protestant Episcopal Theological Seminary in Virginia, Alexandria, Virginia (1823), has been the principal evangelical seminary; and Episcopal Divinity School (established in 1867 in Cambridge, Massachusetts, as the Episcopal Theological Seminary, but merged in 1967 with the one-hundred-five-year-old Philadelphia Divinity School) has represented the broad church point of view and a concern for the role of the church in the larger world. While incorporating all of the emphases of Anglicanism, General Seminary has remained in the high church tradition for most of its history.

Other seminaries with varying versions of the high church tradition have included the School of Theology of the University of the South, in Sewanee, Tennessee (1878), the Berkeley Divinity School in New Haven, Connecticut (founded in 1854 in Middletown, Connecticut but since 1971 affiliated with Yale University), and Seabury-Western Theological Seminary in Evanston, Illinois (formed in 1933 by the merger of Seabury Divinity School of Faribault, Minnesota, and Western Theological Seminary of Chicago). For many decades Bexley Hall in Gambier, Ohio (founded in 1824, but since 1968 part of the Rochester Center for Theological Studies in Rochester, New York), was known for its evangelical orientation. Emphasizing the conservative evangelical tradition while adding charismatic influences to it has been Trinity Episcopal School for Ministry in Ambridge, Pennsylvania (1975). In the university towns of Berkeley, California, and Austin, Texas, two seminaries — the Church Divinity School of the Pacific (1893) and the Episcopal Theological Seminary of the Southwest (1952) — originated in the low and central church traditions.

From the time of their origin until the middle of the twentieth century, the style of life in some of the seminaries was consciously modeled upon Oxford and Cambridge. Numerous Episcopal clergy have also attended such interdenominational seminaries as Chicago, Yale, and Union Theological Seminary in New York. By canon law, bishops have the power to decide which seminaries their candidates may attend. Roman Catholic and Eastern Orthodox priests and ministers from Protestant denominations who wish to become Episcopal clergy often spend a year or more in an Episcopal seminary, so that student bodies have almost always included older students. In the aftermath of the social changes of the 1960s, the number of older students has increased markedly.

A CENTURY OF CHANGE

By World War I, being an Episcopalian was an intellectually more complex matter than it had been one hundred years earlier. In 1817 most Episcopalians had been biblical literalists. They had believed in the Garden of Eden, in the Episcopal Church as a Protestant church, in stately but simple worship, in the divinely ordained exclusion of women from any church vocation, and in the church remaining silent during such political controversies as slavery.

By 1917 belief in a literal Adam and Eve and in churches built like meeting houses had gone the way of the horse and buggy in most Episcopal parishes. Episcopal worship included practices that Episcopalians of one hundred years earlier would have regarded as peculiar to Roman Catholicism. Women served as nuns and deaconesses. Episcopalians were hearing that the kingdom of God was more than a post-mortem reward for piety and that they could not separate their personal religion from the social gospel without being unfaithful to Jesus Christ. In the twentieth century, the challenges posed by these changes would not be resolved, but would only increase.

6

THE EPISCOPAL CHURCH
IN THE TWENTIETH
CENTURY

EPISCOPALIANS AND WORLD WAR I

As might be expected of Christians of largely British heritage, virtually all Episcopalians seem to have supported America's entrance into World War I. Prior to the declaration of war, clerical leaders such as Bishop Brent and William T. Manning of Trinity Church, New York City, openly opposed neutrality. The House of Bishops opposed isolation in 1916 and pledged complete cooperation when America entered the war in 1917.

The few pacifists in Episcopal churches after 1917 generally came from the ranks of clergy who had been influenced by the social gospel. Bishop David Greer of New York opposed America's involvement throughout the war. Bishop Paul Jones of Utah resigned his episcopate in 1918 because of opposition in his diocese to his pacifism.[93] Clergy such as John Howard Melish of the Church of the Holy Trinity in Brooklyn Heights, New York, narrowly escaped losing their rectorates because of their antiwar views.

More typical during World War I were surprisingly jihadistic clergy such as Randolph H. McKim, rector of the Church of the Epiphany in Washington, D.C., who described the war in sermons as "a Crusade. The greatest in History — the holiest. . . . a Holy War."[94] The church's war commission and other agencies supplied Episcopal military personnel with crosses to be worn with dog tags; they also sent Bibles, Prayer Books, and hymnals. More than two hundred Episcopal clergy became military chaplains; Bishop Theodore Dubose Bratton of Mississippi took leave from his diocese and went to France to work for the YMCA. Because General John J. Pershing, commander in chief of the American Expeditionary Force, had become an Episcopalian in the Philippines when

Washington National Cathedral (Cathedral of St. Peter and St. Paul), seat of the presiding bishop of the Episcopal Church, begun on September 29, 1907, and completed on September 29, 1990.

Charles Henry Brent was resident bishop, Bishop Brent was appointed senior chaplain of the AEF. World War I also saw the first regular use of the American flag in Episcopal churches. Since its adoption in 1940, the red, white, and light blue Episcopal Church flag has joined the national flag in the processions and chancels of many Episcopal churches.

144

Following the Treaty of Versailles, the General Convention of 1919, along with many Episcopal clergy and journals, endorsed the League of Nations. The principal opponent of the league, Henry Cabot Lodge, was an Episcopal layman. By 1924 disillusionment about the war (in which eight million were killed and thirty-seven million wounded, most of whom were Christians) had changed attitudes so greatly that antiwar sentiment, whether caused by pacifism or isolationism, continued to be strong among Episcopalians and other American Christians through the 1930s. Pacifist clergy such as Harold Brewster, dean of Gethsemane Cathedral in Fargo, North Dakota, published books (*The Madness of War*, 1928) attacking war. As late as the 1980s, Episcopal clergy who lived through the disillusionment of that period were still writing letters of protest to church journals:

> We were goaded into World War I by stories of atrocities, afterward proven untrue. There was a propaganda war funded by our allies to make sure we became involved in the war. We were! Making us readily a nation of killers because we fell for it. And our young men became its fatalities.[95]

REORGANIZATION, PROHIBITION, AND THE 1920S

In 1917, following seven years of preparatory work by the remarkable Bishop William Lawrence of Massachusetts, the General Convention established the Church Pension Fund, which allowed elderly and disabled clergy and widows as well as dependent children of deceased clergy to receive a pension upon retirement. Previously, most Episcopal clergy had the choice of working until they dropped or of becoming dependent upon charity. The pension fund, which began with an endowment of over $8 million (larger than ever before raised by a denomination through voluntary contributions) influenced the retirement programs of many other denominations.

In 1919 the Episcopal Church attempted to create greater efficiency and corporate consciousness by centralizing its previously uncoordinated denominational boards in the six-story Church Missions House at 281 Park Avenue, South, in New York City. Chaired by the presiding bishop (who from 1925 on was elected for a set term and given an office at what Episcopalians came to call "281"), a twenty-four member National Council consisting of elected bishops, priests, and laity was given the responsibility for carrying on the work of the denomination between sessions of the General Convention. Building upon experience gained from successful fundraising in the previous decade for the pension fund,

"The Circuit Rider of the Shashi": Regina B. Lustgarten, a teacher and nurse
in the Missionary District of Hankow, China, on the "Meracar" she used
to visit outstations, ca. 1926.

the General Convention of 1919 also established a "Nation-wide Campaign" directed at identifying the needs of the church and increasing its financial support. Moderately successful, the campaign made pledge envelopes and the annual Every Member Canvass a regular part of Episcopal life. The church's reorganization was heavily influenced by the patterns of American business life.

During the General Convention of 1919 — the year in which Congress had passed the women's suffrage amendment — Episcopal women sought the right to vote in church assemblies. They also sought representation on the Board of Missions and a pension fund for deaconesses. The all-male General Convention refused the first two requests and voted only to study the third.

In 1919 Episcopalians also confronted the Volstead Act. In previous years, in contrast to mainline Protestantism, the Episcopal Church had remained relatively uninvolved in the temperance and prohibition movements. Most of the nineteenth-century Episcopalians who carried the temperance banner — like Bishop Alonzo Potter of Pennsylvania, a supporter of total abstinence — came from the ranks of the evangelical party.

The majority of Episcopalians saw the use of alcohol as a matter of private morals, accepted the principle of voluntary abstinence, and desired that neither the church nor the nation go further toward coercion. Unlike most Protestant churches, Episcopal churches therefore continued to use fermented wine in their services of holy communion. Even after prohibition, bishops like Junius M. Horner of Asheville directed abstemious clergy that the use of grape juice in services of holy communion was "unwarranted by the action of our Lord."[96] As late as the 1931 General Convention, the House of Bishops tabled a communicant's request for the use of grape juice.

In 1904 the church received widespread unfavorable publicity after a group of reform-minded Episcopalians adopted a visionary scheme of Rainsford (based on similar programs in England) and opened a "reform saloon" on Manhattan's lower east side. In an effort to drive disreputable saloons out of business, they planned a saloon on principles that were rare for the time: they would observe legal hours, serve milder drinks and good food, serve unadulterated alcohol, refuse to give alcohol to minors or to the intoxicated, and make the saloon a place where entire families could come.

The official opening of the saloon included remarks by New York's Bishop Henry Codman Potter, Alonzo's cultured son and an opponent of the national prohibition movement, to the effect that saloons were a refuge for the poor that society should work to improve rather than to destroy. It also included an apparently unplanned singing of the doxology. After the bishop left, the philanthropists and lower east side residents in attendance drank to Bishop Potter's health. Writers and cartoonists from coast to coast had a field day with the short-lived saloon, as did leaders in the prohibitionist movement such as Carry Nation and revivalist "Georgia" Sam Jones. Bishop Thomas F. Gailor of the temperance-minded state of Tennessee, who also served as the chief administrator of the church's national council from 1919 to 1925, was a similar object of attacks.

As national support for prohibition rose, the Episcopal Church reacted with caution. The Church Temperance Society (1881) — which, like earlier temperance societies, initially included both teetotalers and moderate drinkers — refrained from recommending prohibition until World War I. The General Convention of 1916 supported strong legislative action to repress liquor traffic and urged Episcopalians to set an example by refusing alcohol at public functions, but stopped short of supporting total prohibition. When the Volstead Act was passed, however, General Conventions enjoined obedience to the law.

As the 1920s went on, the majority of Episcopalians clearly found prohibition a failure, though many seem to have desired modification instead of complete repeal. Following six years of experience with the Volstead Act, the Church Temperance Society reversed its original support of prohibition.

In the 1920s, too, the General Convention deprecated the Ku Klux Klan, a group that found little support among Episcopalians, but took no official action on the Red Scare or the Sacco-Vanzetti case, over which Episcopal opinion divided. Readers of F. Scott Fitzgerald's novels found that most of his leading figures were Episcopalians, though the male protagonists often had Irish names.

The postwar craze for amusement and the ability to take Sunday drives in the automobile challenged patterns of church attendance. New evangelistic methods included the use of advertising (like many denominations, the Episcopal Church added a department of publicity) and the introduction from England of the Church Army, a society of lay evangelists patterned upon the Salvation Army. The shortage of clergy that dated to the colonial period continued. The heavy emigration from non-British countries meant that the rate of growth of the Episcopal Church from 1900 to 1930 was the smallest since the establishment of the Domestic and Foreign Missionary Society in 1820. Nevertheless, by the 1920s the National Council had begun to overflow its facilities in the Church Missions House, and 1926 saw the first call for a new headquarters building.

Ecumenical advances during the 1920s included a seldom-used concordat patterned upon the Muhlenberg Memorial. It allowed Episcopal bishops to ordain Congregational and other ministers without requiring them to leave their denomination's ministry. Clergy from other denominations, however, continued to become Episcopalians. "Something deep in me responds to the sweet and tempered ways of the Episcopal Church," wrote a noted Baptist minister who became an Episcopal priest in 1925:

> Its atmosphere of reverence, its ordered and stately worship, its tradition of historic continuity, linking today with ages agone; its symbols which enshrine the faith of the past and the hope of the future; its wise and wide tolerance; its old and lovely liturgy . . . the organized mysticism of its sacraments — all these things of beauty and grace move me profoundly.
>
> More vital still, if possible, is the central and strategic position which the Episcopal Church holds in the confused religious situation of our time. It is the roomiest Church in Christendom, in that it accepts the basic facts of Christian faith as symbols of transparent truths, which each may interpret as his or her insight explores their depth and wonder.

Midway between an arid liberalism and an acrid orthodoxy, it keeps its wise course, conserving the eternal values of faith while seeking to read the Word of God revealed in the tumult of the time. If its spirit and attitude were better understood, it would be at once the haven and the home of many vexed minds torn between loyalty to the old faith and the new truth.[97]

In international ecumenical affairs, the landmark World Conference on Faith and Order, which met in 1927 in Lausanne, Switzerland, owed much to the vision of Bishop Brent. It owed much more to the years of selfless preparatory work by layman Robert Hallowell Gardiner of Gardiner, Maine. Scion of an old Episcopal family and a deputy of quiet influence in General Conventions, Gardiner served as secretary of the commission of the Episcopal Church charged with assembling the conference. Scholars have yet to assess his contributions to the cause of Christian unity. At Lausanne four hundred representatives from more than one hundred Protestant, Eastern Orthodox, and Old Catholic churches met to discuss Christian unity.

Theologically, the controversy over fundamentalism and evolution had few ramifications in the Episcopal Church. Whatever might be the views of some laity and older clergy, most Episcopalians had accepted Darwinism and the need for biblical criticism by the 1920s. In 1923 the House of Bishops declared that Episcopal clergy and laity must believe in the literal interpretation of the virgin birth and the physical resurrection of Jesus. The resulting dispute between the "modernist" faction (or the clergy and laity who believed that modern thought demanded radical reinterpretations of dogma) and the defenders of traditional orthodoxy subsided more quickly in the Episcopal Church than did similar controversies in other denominations. Although an extreme form of modernism appeared in such clergy as Bishop William Montgomery Brown of Arkansas, who was deposed from the episcopate in 1924 after publicly denying many traditional tenets of Christianity, modernism found fewer advocates in the Episcopal Church than in the Church of England.

"Bad plumbing, bad food, bad air, bad social conditions, bad legislation, bad education, as well as bad morals are distinctively unchristian," a Pittsburgh rector declared in a lecture during World War I.[98] While the Protestant adoption of business techniques and outlook that some church historians have titled "the Babbittonian captivity of the church" failed to engulf the Episcopal Church in the 1920s, only a small minority of its clergy and laity remained actively involved in the concerns of the social gospel after the war. The national church's department of Christian social service and similar diocesan offices continued to affirm the message of social Christianity. Especially active in social concerns were William B. Spofford, secretary of the Church League for Industrial Democracy, and William Scarlett, dean in succession of Trinity Cathedral, Phoenix, and Christ Church Cathedral, St. Louis. Scarlett later became the bishop of Missouri.

THE DEPRESSION

The Episcopal Church suffered seriously from the economic collapse of the Depression. In some parishes, virtually the entire congregation became unemployed. Churches reduced staff and salaries; deaconesses (who had no job security) became one of the prime casualties. Seminary enrollment declined, and young men graduating from seminary found few positions.

The giving of dioceses to the national church plummeted; that of the Diocese of North Carolina declined from a high of $37,000 in 1922 to only $12,000 during some of the Depression years. In the dollar equivalents of the time, contributions to missions declined from $2.25 per capita in 1930 to 96 cents in 1940. Despite a requirement for a balanced budget, the National Council fell into increasing debt and had to slash staff and salaries and appeal to the dioceses for assistance. On the parish level, churches sometimes fell months behind in the payment of their clergy. In Grand Forks, North Dakota, St. Paul's Church had $350 in the bank in 1940, but its outstanding bills totaled $3,000.

Dioceses and parishes were forced into the most rigorous economics. The bishop of Georgia asked the council to reduce his own salary rather than cut the missionary budget. The missionary district of North Dakota suspended publication of its newspaper and began to mimeograph, rather than print, the journal of its annual convocations. Churches that had embarked on major building programs during the 1920s encountered difficulty in meeting mortgage payments in the 1930s. The Diocese of Olympia laid the cornerstone for St. Mark's Cathedral in 1930, dedicated it in 1931, and lost it to foreclosure in 1941 after ten years of struggle to pay indebtedness. Other churches, such as Trinity Church in Huntington, West Virginia, abandoned building plans altogether. Dioceses such as New Jersey — which not only grew in communicant strength and financial support during the 1930s but also laid the cornerstone of its cathedral — were rare.

Although many parishes expended substantial energy simply to maintain solvency, money was available during the Depression for some purposes. In 1934 a successful campaign for funds by the laity of the church erased the approximately $1 million debt of the National Council and provided the impetus for the "Forward Movement" in the church. Commissioned by the 1934 General Convention, this group of clergy and laity sought to inject new life into the Episcopal Church and to move it forward, both spiritually and financially. They designed conferences for youth, clergy, and laity to address important questions:

> Has this parish a large number of lost or casual communicants? . . . Are we awake to needs of our community? . . . What proportion of our members are taking their Christianity seriously and expressing their loyalty by regular giving . . . ?[99]

The group began publishing mission and devotional materials, a function which survives today under the name Forward Movement Publications.

During the Depression, the majority of Episcopalians probably continued to vote Republican; the leading Republican challengers to Franklin Delano Roosevelt — Wendell Wilkie, Thomas Dewey, and Robert Taft — were Episcopalians. One survey has shown that the majority of Episcopal clergy seem to have viewed the New Deal favorably, but were somewhat less favorable toward it than the general clergy population of America.

A significant minority of the denomination, however, swung to the left in social and economic thought. Both Franklin and Eleanor Roosevelt were Episcopalians, as were two of the most influential members of Roosevelt's cabinet, Frances Perkins and Henry A. Wallace. Several Episcopal periodicals and unofficial organizations took strong pro-labor stances, as did the General Convention of 1934.

PARTY CONTROVERSIES AND ECUMENICAL ACTIVITY

One hundred years after the start of the Oxford Movement, the often bitter controversies it created in the Episcopal Church had declined but not entirely ceased. What had become known as liberal evangelicalism and liberal catholicism — twentieth-century descendants of the evangelical and Oxford movements that accepted biblical criticism and modern scientific thought — were increasingly dominant; the two parties gradually learned from each other. "Prayer Book Churchmen" — Episcopalians who strictly followed the rubrics of the Book of Common Prayer and so walked the *via media* between the two parties — proved a mediating group.

In an effort to show parishioners how to deal with the bewildering variety of clerical titles that had developed within the Episcopal Church since the evangelical and Oxford movements, one Prayer Book churchman wrote what he called a "little jingle":

Call me "Brother" if you will;
Call me "Parson," better still;
Or if perchance the Catholic frill
Doth your heart with rapture fill,
Though plain "Mister" fills the bill,
Even "Father" brings no chill
Of hurt or rancor or ill will.
To no degree do I pretend,
Though "Doctor" doth some honor lend.
"Teacher," "Pastor," "Preacher," "Friend,"
Titles almost without end,
To all a willing ear I lend
And none disturb and none offend;
But how the man my heart doth rend,
Who blithely calls me "Reverend."[100]

But divisions between Anglo-Catholics and evangelicals (or low churchmen, as they were more and more called after the 1870s) remained sharp and carried beyond parishes into denominational life. Resolutions to drop the name "Protestant" — a term that Anglo-Catholics opposed on the grounds that it failed to describe the unbroken Catholic heritage of Anglicanism — became routine in the triennial General Conventions.

"The extremes are far apart and often seem impossible to reconcile," the House of Bishops candidly declared in 1928 of the division among church parties:

The tension is at times severe. . . . One group seeks a fuller measure of what it counts Catholic. Another group is sick at heart lest some of those great values which we gained at the Reformation may be lost. One prays hopefully for reunion with the Church of Rome; the other seeks continually closer relations with Protestantism.[101]

Although the 1928 pastoral letter asserted that the extremes "witnessed [to] the great truth that Christianity is not . . . narrow [or] one-sided," the tensions between Anglo-Catholic and low church Episcopalians kept the Episcopal Church from voting full membership in the Federal Council of Churches until 1940, thirty-two years after that cooperative council was formed. One could never guess where the tensions would end.

152

The Roman Catholic chaplain at Columbia University — a priest who was so often at odds with Francis Cardinal Spellman, the archbishop of the Roman Catholic Archdiocese of New York, that he had become the friend of many low church Episcopalians in the Diocese of New York — sat with the low church party at the diocesan convention that elected Charles Gilbert as suffragan bishop in 1930. "All were so eager to have him elected," Father George Ford later wrote about Gilbert, "that I remember having thought at the time that if any way could be found to make it legal, I would have voted for him."[102]

In 1946, the tensions also caused the General Convention abruptly to terminate negotiations for organic unity with the Presbyterian Church in the U.S.A. The discussions had begun in 1929 with an invitation from the General Convention to the Presbyterians and Methodists to discuss unity on the basis of the Chicago-Lambeth Quadrilateral. The Methodists withdrew from the discussions in order to concentrate on uniting their own divisions. But in 1937, the General Convention — followed in 1938 by the Presbyterian General Assembly — adopted a declaration that showed a serious intention to unite:

> The two churches, one in the faith of the Lord Jesus Christ, the Incarnate Word of God, recognizing the Holy Scripture as the supreme rule of faith, accepting the two Sacraments ordained by Christ, and believing that the visible unity of Christian Churches is the Will of God, hereby formally declare their purpose to achieve organic union between the respective churches.[103]

The declaration indicated agreement on three points of the quadrilateral, but omitted any mention of the Anglican requirement for the historic episcopate.

In 1938 both churches published "Proposals Looking Toward Organic Union." In 1939 the Episcopal Joint Commission on Approaches to Unity and the Presbyterian Department on Church Co-operation and Union proposed a concordat of principles for the union which included "a mutual extension of ordination." Moderators of presbyteries would lay hands on Episcopal clergy; Episcopal bishops would lay hands on Presbyterian clergy. To the Anglo-Catholic party, led by Manning (by now bishop of New York), by Bishop Frank E. Wilson of Eau Claire, and behind the scenes by Bishop Wallace E. Conkling of Chicago, the concordat cut the roots of the doctrine of apostolic succession, for it placed ordinations performed by Presbyterian ministers on the same level as those performed by Episcopal bishops. To supporters, led by Bishop Edward L. Parsons of California and Dean Alexander C. Zabriskie of Virginia Theological Seminary, the Anglo-Catholics were requiring Presbyterians to accept a doctrine of ordination that neither the Book of Common Prayer nor early Christianity taught.

In an atmosphere of intense and frequent acerbity, Episcopalians discussed the proposals for union for nine years. In 1946, after a debate in the House of Deputies that Bishop Henry Knox Sherrill of Massachusetts described as "not a happy one, with many low points," the proposed reunion with the Presbyterians was voted down.[104] Anglo-Catholics saw the decision as a victory that safeguarded the Catholic teachings of the Episcopal Church. Other denominations viewed the discussions as giving Episcopal ecumenical intentions a bad name. The doctrine of apostolic succession and the sense of superiority over other forms of ministry that it assumes continued to be a major obstacle for the Episcopal Church in all discussions of unity with Protestant denominations. In 1991 it caused the suspension of discussions toward a proposed concordat intended to lead to full communion and possible union between the Episcopal Church and the 5.3 million-member Evangelical Lutheran Church in America, two churches that otherwise have much in common.

OTHER MOVEMENTS

Another issue that sparked controversy in the early years of the twentieth century, faith healing, was foreshadowed in the Episcopal Church by the medical ministry of Episcopal layman Charles Cullis in Boston in the nineteenth century. It entered the church more fully in the first decade of the twentieth century through Elwood Worcester's Emmanuel movement, which combined modern science with a modernist approach to biblical religion. Worcester's movement was named for the church of which he was rector in Mary Baker Eddy's Boston.

A movement for personal and national spiritual reconstruction that began in England in the 1920s, the Oxford Group movement (named Moral Re-Armament after 1938, and often called "Buchmanism" after its American founder, Frank Buchman), gained more support from Episcopalians than from the members of any other American denomination. Its Episcopal support stemmed partially from its English origins, partially from its adaptation of evangelistic methods to the lifestyle of the upper class, and partially because it maintained its American headquarters until 1941 in the new parish house of Manhattan's Calvary Episcopal Church. After the evangelical rector of Calvary Church, Samuel M. Shoemaker (who had served as the movement's American leader), expressed "increasing misgivings" and left the movement amidst national publicity in 1941, the number of Episcopalians in Moral Rearmament began to decline.

The Emmanuel movement, the Oxford Group movement, and Shoemaker all contributed to the philosophy of Alcoholics Anonymous (founded 1935). Having come into contact with Calvary's Church's rescue mission, one of the organization's founders subsequently attended Oxford Group meetings at the parish; Shoemaker assisted in formulating the Twelve Steps of Alcoholics Anonymous.

WORLD WAR II

On the eve of World War II, the majority of Episcopalians, like the majority of Americans, seem to have wished to stay out of another European war; on Armistice Day, 1939, the Episcopal Pacifist Fellowship was founded. Two years later the Japanese attack on Pearl Harbor not only created a national consensus but also neutralized most theological opposition; Christians could now view World War II as a defensive (and hence just) war.

In countries such as Japan and China, the war devastated Episcopal missionary work. In the Philippines the two American bishops and virtually every other American Episcopal missionary were imprisoned. In the United States Episcopal parishes lost young men and women to the armed forces. The war industries that sprang up in metropolitan areas attracted parishioners from rural parishes. Gas rationing curtailed the number of church meetings and pastoral calls. Churches organized letter-writing campaigns and Saturday evening dances and Sunday open houses for servicemen. Most Episcopal churches opened for special services on D-Day (the day of the Allied invasion of the European continent), V-E Day (the day of the surrender of Germany), and V-J Day (the day of the surrender of Japan).

More than five hundred Episcopal clergy served in the war as chaplains, creating a shortage of civilian clergy. To meet the need, many of the church's seminaries went on a year-round schedule. Bishop Sherrill, who had served as a hospital chaplain in France in World War I, not only supervised the work of Episcopal military chaplains but also chaired the General Commission on Chaplains, which coordinated the work of all Protestant, Anglican, and Eastern Orthodox military chaplains. Sherrill's visits to military units from the Aleutian Islands to Europe prepared him

"A curious contradiction," Bishop Sherrill commented about General George S. Patton, an Episcopalian (here shown at his World War II headquarters). "He attended church regularly, had considerable interest in religion, but was exceedingly profane."

for his post-war duties as presiding bishop of the Episcopal Church and as president of the World Council of Churches.

THE POSTWAR RELIGIOUS REVIVAL

Unlike most wars in American history, World War II was followed by a nationwide religious revival. Critics questioned the theological depth of the revival, but the Episcopal Church benefited greatly from it in terms of sheer numbers. By 1960 the number of baptized Episcopalians had risen to over 3.4 million. The ratio of Episcopal communicants to the general population increased from one to one hundred two in 1900, to one to ninety-two in 1950, to one to eighty-six in 1960. The postwar religious revival seemed to be accomplishing what Episcopal domestic missions had been unable to do. Contributions flowed in, and new Episcopal churches appeared throughout the nation. Like many other churches which suffered through the Depression, the Diocese of Olympia was able to redeem its foreclosed cathedral and erase its debts.

As veterans and converts packed the denomination's seminaries, candidates for the ministry doubled, and many seminaries enlarged their faculties and established their first dormitories for married students. In Austin, Texas, the first Episcopal seminary since the nineteenth century — The Episcopal Theological Seminary of the Southwest — was established. By the late 1950s, the Episcopal Church had more clergy than parishes for the first time in its history. Yet as late as 1961 a report in the *Episcopal Church Annual* declared that the church needed at least twelve hundred more clergy to carry on its work in the more than seven thousand congregations in the continental United States.

The postwar increase in membership prompted not only the construction of a new twelve-story Episcopal Church Center at Second Avenue and 43rd Street in New York City, but also the founding of the denomination's first official publishing house, the Seabury Press, which remained under church ownership until 1984. Before constructing its new building, the National Council resisted strong pressure to move to the new Interchurch Center on Manhattan's Morningside Heights. The decision showed that the Episcopal Church still considered itself distinct from the mainline of American Protestantism. In the 1980s the executive council also resisted the trend among other denominations to move its headquarters to a city more geographically central than New York City.

Following World War II, women continued to seek voting rights within the church. In 1946, when a female deputy-elect from the Diocese

This 1962 photograph not only shows the extensive programs for youth
at an institutional church (St. George's, Manhattan) but also gives
a sense of the post-war revival of religion in America.

of Missouri arrived at the General Convention, the House of Deputies
voted to seat her following debate over the definition of the constitutional term *layman*. In 1949 the house voted differently, refusing 321 to
242 to seat three women deputies-elect from the Dioceses of Missouri,
Nebraska, and Olympia on grounds that the word *laymen* did, in fact, ex-
clude *laywomen*. When the house offered the three women seats without
voice or vote, they refused the offer, declaring that "the question is not one
of courtesy to women, but that of the right of women to represent . . . the
church they are proud to serve."[105] The convention then appointed a joint
commission to study "the Problem of Giving the Women of the Church
a Voice." Not until 1967 would the General Convention grant women
legislative representation in the church.

Growth in the mushrooming suburbs following World War II raised
questions (such as those covered in 1961 by Episcopalian Gibson Winter

in *The Suburban Captivity of the Churches*) about the denomination's role in urban areas. Prior to World War II most Hispanic Episcopalians lived in the church's missionary dioceses in Central America, South America, and the Caribbean. When Puerto Rican and other new immigrant groups began to appear in the 1940s, missions among them were pioneered by such inner-city parishes as Grace Church, Jersey City. Every decade after the 1950s saw the number of Hispanic clergy and laity increase. By the mid-1980s they represented three percent of Episcopal membership and were the fastest-growing ethnic group in the church. By the 1990s the number of Americans of Hispanic background preparing for the Episcopal priesthood rivaled the number preparing for the Roman Catholic priesthood. In its ministry to the nation's Hispanic population, the church showed signs of having learned from the mistakes it made in its domestic missionary enterprise of the nineteenth century.

If the Episcopal Church had a figure to rival Norman Vincent Peale, Fulton J. Sheen, and Billy Graham during the post-World War II resurgence of religion, it was the maverick convert from Roman Catholicism, James A. Pike. Although initially a spokesperson for orthodox Anglicanism, Pike became increasingly controversial as he called for the reformulation of certain Christian beliefs and maintained a high profile in the social causes of the 1960s. His ministry began in the 1940s on the eastern seaboard and ended in the 1960s in California. During the same period the center of Episcopal Church membership began to move westward from the old eastern dioceses as well. As the years went on, more and more of the largest Episcopal parishes were found west of the Mississippi.

EPISCOPAL THEOLOGY IN THE POSTWAR DECADES

The two Anglican theologians who have had the most influence on Episcopal clergy and laity since World War II have had strong associations with Great Britain. New Jersey-born W. Norman Pittenger, a graduate of the General Theological Seminary who taught at the seminary from the mid-1930s until moving to Cambridge University in 1966, co-authored (with Pike) the volume in the Episcopal Church's Teaching Series entitled *The Faith of the Church* (1951). An exponent of process theology (a form of theology that emphasizes the interplay between the nature of God and the evolving cosmos) and a prolific author, Pittenger aimed his writing for practical consumption and reached a wide audience of Episcopalians. He was aware of deep indebtedness to DuBose, "the only important creative theologian," he wrote, "that the Episcopal Church in the United States has produced."[106]

The theology of the second influential figure from Great Britain, John Macquarrie, was more systematic. A minister and theologian in the Church of Scotland, the Presbyterian Macquarrie joined the faculty of New York's Union Theological Seminary in 1962. The conversion to the Episcopal Church of the seminary's leading New Testament scholar, John Knox, influenced Macquarrie to seek and receive ordination to the Episcopal priesthood. Although he moved to England in 1970 to accept a distinguished chair at Oxford University, he retained his canonical ties to the Diocese of New York (as did Pittenger) and so technically remained an Episcopalian.

Existentialist in his underpinnings and influenced by the New Testament scholarship of Rudolf Bultmann and the metaphysics of Martin Heidegger, Macquarrie sought to write a new form of natural theology (or theology that asserts that human reason is able to arrive at some knowledge of God). He writes:

> Any faith must let itself be exposed to the observable facts of the world in which we live. The business of natural theology is to show that these acts are not incompatible with the convictions of faith, and may even tend to confirm these convictions.[107]

Crisp and clear, Macquarrie's *Principles of Christian Theology* (2d ed., 1977) and other writings continue to be widely assigned not only in Episcopal seminaries but also in interdenominational seminaries.

A contemporary author has noted that "very little *criticism* as such survives the generation in which it is written. The same is true . . . of most philosophy and theology."[108] While other Episcopalians have written theological studies (and some are currently contributing to the ecumenical theology and feminist theology that has characterized much of Christian thought since the 1960s), no recent figures seem to have attained the stature of DuBose or Hall. Although the Protestant theologian Paul Tillich influenced many in the Episcopal Church following World War II, Tillich's influence faded after the 1960s. Today Episcopalians are attracted to some of the more progressive Roman Catholic theologians, to contemporary Lutheran systematic theologians, or to the theology of the Reformed theologian Karl Barth — a figure whose theology seems to have survived "the generation in which it was written."

Barth was Swiss; Tillich was German; Macquarrie was a native of Scotland. Only Pittenger was born in the United States. Like the Church of England during the reigns of Henry VIII and Edward VI, the Episcopal Church has generally been dependent on theologians from other countries and communions. Why has it produced so very few theologians? The answer seems to divide into four points.

First, the church has lacked the university base from which Christian theology has generally emerged. German universities, for example, have both Protestant and Roman Catholic theological faculties, where theologians are expected to publish at the same level as their secular colleagues. In the Church of England clergy who produce works on theology generally teach at research-oriented Oxford or Cambridge. In the United States theological writing has tended to emerge from the great universities such as Yale or Chicago, or from the leading interdenominational seminaries adjacent to them. The one Episcopal college that developed into a research university — Columbia University — severed its ties to the Episcopal Church early in the twentieth century and never had a theological faculty.

Instead of teaching in a university setting, most Episcopal theologians have therefore taught at the free-standing seminaries of the church. Regardless of where its seminaries are located, however, the Episcopal Church has viewed all of them in a highly practical way — which is the second reason the church has produced so few theologians.

Rather than encouraging its theological professors to write systematic theologies, the church has assigned them the task of preparing students for the parish ministry. It has given them not only a wide spectrum of duties teaching the theology of others, but also time-consuming supportive roles on diocesan and national church committees. So prevalent has this orientation toward the parish been that even the Episcopal Divinity School, viewed from its founding until the 1960s as the most academic and scholarly of Episcopal seminaries, has never had an internationally known theologian on its permanent faculty.

Third, the Episcopal Church has remained dependent upon its mother church. Just as Lutherans have often looked to Germany for their theologians, so Episcopal seminaries have often turned to the Church of England for systematic theologians. If the prestigious British theologians recruited for Episcopal seminaries have continued to write theology while in the United States, they have often written with British audiences in mind. Their books have usually been viewed as a product of the Church of England rather than of the Episcopal Church.

All of these causes have contributed to the dearth of theologians produced by the Episcopal Church. But the overriding reason involves the nature of the Anglican tradition. Because of the character of the Reformation Settlement in England, Anglicanism lacks the kind of sharply defined teaching tradition that produces systematic theology. Unlike Roman Catholicism, Lutheranism, or Calvinism, it has no oracular central figure or reformer; unlike Eastern Orthodoxy, it is not tied tightly to the teachings of church councils. Instead of a common theology, it has found its identity in a tradition of common worship and prayer.

The advantage of this avenue to Christian orthodoxy is clear: no Episcopalian is obliged to believe that the sum of theological wisdom is found in one dominant figure or office, in a series of church councils, or in a confession of faith. Instead, the Anglican tradition places a high value on spiritual freedom and holds broad positions that will attract, rather than repel, the highest number of followers. Yet this comprehensiveness also has its disadvantages, for Anglican theologians have been able to avoid wrestling with the teachings of great Christian theologians and central Christian councils. And it is precisely from this wrestling that the kind of philosophical or systematic theology that seeks a viable intellectual basis for religious claims emerges.

What has taken the place of systematic theology in Anglicanism? Anglican theological writing has been directed primarily toward clarifying the faith of the "True Church" — the Holy Catholic Church affirmed in the early Christian creeds.

Much Anglican scholarship has focused on biblical studies, for example, for Anglicanism claims biblical authority for its teaching. Since the fundamental formularies of Christianity emerged in the period of the church fathers, Anglicans have excelled in patristic scholarship; at one time virtually all of the outstanding patristic scholars in the world were Anglicans. Because of the sixteenth-century legacy of the Church of England, Anglicans have made vital contributions to Reformation scholarship. In recent years the writings of Anglicans have become increasingly influential in the field of spirituality and spiritual direction. Finally, because Anglicanism has found its focus of unity in the liturgy, it has produced a disproportionate number of liturgical scholars, even among laity and parish clergy. The faculties of Episcopal seminaries as well as their publications have mirrored these built-in tendencies of Anglicanism. For the church to produce systematic theologians now would require major shifts in its values.

A final area of twentieth-century Anglican thought involves psychoanalytic theory. If the teachings of any psychiatrist have found proponents in the Episcopal Church, they are those of Carl Gustav Jung, the son of a Swiss Protestant pastor.

Jung's appeal to Episcopalians may have a strong liturgical basis. Respectful in his teachings toward worship (as Freud was not), Jung did not display the common Protestant desire to simplify the western liturgical tradition. Instead, he viewed liturgical symbols as meaningful signs of inner realities. Thus he saw the preservation of a symbolic richness in worship as a way that humans could acknowledge their deep connectedness to the inner needs of the spirit. This high value placed upon worship may be one of the principal reasons a significant number of Episcopal clergy since the 1960s have undergone the extensive training required to become Jungian analysts. From the 1980s on, the teachings about healing the inner child offered by psychotherapist John Bradshaw, a Roman Catholic who became an Episcopalian, also became increasingly influential among Episcopal counselors.

A DECADE OF CHANGE

The 1960s ushered in a period of ferment and change in the church. The decade began in the confident spirit of the 1950s, with a call by Presbyterian Eugene Carson Blake in San Francisco's Grace Episcopal Cathedral for a united church that would be "truly catholic, truly reformed, and truly evangelical." Out of the proposal came the Consultation on Church Union, in which the Episcopal Church and other major denominations in America continue to participate as discussants or observers. In more recent years, however, ecumenism in the Episcopal Church has moved away from ideas of governmental mergers with other bodies toward what the General Convention has called "one Eucharistic fellowship . . . a communion of communions." The Lutheran-Episcopal Agreement of 1982 allows an interim sharing of eucharistic fellowship while discussions (temporarily suspended in 1991) continue toward full communion, or the time when clergy of one denomination can replace those of another denomination at the altar. Although the ordination of women (and the consecration of women bishops) strains ecumenical dialogue with those churches that claim the apostolic succession, it also facilitates discussions with other Protestant bodies, most of whom have women as clergy.

The open, positive spirit of Pope John XXIII and the reforms of the Second Vatican Council (1962–1965) also had a major impact on the Episcopal Church. Vatican II's concern with such issues as the role of the laity in parish work, the church as a community rather than an institution, and the challenges of the modern world intensified the examination of the same topics in Anglicanism. Vatican II's revision of the Roman Catholic liturgy encouraged the General Convention of 1964 to authorize a revision of the Book of Common Prayer. The irenic, liberal, and ecumenical spirit of the council also brought the Roman Catholic and Episcopal churches much closer. Pulpit exchanges, consecrations of Episcopal bishops in Roman Catholic cathedrals, shared theological seminaries and churches, and a continuing ecumenical dialogue were all signs of that change. A new spirit of self-examination and openness to Protestants and to other schools of Anglicanism also developed among many American Anglo-Catholics. The liturgical movement caused Anglo-Catholicism, like Roman Catholicism, to reduce the number of devotional practices that dated only to the medieval or Counter-Reformation periods.

In the 1960s the church also witnessed the emergence of renewal movements. Led by such clergy as Dennis J. Bennett of Seattle and Terry Fullam of Darien, Connecticut, the Episcopal charismatic movement spread to many dioceses and created some of the largest parishes in the church. Conservative evangelicalism — which had remained strong in the Church of England but had been muted in the Episcopal Church since approximately 1900 — reappeared as a force, establishing its own seminary in Ambridge, Pennsylvania and electing bishops for an increasing number of dioceses. Organizations and movements such as the Episcopal Charismatic Fellowship, Cursillo and Tres Dias (long weekend conferences on spiritual values), the Anglican Fellowship of Prayer, the Bible Reading Fellowship, and Faith Alive (weekend witnessing in parishes by invited teams of trained laypeople) added to the vitality and comprehensiveness of the church but divided some parishes. Episcopalians sometimes benefited from the divided parishes of other denominations. In several states Pentecostal congregations who left the Assemblies of God affiliated with the Episcopal Church.

During this period of national changes the Episcopal Church was deeply involved in the struggle for social justice. In 1957 the presiding bishop, Henry Knox Sherrill of Massachusetts, transferred the General Convention to multiracial Honolulu when Houston, the scheduled city, appeared to be unable to live up to its desire to provide equal accommodations. In 1959 clergy and laity organized the Episcopal Society for Cultural and Racial Unity (ESCRU). Partially as a result of its activism, Episcopal clergy and laity participated in sit-ins and marched with Martin Luther King, Jr., in the early 1960s. In 1964 the General Convention formally prohibited racial discrimination in Episcopal churches. In the summer

Former Presiding Bishops Arthur Lichtenberger (1900–1968) and
Henry Knox Sherrill (1890–1980) converse with John E. Hines (1910–)
at his consecration as presiding bishop in 1965.

of 1965, Jonathan M. Daniels — a student at the Episcopal Theological
School and member of ESCRU — was killed by a segregationist while
working for the cause of civil rights in Alabama.

Finally, in 1967, under the leadership of Presiding Bishop John E.
Hines — who as a young priest had come under the influence of Bishop
Scarlett — the General Convention announced a special program "of assisting the poor to organize themselves so that they may stand on their
own feet, rise out of their degradation, and have a full share in determin-
ing their own destiny."[109] The program came as a result of Bishop Hines's
call for the Episcopal Church to "take its place, humbly and boldly, along-
side of, and in support of, the dispossessed and oppressed peoples of this
country."[110] It included channeling $3 million during each of the fol-
lowing three years to African American, Native American, and Hispanic
organizations. Over $2 million of the sum came from the United Thank
Offering of the woman's auxiliary — a group which had changed its name
to Women of the Church in 1958.

Hines was theologically in the orthodox mainstream of Episcopal
thought. He was also one of the great, prophetic preachers in the church's

history. Under his leadership, the Episcopal Church became more involved in social concerns than at any time in its history. By the late 1960s, the church again led other denominations in the quest for social and economic justice for American citizens. The decade of his presiding episcopate must be seen in the context of the church's earlier role as a pioneer in the social gospel.

A reaction among conservatives and traditionalists soon occurred. In 1963 a North Carolina rector renounced his ordination and established the Anglican Orthodox Church. In 1964 an all-white parish in Georgia left the Episcopal Church. The dissidence increased during the social and political revolution that swept America from approximately 1965 through 1973. To find a period of similar controversy in the Episcopal Church, one must go back to the struggles of almost precisely one hundred years earlier regarding church style and practices. Contributing to the conflict were the financial support by the General Convention special program of minority empowerment groups (a few of whose leaders had committed violence) and the activities of some bishops and clergy in opposition to the Vietnam War. (The Episcopal Church was sufficiently divided that the General Convention could agree upon no statement about the war.) Also important were the liberalization during this period of Episcopal teaching about divorce (now fully and clearly acknowledged), remarriage (now permitted with fewer restrictions), and abortion (now permitted under certain circumstances).

In reaction, conservative and traditionalist Episcopalians began to withhold financial support from their dioceses, which in turn (approvingly or otherwise) withheld it from the national church. In protest of the General Convention's support of a militant Hispanic group, a southwestern bishop cut the contributions of his diocese to the national church from $80,000 to $1. By 1970 diocesan support for the national church had fallen $3.5 million short of its needs. The decline caused the staff at the Episcopal Church Center in New York to be reduced and reduced again. The Episcopal Church had front-page problems.

Membership declined from the mid-1960s through the 1980s and gradually stabilized. At the same time — partially because of the smaller membership, partially because of the ordination of women, and partially because of the accession of many ex-Roman Catholic priests in the years following the Second Vatican Council — the number of clergy increased. A surplus of clergy and a shortage of positions resulted. Over two hundred years after Bishop Seabury ordained its first clergy, the Episcopal Church still lacks a central authority to control the number of ordinations. Confronted with an oversupply, bishops began to enforce increasingly rigorous standards for ordination.

AN ERA OF CONTROVERSY
AND SCHISM

The three issues that caused the most controversy in the Episcopal Church during the 1970s and 1980s were the ordination of women, the rights of homosexuals, and the revision of the Book of Common Prayer. Other issues such as abortion and inclusive (gender-free) language in the liturgy caused recurrent debates in conventions, but failed to reach the level of a national debate among Episcopalians.

The Ordination of Women

The controversy over women's ordination to the priesthood began in the 1960s. Supporters argued that God could call women as well as men to the ministry. Jesus Christ was fully human, the proponents asserted. His priesthood is an office of his humanity. To deny women the priesthood would be to deny their humanness. Just as the Christian priesthood changed from orthodox Jews to Gentiles, so it could now incorporate women as well as men. Proponents argued that the Episcopal Church was running the risk of denying the Holy Spirit and of alienating large numbers of women who were current or potential communicants.

The opponents based their arguments on the biblical distinction between male and female roles and on the maleness of Jesus. Just as the priest represents Christ at the altar, so a woman by definition could not be a priest; the apostles were male, so the apostolic succession must remain male. Women's ordination, their argument continued, would break with more than four hundred years of Anglican tradition and almost two thousand years of Christian tradition. It would represent only "a product of the wacky Vietnam War years, as an example of the Church's willingness to buy the standards of this world."[111] Practical reasons cited by opponents included the fear of schism, the collapse of ecumenical discussions with the Eastern Orthodox and Roman Catholic churches, and the creation of a surplus of clergy.

In 1970 the House of Deputies debated a proposal authorizing the ordination of women to the priesthood. The defeated proposal did not reach the upper House of Bishops, but unofficial votes in 1972 and 1974 indicated that a majority of bishops favored women's ordination. When the resolution was presented to the House of Deputies in 1973, it received more ayes than nays but was again defeated because of a rule that counted tie votes in any diocesan delegation as nays.

Nevertheless, in the summer of 1974, in Philadelphia's Church of the Advocate, eleven women deacons were ordained to the priesthood by three Episcopal bishops. Two of the bishops were retired; the third had resigned as bishop of Pennsylvania earlier in the year. Neither the bishops, nor the deacons, nor the parish had authorization for the ordinations. In an emergency session, the House of Bishops declared the ordinations invalid and rebuked the ordainers.

Following two more years of conflict, the General Convention approved the ordination of women to the priesthood in 1976. Throughout the following year, individual bishops regularized the 1974 "Philadelphia Eleven." Rachel Hosmer remembers her feelings on the day prior to her ordination in 1977:

> I had an experience . . . that is apparently common to many women at some point before their actual ordination to the priesthood. I was praying in the chapel when suddenly it seemed as if the place was filled with thunder, and a voice said to me, 'Are *you* going up there behind that altar, you, a *woman?* You're going to stand up there and celebrate the Eucharist?' And it roared on and on and on like a thunderstorm, accusing and menacing.
>
> 'Well,' I said, looking towards the altar and thinking about it, 'Yep, I am. I've gotten this far and I'm going to go through with it.' The next day dawned bright and lovely, and the voice had died completely away, never to return.[112]

A conscience clause has allowed bishops to refuse to ordain women if they so choose. John M. Allin of Mississippi, who became presiding bishop in 1974, was among those who so chose, but Edmond L. Browning, who succeeded Allin in 1986, endorsed the right of women to be ordained not only to the priesthood but also to the episcopate.

Browning's election by the House of Bishops was an indication of the degree of support for women's ordination among bishops. By 1991 American bishops had ordained over one thousand women to the priesthood. In that year fewer than ten dioceses still refused to ordain women to the priesthood, and the number was steadily declining. That dioceses frequently elected bishops who supported women's ordination to succeed opponents who were retiring also indicated the degree of support among laity and clergy. To be sure, female priests continued to encounter more difficulty than male priests in securing rectorates (rather than assistantships), but polls indicated that an increasing majority of Episcopalians felt comfortable with women clergy.

The maleness of Jesus and the apostles, the election of women bishops, and the effect of women's ordination upon union with the Roman Catholic and Eastern Orthodox churches dominated the concerns of Episcopalians who continued to oppose women clergy. Although the Anglo-Catholic wing of the Episcopal Church provided the largest number of opponents, support for the ordination of women was also found among Anglo-Catholic clergy and laity, and some of the women priests considered themselves Anglo-Catholics.

A final step remained for women in the Episcopal Church: the episcopate. In 1986, a woman priest who was herself the daughter of a bishop ran a strong second in the election of a suffragan bishop for the Diocese of Washington. In September of 1988, a convention of the Diocese of Massachusetts elected Barbara C. Harris as suffragan bishop. An African American priest from Philadelphia who edited the Episcopal social action journal *The Witness*, Harris had served as crucifer at the ordination of the "Philadelphia Eleven."

Harris's election sparked controversy. She was not only a woman but also the editor of a journal some Episcopalians considered "radical." Although some opponents had declared that a majority of diocesan standing committees and diocesan bishops would not confirm her election, the required approvals were received. In February 1989, in a ceremony in a Boston auditorium marked by both protest and celebration and witnessed by over 8500 persons — including more than fifty Episcopal bishops and representatives from denominations ranging from Roman Catholic to Baptist — Harris was consecrated as the first female bishop in a church claiming the historic episcopate.

Coming one hundred years after the Episcopal Church sanctioned the office of deaconess as the first church vocation available to women, the consecration of Bishop Harris represented for many Episcopal women, finally, full acceptance. For parishes who objected to visitations from women bishops, the 1988 General Convention designed the episcopal visitor's clause, which allows for a substitute bishop. Requests for an episcopal visitor must be made at the parish level, sent to the diocese, and finally approved by the presiding bishop.

An unwritten rule of thumb in the Episcopal Church is that clergy should have at least ten years of experience as a priest before being considered for the episcopate. As more and more women reached that level of experience after 1990, dioceses increasingly began to nominate women for the episcopate. The second woman elected was Jane Holmes Dixon, who was consecrated as suffragan bishop of the Diocese of Washington in

Mary Adelia McLeod (1938–) during her interview for the office of Bishop of Vermont. In 1993 she was elected first woman diocesan bishop in the Episcopal Church.

1992. In the meantime, the House of Deputies had elected its first woman president, Pamela P. Chinnis of Washington, D.C. In 1993, the Diocese of Vermont elected Archdeacon Mary Adelia McLeod of West Virginia as Bishop of Vermont — the first woman to hold the office of diocesan bishop in the church. Since the opponents of women bishops now make up a small percentage of Episcopal communicants, and since a woman has now been elected to the highest position open to a layperson, there is every indication that women bishops will become as familiar a part of the Episcopal Church as women deacons and priests have become.

Ordination and Homosexuality

In 1975 the standing committee of the Diocese of New York, composed of clergy and laity, approved the ordination to the diaconate of a seminary graduate who acknowledged a lesbian orientation. The committee reasoned that it would be hypocritical to deny ordination for an honest answer when they and other standing committees had in the past approved homosexuals for ordination after dishonest answers. When Bishop Paul Moore of New York ordained the candidate to the priesthood in 1977,

170

the Episcopal Church was again engulfed in publicity and controversy. The ordination contributed to the loss of confidence in the church's leadership among some members. It also called into question the doctrine and discipline of the church.

Although the House of Bishops in its next meeting declined by a vote of sixty-two to forty-eight to censure Bishop Moore, the bishops declared their opposition to the ordination or the marriage of practicing homosexuals. Two years later the General Convention adopted a resolution that recognized "marriage, marital fidelity and sexual chastity as the standard of Christian sexual morality." After differentiating between homosexual orientation and homosexual practice, the resolution declared that "we believe it is not appropriate for this Church to ordain a practicing homosexual, or any person who is engaged in heterosexual relations outside of marriage."[113]

Succeeding General Conventions have not changed these guidelines. But the volcanic question of homosexual ordination has simmered beneath the surface and occasionally erupted. In 1974, Integrity, Inc., a gay and lesbian organization of Episcopalians, was formed to eliminate all barriers to full homosexual participation in the life and work of the Episcopal Church, and since that time a number of bishops in addition to Moore have ordained openly gay or lesbian candidates. Yet opposition remains strong, and joined to the issue of ordination has been the question of church blessings for unions of gays and lesbians. In 1990 a Gallup survey showed that twenty-one percent of Episcopalians approved of church sanctions for these same-sex unions, while sixty-four percent disapproved and fifteen percent had no opinion.

The question of the ordination of homosexuals has had an impact on ecumenical relations as well. Citing the ordinations of homosexuals that had already occurred, for example, the Greek Orthodox Archdiocese of North and South America broke theological dialogue with the Episcopal Church in 1991. And discussions concerning homosexuality during this period have also raised questions concerning the sexual conduct of all clergy. Paralleled by widespread reports of serious problems in other churches, the question of professional sexual misconduct — both heterosexual and homosexual — by clergy became a concern of the Episcopal Church in the 1990s.

Prayer Book Revision and Schism

After approving a new standard Book of Common Prayer in 1928, the General Convention established a standing liturgical commission of clergy and laity to prepare for future revisions. In 1964, following the major liturgical reforms of the Second Vatican Council, the General Convention directed the commission to begin the process for a new revision. From 1967 to 1976 the commission submitted a series of rites for trial use and discussion by Episcopal congregations. The process allowed parishes not only to experiment with the new services but also to respond with comments and suggestions. During the process the liturgical commission remained in close communication with the liturgical committees of other denominations, in order that the new Prayer Book might serve as an instrument of unity.

In 1976 the General Convention approved the full report of the commission (entitled *Draft Proposed Book of Common Prayer*) by an impressive majority. At the 1979 General Convention, the proposed book was adopted as the new, standard Book of Common Prayer. Based upon Scripture, the church fathers, and the historic Christian liturgies, the 1979 Prayer Book incorporates the teachings of the liturgical movement following World War I. It keeps many of the forms of the 1928 Book of Common Prayer, but uses contemporary language and adds new material. In the 1980s the new Prayer Book was joined by the new *Hymnal 1982,* the result of many years of similar study and discussion.

Although opposition had greeted the Prayer Book revisions of 1892 and 1928, it was minor compared to the outcry that attended the process of revision in the 1960s and 1970s. For some Episcopalians, revision of the familiar 1928 Prayer Book and its "incomparable English" during an era of social turmoil was the last straw. For older Episcopalians, the changes in inherited worship habits were unsettling; people who have worshiped the same way for decades rarely like their devotional habits disturbed. For conservatives and traditionalists, the addition of gender-free language and prayers for social concerns was troubling. To them, the revision seemed to show that the same liberals who had led the church into social action and women's ordination were now forcing their views on its worship life.

Through lobbying, mailings, and organized protests, the well-funded Society for the Preservation of the Book of Common Prayer attempted to stop the process of revision. After the General Convention adopted the new book, those members of the society who remained within the Episcopal Church worked unsuccessfully for the retention of the 1928 Prayer Book as an alternative rite. A number of Episcopalians chose to leave the church and create places of worship with others who preferred the 1928 Prayer Book.

Schism was not a new experience for the Episcopal Church. In 1873 assistant bishop George D. Cummins of Kentucky, a leading evangelical, and more than twenty other evangelical clergy and laity organized the Reformed Episcopal Church. A protest against the "de-Protestantizing" of Episcopalianism after the rise of ritualism and Anglo-Catholicism, the new denomination hoped to attract other evangelical Episcopalians and to serve as a center for the union of all evangelical Protestants. Its high hopes went unrealized. Since the time of its founding, its membership has declined and today approximates seven thousand. In recent years, however, it has made common cause with the Anglican churches that emerged from the dissatisfaction with the Episcopal Church from the 1960s on.

"Faithfulness to Scripture and Tradition" is the rallying cry of tra ditionalist Episcopalians. They believe they are witnessing to powerful moral and theological principles that the church has abandoned. Within the Episcopal Church the Evangelical and Catholic Mission, an organization of clergy and laity, firmly upheld those values from 1976 to 1989. It was succeeded in 1989 by the Episcopal Synod of America, whose some 18,000 members reject "alteration of this faith demanded by those who question the authority of Holy Scripture in order to advocate twentieth century secular values."

It is too early to say what the future holds for the churches formed by traditionalists who left the Episcopal Church. The Anglican Church in America, the Anglican Catholic Church, the Anglican Rite Jurisdiction of the Americas, the Province of Christ the King, the United Episcopal Church of America, and the Episcopal Missionary Church — all have bishops, priests, and active parishes. Some have theological seminaries. Most represent conservative political views. Many maintain working relationships with each other as well as with Anglican traditionalist churches in other countries. Most began with older constituencies.

In style and practice, the new groups range from the low church tradition to an Anglo-Catholicism that seeks uniate status with Roman Catholicism. Most use the 1928 Prayer Book and prefer the standards of worship that existed prior to the liturgical movement. Although the Book of Common Prayer goes back to the liturgical revisions and language of the sixteenth and seventeenth centuries, there is some truth in the assertion of one historian that many "Anglican traditionalists have preferred to remain in the Victorian period, whether of the Anglo-Catholic style or the evangelical style."[114]

After a series of protest meetings following the approval of women's ordination by the General Convention in 1976, one leader of the disaffected Episcopalians declared that a half million clergy and laity would secede from the Episcopal Church. Sixteen years later the decision of the mother Church of England — joined by an increasing number of national churches within the world-wide Anglican Communion — to ordain women as priests (and inevitably as bishops) caused additional parishes, individuals, and clergy to leave the Episcopal Church. Some have affiliated with Eastern Orthodoxy, others with Roman Catholicism, but most with one of the traditionalist Anglican churches.

Although there are no authoritative figures for membership in the new Anglican churches, the total of former Episcopalians who have united with them appears not to exceed five percent of the number of secessions predicted in 1976. To date the record seems to indicate that the traditionalist Anglican churches may follow the pattern of the Reformed Episcopal Church, whose numbers and influence have steadily declined. But much will depend upon the avenue followed by Anglicans who oppose women's ordination in England. The election of an archbishop of Canterbury who firmly supports the admission of women to priestly and episcopal orders, the decision in 1992 of the mother Church of England to ordain women to the priesthood, and the increasing number of provinces of the Anglican Communion who approve the ordination of women has placed a significant international dimension upon the future of Anglican traditionalism.

A STATISTICAL PROFILE

Statistics can be deceptively authoritative when applied to a religious group, for numbers cannot reflect the inner life or the commitment of a Christian church. In addition, figures can mislead, for parochial reports are subject not only to reporting error but also to methodology that varies from decade to decade. Moreover, church statistics tend to be out of date even before they appear in print, in that parochial reports can take up to two years to be submitted and tabulated. But if readers approach the numbers with caution, statistics can provide a broad profile of a church.

Numerically, the Episcopal Church is smaller than the Roman Catholic Church and various denominations stemming from the Baptist, Methodist, Lutheran, and Presbyterian traditions. As of 1992, inclusive Episcopal membership seemed to rank somewhere between twelfth and fourteenth among church bodies in the United States. The church's baptized membership began to decline in the mid-1960s, as did membership in most mainline denominations. Membership peaked in 1966 at 3.4 mil-

174

lion, declined steadily until the late 1970s, and stabilized somewhat below 3 million baptized members in the 1980s. In 1992 baptized membership in the Episcopal Church approximated 2.49 million; communicants — or persons who had received holy communion and retained an active parish membership during the previous year — numbered 1.76 million; and ordained clergy (including bishops) numbered roughly 15,000.

During the same years, from the mid-1960s through the early 1990s, the number of members over sixty-five years of age in Episcopal congregations increased and the ratio of known, baptized Episcopalians to the American population steadily declined. By 1990 that ratio was approximately 1 in 102. The parochial reports from these years showed that the Episcopal Church was losing members steadily in its traditional stronghold of the northeast. Only in the southeast and southwest was its growth remaining within sight of the overall increase in the American population.

Of the fifteen largest parishes of the Episcopal Church in 1991, more than half were in the southeast, southwest, or west. Led by All Saints' Church in Pasadena, California (with a baptized membership of 7,103), the largest parishes included two in Dallas, Texas (St. Michael and All Angels, and Incarnation), two in Houston, Texas (St. Martin's and St. John the Divine), two in California (All Saints', Pasadena, and Holy Family, N. Hollywood), and one apiece in Arizona (St. Philip's-in-the-Hills, Tucson), Colorado (St. John's Cathedral, Denver), Connecticut (St. Luke's, Darien), Georgia (St. Philip's Cathedral), Massachusetts (Trinity Church, Boston), Maryland (Redeemer, Baltimore), New York (St. Mark's, Brooklyn), South Carolina (Christ, Greenville), and Virginia (St. Stephen's, Richmond).

All of these churches had over 2500 baptized members. As those figures indicate, the statistical picture contained some bright spots for the Episcopal Church. Though size and spiritual vitality should not be confused, one survey showed that the number of persons worshiping in Episcopal churches increased thirty-one percent from 1974 to 1986: from 884,400 to 1,107,500. In annual giving, too, Episcopalians ranked well among American churches, contributing $722 million to their churches in plate and pledge offerings in 1991 and increasing their gifts nineteen percent between 1974 and 1986.

A study of church growth in post-baby-boom America identified the six marks of "growing churches" as commitment, discipline, missionary zeal, absolutism, conformity, and fanaticism.[115] Pentecostal, Holiness, Independent Baptist, and similar denominations exhibited those marks; like most denominations in the mainstream of American Christianity, the Episcopal Church exhibited only a few. From the nineteenth century on, the evidence has been fairly consistent that a substantial minority of Episcopalians are relatively unconcerned with church growth. A 1990 study of an Episcopal diocese that continued to outgrow population increases identified contributors to its growth as: widespread use of the diocesan camp, extensive investment in ministries to high school and college students, thorough education of communicants in the meaning of stewardship, voluntary financial support to the diocese, considerable commitment to outreach and poverty relief, close relations with an overseas diocese, financial support of communicants who volunteer for church work overseas, Cursillo weekends, team ministries to prisoners, diocesan sponsorship of study programs on the new Book of Common Prayer, active participation of bishops in all aspects of diocesan life, high clerical salaries, and a diverse body of clergy.[116]

Three surveys of the 1980s identified some trends in the Episcopal Church. According to the 1987 Gallup "Religion in America" survey, the Episcopal Church is numerically strongest in the east and in urban areas, while weakest in the midwest and rural areas. The survey reported that thirty-four percent of Episcopalians had a college education and that thirty-one percent had annual household incomes of over $40,000 in 1987 dollars. Forty-one percent of church members in that year were over fifty years of age, fifty-one percent were women, and ninety-two percent were white. The Gallup poll also found that forty-four percent of Episcopalians considered themselves Republicans, twenty-six percent considered themselves Democrats, and twenty-nine percent called themselves independent. (Other surveys indicate that the percentage of Democrats is higher among clergy.) Previous polls had also reported that up to three times as many Americans think of themselves as Episcopalians than are listed on the church's rolls.

A 1987 study, Wade Clark Roof and William McKinney's *American Mainline Religion: Its Changing Shape and Future,* asserts that Episcopalians rank third (behind Unitarian-Universalists and Jews) "on all the status indicators — education, family income, occupational prestige, and perceived social class." Among the over two dozen religious groups surveyed, Roof and McKinney placed Episcopalians first in their willingness to grant rights to racial minorities, third in support of women's rights, and fifth in support of civil liberties and toleration of the new sexual attitudes of the post-Vietnam era. In the last two categories, Unitarian-Universalists, Americans of no religious preference, Christian Scientists, and Jews ranked ahead of Episcopalians.

In 1984 a survey of statistics reported by the presiding bishop indicated that more than half of the membership of the Episcopal Church came into the church as adult converts. According to the report, over eighty thousand of the adults received into the church in the seventeen previous years, including hundreds of priests, came from Roman Catholicism. By 1991 a number of Episcopal dioceses had former Roman Catholic clergy as bishops. Well known to Episcopalians active in parish life, the trend of Roman Catholic clergy, nuns, and laity becoming Episcopalians in large numbers prompted a letter to a church magazine from a Roman Catholic monk urging against either church tabulating a "convert score":

> Certainly many . . . have journeyed from Rome to Canterbury, and vice versa, through the years. . . . But if . . . our two churches are called to be sister churches . . . then perhaps we are challenged to discover another interpretive model. Every 'conversion story' is extraordinarily unique. . . . Perhaps Christians on both 'sides' are called to rejoice when a pilgrim truly finds his or her new ecclesial home, where she or he can more fruitfully serve our one Lord.[117]

Episcopalians have long played leading roles in American society. Such diverse figures as Fiorello La Guardia, Oliver Hazard Perry, Margaret Mead, John Jacob Astor, Robert E. Lee, George Gallup, Nat "King" Cole, Eli Lilly, Eleanor Roosevelt, Richard Upjohn, Nicholas Murray Butler, Queen Liliuokalani, Jefferson Davis, George Marshall, and J. Pierpont Morgan have been Episcopal laity. In literature the denomination has been represented by such authors as William Byrd, Washington Irving, Annie Dillard, James Fenimore Cooper, Clement Clarke Moore, Francis Scott Key, Thomas Nelson Page, Willa Cather, John Dos Passos, John Cheever, and Louis Auchincloss. Harriet Beecher Stowe, Henry Clay, Daniel Webster, Richard Henry Dana, John Cogley, John Updike, and Mortimer Adler are among the many Americans who entered the church during their later years.

Of the first forty-two presidents of the United States, eleven — George Washington, James Madison, James Monroe, William H. Harrison, John Tyler, Zachary Taylor, Franklin Pierce, Chester A. Arthur, Franklin D. Roosevelt, Gerald R. Ford, and George Bush — have been Episcopalians. If Thomas Jefferson is counted, the number rises to twelve.[118] Thirty-three of one hundred six Supreme Court justices (including seven of the sixteen chief justices) have been Episcopalians. In the 101st Congress (1988–1989), approximately twenty percent of the Senate and twelve percent of the House of Representatives were members of the Episcopal Church. Episcopalians ranked third (after Roman

Catholics and Methodists) in the number of senators and representatives who claimed membership.

Families such as the du Ponts, Vanderbilts, Whitneys, Roosevelts, Astors, Mellons, Harrimans, and Morgans have traditionally been Episcopalian. In 1976 *Fortune* magazine reported that Episcopalians headed twenty percent of the Fortune 500 companies. Although its inclusive membership currently ranks no higher than twelfth among churches in the United States, the denomination that first appeared in the colonies as the Church of England four hundred years ago has become substantially Americanized. The Episcopal Church has never quite been able to secure the loyalties of the lower social and economic classes, but it may be second to none in the nation in terms of power and influence.

HENRY VIII'S QUEST FOR
AN ANNULMENT

"A detestable villain. . . . a disgrace to human nature and a blot of blood and grease upon the history of England" — so Charles Dickens described King Henry VIII of England.[119] Writers often praise Martin Luther for his courage in precipitating the Reformation and for refusing to recant in the face of the combined opposition of papacy and the Holy Roman empire. Just as frequently, they deride his contemporary, Henry VIII, as a lustful and self-indulgent king who started a new church because an honorable and righteous pope would not annul his marriage. There is nothing wrong with this interpretation of Henry VIII and the pope, except that it is historically insupportable.

Those who hold this interpretation have assessed Henry's quest for an annulment outside of the essential backdrop of his times. They have forgotten that Henry VIII lived in an era when kings promised daughters in marriage for political gain, princes murdered their way to kingship, infidelity characterized royal marital relationships, and monarch after monarch discarded spouses for someone better in the political or sexual line. Denounced by Protestant and Roman Catholic reformers alike, the church of Henry's time was rich and worldly. Clergy wearing hairshirts moved in worlds of velvet and furs, royalty played fast and loose with holy things, and politics, bribery, and duplicity characterized negotiations for the dissolutions of marriages. Only by understanding the teachings about annulments as well as the marital practices of the Middle Ages and Henry VIII's time can someone who lives in the twentieth century place his quest in the proper perspective.

Anyone considering the teachings about annulments in Henry's day must first look to the Christian tradition. What does the New Testament say about marriage and divorce? Although it records the original teachings of Jesus on the subject as strict (see Mk. 10:2–12; Mt. 5:31–32, 19:3–9,

Lk. 16:18; and 1 Cor. 7:10), organized Christianity very early found ways for its members to end a marriage and to marry again. It is significant that the two churches that claim to have existed at the time of the apostles — the Eastern Orthodox Catholic and the Roman Catholic — continue to do the same thing.

Eastern Orthodoxy has traditionally permitted divorce; its laity may marry up to three times. Roman, or western, Catholicism for some centuries permitted marriages to be dissolved, but gradually adopted the teaching that Christian marriage is indissoluble. Henry VIII was born into western Catholicism after the teachings about indissolubility had been a part of canon law for many centuries. Yet he was not born into a church that categorically refused to dissolve marriages. In the sixteenth century as in the twentieth century, the Roman Catholic Church provided ways out of marriage.

"No human power," declares an authoritative twentieth-century dictionary of Roman Catholic doctrine, "can dissolve the bond of marriage when ratified and consummated between baptized persons. But.... "[120] The dictionary then lists three grounds on which popes and bishops may *annul* marriages. And while they have the same effect of dissolving marriages, annulments differ from divorces. A *divorce* is a declaration that a true marriage has failed; an *annulment* is a declaration that a true marriage has never existed.

Henry VIII sought an annulment — a declaration from the pope as vicar of Christ, or from a lesser church official or court authorized by the pope to make such decisions for him — that his first marriage had never been valid. Such dissolutions of marriage were relatively common in Henry's time. If Christian officials in the west gradually became unwilling over the centuries to permit Christians to end marriages with divorce, they nevertheless remained willing to say that some marriages had never begun.

To understand Henry's pursuit of an annulment, a twentieth-century reader must also understand the marriage customs of his time. In the medieval period, property married property and kingdom married kingdom. Parents arranged engagements when their children were infants. And the negotiations for such marriages were usually conducted with little concern for the personal feelings of the prospective bride and groom.

The royal marriages of Spain and England during Henry VIII's youth exemplify this pattern. After their own marriage had united the Spanish kingdoms of Aragon and Castile, King Ferdinand and Queen Isabella married two daughters into the royal families of Portugal and England.

They also married a son and another daughter into the family of the Holy Roman emperor.

In England, Henry VIII's father, Henry VII — the first of the Tudor dynasty (Henry VIII's daughter Elizabeth I was the last) — sealed his claim to the English throne by marrying a princess of a rival house. He then assisted England's foreign policy by marrying two sons and two daughters into the royal families of Europe — Mary into the royal family of France, Margaret into the then-separate royal family of Scotland (a marriage that was accompanied by a quickly broken treaty of "perpetual peace"), and Arthur and Henry in succession into Ferdinand and Isabella's royal family.

Since such unions sealed alliances, royalty understood that political necessity might place an unattractive foreign mate in their marital chambers. While queens and princesses generally lacked the freedom to pursue their passions after marriage (although heiresses to notable kingdoms could sometimes exercise some choice in marriage), male monarchs often had affairs of the heart. A king's or prince's wife, subjects, and clergy understood that he might take mistresses.

But mistresses were only one way that arranged marriages were made more palatable in the era of Henry VIII. It was also standard for kings and nobles to enter into political marriages knowing that the arrangement was not permanent and that they could shed their spouses in later years. The means employed was a decree of nullity — a ruling that no true marriage had occurred — from an ecclesiastical court.

To argue his or her case for an annulment before a church court, a married person (generally, though not invariably, a husband) would hire one or more ecclesiastical lawyers who specialized in marriage law. Although very human reasons might lurk behind a spouse's desire for an annulment, the lawyers would present arguments to the church court based upon a supposed flaw, or impediment, that had rendered the marriage null and void from its inception. If such grounds as consanguinity (too close a blood relationship), affinity (too close a relationship to blood relatives of a former spouse), spiritual relationship (such as godfather and goddaughter), insanity, coercion, impotency, or a pre-existing valid marriage could be shown to have existed at the time of marriage, a church court could declare that a true marriage had never existed. If a marriage was not consummated, or if either partner entered a religious order, a church court could annul a marriage.

In Henry VIII's time England had twenty-six such courts at the diocesan, or bishop's, level authorized by the pope to nullify marriages and to free successful petitioners to remarry. Applicants for annulments whose cases failed in such a diocesan court could hire expensive specialists and appeal to the sacred Roman rota, the papal court that handled matrimonial cases. Petitioners who possessed money and influence found annulments a fairly simple matter. Arranged annulments were as much a part of the royal expectation of the time as arranged marriages. To make an annulment even easier, in fact, some of the nobility concealed impediments when they were married, in order to use them if necessary as the basis for later annulments. Although diocesan courts and the rota granted annulments less routinely than some historians claim, the ease with which they were obtained constituted one of the ecclesiastical scandals of the late Middle Ages.

Two developments seem to have increased the traffic in annulments as the Middle Ages progressed. First, an ever-growing body of papal decrees, theological commentaries, and precedents from earlier decisions of ecclesiastical courts had so bled the supposedly indelible sacrament of holy matrimony that canon lawyers could find grounds for declaring almost any marriage invalid. In Scotland, for example, the church laws governing marriage became so intricate that one archbishop of St. Andrews complained to the pope that few men and women of social standing could validly marry.

Second, the popes of the Middle Ages were also monarchs who ruled the papal states extending from France to Italy. Like royalty, medieval popes wore purple. They maintained armies. They entered into wars and treaties, dressed in armor and led their troops, married their illegitimate children into other royal families for political advantage, and supported immense courts. Pope Leo X (the pope who excommunicated Martin Luther), for example, had a court consisting of 683 people, including his own private archbishop, his own poets, his own painters, his own court jesters, and even his own keeper of elephants.

To achieve their religious and political ends, popes needed the good will of other rulers. Hence they generally thought twice before denying annulments to royal or noble families. Sometimes, in fact, an annulment — like the royal marriage before it — became part of statecraft. In 1499, for example, Pope Alexander VI (pope from 1492 to 1503) annulled the twenty-three-year marriage of King Louis XII of France so that he might marry the heiress of Brittany and unite that land with France. In return, the pope received military support for the papal states and a princely marriage for his illegitimate son, Cesare Borgia.

To be sure, this trade in annulments did not flow free of protest. In 1351 an Irish synod protested that "false and feigned reasons" and "corrupt and suborned witnesses" turned annulment proceedings into farces.[121] In 1460 the Canterbury Convocation called annulments "the scandal of the whole Church."[122] In France public opinion was shocked by the annulment of Louis XII's first marriage. In Italy public laughter greeted Pope Alexander VI's annulment of his daughter's four-year marriage on the grounds (indignantly challenged by her former husband) that it had never been consummated.

Thus readers with twentieth-century perspectives on marriage must tread cautiously in assessing Henry VIII's petition for an annulment. That Henry was "a detestable villain" is not in question. But few approaches to history stray further from the truth than the portrayal of a righteous pope protecting the sacrament of Christian marriage against the concupiscence of a dissolute king. Seeking primarily to protect his political interests (by securing an heir to succeed him on the throne), Henry VIII chose what had become a standard vehicle for achieving political aims — an annulment. The history of annulments gave him every reason to expect that the pope would free him to remarry. And he had reason to be stunned and angered when what should have been a relatively routine matter became immensely complicated.

The saga of Henry VIII's annulment begins with the marriage of his older brother, Arthur. In 1501 Henry VII had diplomatically arranged for Arthur, his oldest son and heir, to marry Catherine of Aragon, daughter of the powerful King Ferdinand and Queen Isabella of Spain. The sickly Arthur was then fourteen and apparently dying; Catherine was fifteen. Although Henry subsequently based his case on the opposite interpretation, the evidence is persuasive that Arthur (though he said otherwise) was never able to consummate his marriage with Catherine.

When Arthur died only five months after the wedding, Henry VII, Ferdinand, and Isabella decided to preserve the alliance between England and Spain by marrying Catherine to Henry, the new heir to the throne. But the proposed union ran into an impediment: the marriage laws of western Christendom followed the prohibition of Leviticus 20:21: "If a man takes his brother's wife, it is impurity; he has uncovered his brother's nakedness; they shall be childless." Just as John the Baptist affirmed this law when he forbad Herod from marrying his brother's wife (Mt. 14:3–4), so canon law prohibited Henry from marrying his brother's widow.

For Henry and Catherine to marry, a papal *dispensation* (or exemption from church laws) was therefore required. Scholars still debate whether any earlier pope had given such a dispensation, but a number of theologians and church officials of the time said that the then-pope, Julius II (pope from 1503 to 1513), lacked the authority to set aside a biblical inter-diction. Even the Archbishop of Canterbury, William Warham, and Julius himself initially expressed doubt that Henry and Catherine could validly marry. But under the pressure of England and Spain, Julius granted the dispensation in 1503 and sent it to England the next year. Upon assuming the throne in 1509, the eighteen-year-old Henry married Catherine, then twenty-three.

By all outward appearances, the marriage between the king of England and the princess of Spain was happy. To be sure, Henry had mistresses and an illegitimate son (whom he had named Duke of Richmond), but that was the royal practice of the time. Yet by at least 1527, and perhaps as early as 1514 (though this date is much less probable), he had begun to contemplate seeking an annulment of his marriage to Catherine.

Why did Henry seek this annulment? The answer is clear to scholars: succession to the throne, not passion for a woman, was the principal problem. Three considerations seem to have caused Henry to seek an annulment.

Above all, Henry seems to have been propelled by an urgent, almost desperate desire for a male heir who would continue the Tudor dynasty. Providing for a successor ranked among the most important duties of monarchs in late medieval and early modern Europe, and Henry took his duty seriously. His father and two brothers were dead; he was the only surviving Tudor male. He fathered six children by Catherine, but only one — the Princess Mary (born in 1516 and later to rule as Queen of England from 1553 to 1558) — survived. By Catherine's fortieth year miscarriages, sorrow, and age had taken such a toll that her physicians believed that she could bear no more children.

Since England's one previous experience with a female ruler (the twelfth-century Eleanor of Aquitaine) had been unsuccessful, the absence of a male heir seemed to endanger the young Tudor dynasty. In 1486 Henry's father, Henry VII, had ended the Wars of the Roses — the series of dynastic civil wars between the houses of Lancaster and York that had disturbed the peace of England in the fifteenth century — by marrying a princess of the house of York. But various Yorkist revolts had broken out during his reign. If Henry VIII were to pass his throne to the Princess Mary, he and his advisors believed, civil war might erupt again as the various factions in the English aristocracy sought to overthrow the new half-Spanish queen, to control her, or to influence her selection of a mate.

Yet if Mary assumed the throne and decided (with her advisors) to circumvent factional struggles by choosing a husband from outside the kingdom, the foreign consort might attempt to place England's foreign policy in the service of his own country. (Precisely that did occur in the 1550s when Mary took the throne, married Philip II of her mother's native Spain, and as a result took England into a war with France, Spain's great rival. Mary's experience with a foreign mate undoubtedly contributed to her half-sister Elizabeth I's decision to remain unmarried.) Thus a male heir seemed essential for the peace and security of England. No one in the first decades of the sixteenth century knew of the long and stable reigns of Elizabeth I, Victoria, and Elizabeth II that lay hidden in the future.

As early as 1514, rumors circulated in royal circles on the continent that Henry VIII was considering an annulment because of Catherine's failure to bear a son. The rumors appear to have had little basis, for Catherine was pregnant at the time, and Henry was joyfully awaiting the birth of what he hoped would be a son, but the stories do indicate that Henry's contemporaries knew of his longing to continue the Tudor dynasty. They also show that his concern for a male heir predated by many years Anne Boleyn's appearance in the English court.

In December 1514, Catherine gave birth to a boy, but the child lived less than two months. In 1516 the birth of a healthy Princess Mary renewed Henry's hopes that Catherine might give him the male heir he needed. But in 1517 she miscarried. In 1518 — it was her last pregnancy — she delivered a stillborn girl. In the 1520s, when Catherine's age and declining physical condition cast serious doubts on her ability to have more children, Henry and his advisors began planning for an annulment in earnest.

If Henry was troubled by the lack of a male heir, it is also clear that the Leviticus passage pricked his remarkably elastic conscience, for it suggested that God had cursed his union with Catherine. He asked himself: were not the stillbirths and miscarriages — more than any previous English king had experienced — signs of divine displeasure with his marriage? After all, Leviticus 20:21 read: "if a man takes his brother's wife, it is impurity. . . . they shall be childless." And in terms of a male heir, Henry was childless.

Despite his later reputation for pubescence and gluttony, Henry was one of the most scholarly of the kings of his time. Immersing himself in the canon law of annulments, he concluded that Christ had not given the authority to a pope to dispense couples from the law of God as revealed in Leviticus. While the world viewed the king of England as married, Henry's research led him to believe that God viewed him as a bachelor. And since God had seen fit to punish him by the deaths of all of those babies for living in sin with Catherine, Henry decided that he must make matters right with God. This apparently sincere but utterly self-serving theological opinion of the king involved no searching self-appraisal, but it clearly contributed to his decision to seek an annulment.

Finally, by the late 1520s, Henry had also fallen in love with a lady-in-waiting, Anne Boleyn, who for a period of time insisted upon marriage as a prerequisite for other favors. Charming, well-connected, raised for some years at the French court, and twenty years old (as of 1527), Anne had many childbearing years ahead and seemed to promise the end of the Tudor king's anxieties about succession.

That Henry's desire for a legitimate successor came before any fleshly desire for Anne seems clear. Members of the nobility typically took mistresses and received the tacit approval of the clergy in doing so. Thus Henry had no need to annul his marriage and to remarry in order to enjoy sexual gratification. If he wished to ensure the birth of a legitimate male heir, however, an annulment and remarriage was essential.

That Anne's failure to present him with a son — she gave birth to one daughter, the later Queen Elizabeth I, and had many miscarriages — caused Henry to think of taking a third wife is a further illustration that the king placed more emphasis on Anne's fertility than on her sexual charms. Contrary to the depiction of popular history, Anne was neither the only cause of Henry's break with Rome nor even the principal one. Her accessibility in 1527 clearly precipitated the timing of Henry's nullity suit, however. If Anne had not been willing, available, and fertile, Henry's suit probably would have been postponed until he found another young woman who was.

All of these considerations pushed Henry and his advisors to seek an annulment. And they had many reasons to believe that he would be successful in receiving one. Four reasons stand out.

First, Henry had on his side the substantial theological arguments just summarized. According to the teaching of Leviticus, he could argue that his marriage had been null and void from the start. That argument alone could win him an annulment.

Second, in 1521 Henry had won favor in the courts of Rome by writing a defense of the seven sacraments against the teachings of Martin Luther, who had asserted that Christ had instituted only two sacraments. As a result, Pope Leo X had conferred upon Henry the title of "Defender of the Faith." Henry had also assisted both earlier popes and the current pope, Clement VII (pope from 1523 to 1534), in their recurrent conflicts with the Holy Roman emperor. Such devotion to the Holy See usually did not go unrewarded. An annulment, especially when the arguments supporting it were compelling, was scant repayment.

Third, Henry held one of the more powerful crowns in Christendom at a time when popes had every reason to fear that any monarchs they offended might in pique carry their nations into the rapidly growing Protestant camp.

Finally, if theological arguments, papal favors, and kingly power were not enough, Henry also had strong legal precedents for annulment on his side. To the canon lawyers who argued the cases and to the ecclesiastical courts who decided them, precedents were crucial. If it could be shown that a pope or matrimonial court had ruled favorably in similar cases, the precedent could tip the balance in a suit. Since these precedents place a different light on the understanding of what the English court called Henry's "Great Matter," they require discussion.

The precedents Henry and his canon lawyers cited dated back to suits for annulments filed and won by English and Spanish monarchs centuries before. One precedent well known to Henry and his advisors involved the prominent queen of England, Eleanor of Aquitaine. In 1152 Pope Eugene III ruled that Eleanor's marriage to Louis VII of France was null and void, although the couple had been married for fourteen years and had two daughters. Three months later Eleanor married King Henry II of England. Also well known were the two successive annulments Pope Innocent III (pope from 1198 to 1216) had granted King Alfonso IX of Leon.

But Henry really needed to look no further than his contemporaries for precedents. During Henry's lifetime, the list of annulments included one in which a pope dissolved the marriage of his own illegitimate daughter in order to marry her into the royal house of Naples. And in the less than forty years Henry had lived, his own family had been the beneficiaries of at least four annulments.

Henry's sister Margaret, for example, who became Queen of Scotland through her first marriage (and became generally known as Margaret of Scotland), continually became involved in marriages requiring annulments. Shortly after she reached puberty (in 1503), Henry VII attempted unsuccessfully to improve England's relations with the then-separate kingdom of Scotland by marrying her to King James IV of Scotland. After James was killed by the English in the battle of Flodden in 1513, the widowed Margaret married Archibald Douglas, Earl of Angus.

After thirteen years of this second marriage, however, Margaret became the mistress of a young courtier — Henry Stewart, Lord Methven —

who was also married. The couple decided to marry, but the marriage depended upon both receiving annulments.

Margaret of Scotland now petitioned the pope to have her marriage to Angus annulled on the basis of two supposed impediments. The first: she and her canon lawyers argued that Angus had been subject to a pre-marital contract to another woman at the time he married Margaret — and so had in fact not been free to marry. The second: they asserted that Margaret's first husband, James IV, had actually survived the battle of Flodden and lived three additional years. Because James IV had been very much alive at the time Margaret remarried, Margaret and her ecclesiastical lawyers argued, her marriage to Angus had been invalid from the start. Since James IV's death at Flodden (along with one-third of his army) was well attested, the assertion was outrageous. Henry VIII, for example, found Margaret's arguments for the annulment so flimsy that he scolded her. Nevertheless, the influential French ambassador to the papal court agreed to oversee Margaret's suit for her.

In March 1527, just two months before an ecclesiastical court in England began to consider Henry's suit, the sacred Roman rota granted Margaret an annulment. She then married Methven, who had likewise secured an annulment. Yet in time this marriage, too, was annulled when Margaret presented evidence that Methven bore the relationship of a cousin, eight degrees removed, from her second husband, Angus. Thus Henry's older sister succeeded in having two marriages annulled — both on seemingly rickety grounds — and one of her husbands also had a marriage annulled.

In addition, both of the husbands of Henry's younger sister, Mary, had received annulments. In 1514 Mary, then eighteen, married the fifty-two-year-old Louis XII of France, whose annulment in 1499 has already been described. After marrying Mary, the enfeebled Louis had lived less than three months. As a widow, Mary was free to remarry. And given the marital histories of medieval royalty, it is not surprising that the person she now chose to marry — Charles Brandon, the Duke of Suffolk and Henry's courtier *par excellence* — had marital complications that required the hand of a pope to unravel.

The arguments Suffolk and his lawyers presented to the pope for an annulment closely paralleled those on which Henry was basing his case. Like Henry, Suffolk had received a dispensation from Pope Julius II to marry a close relative — in his case, a blood relative named Margaret Mortimer. When, like Henry, Suffolk decided (or so he said) that his marriage was cursed because of his blood relationship to his wife, he left Margaret

Mortimer. Receiving a declaration from the archdeaconry of London — an annulment of sorts — that the impediment of consanguinity had rendered his first marriage invalid from the start, he married again. When his second wife died, he married Henry's sister Mary in 1515.

But the edicts of the archdeaconry about Suffolk's first marriage were of questionable validity, and Suffolk's first wife was still alive. To assure that there was no question of the legitimacy of any children he might have by Mary (for they could become heirs to the throne of England), Suffolk asked Pope Clement VII to declare that his first marriage had not been a true marriage.

Here the parallels to Henry's case were striking. Like Henry, Suffolk and his lawyers argued that his relationship to his first wife was closer than God's law allowed. Like Henry — and at virtually the same time — they asked Pope Clement to declare that Pope Julius II's dispensation that allowed Suffolk to marry Margaret Mortimer should never have been granted.

It seemed a forecast of what was to come for Henry VIII that Suffolk's petition was successful. In 1528, at precisely the time that Henry's similar suit was pending in Rome, Clement VII issued a bull annulling Suffolk's first marriage and censuring any one who questioned the validity of his marriage to Mary Tudor.

Initially Henry and his advisors planned to follow the same strategy that Suffolk and his canon lawyers had employed. According to their plan, an ecclesiastical court convened by Henry's principal advisor, Lord Chancellor Thomas Cardinal Wolsey, would hear testimony and declare Henry's marriage to Catherine void. Clement VII would then confirm the annulment and place under censure any Christians who disputed the validity of his second marriage. Thus any male children born to Henry and Anne would have an uncontested right of succession to the throne of England. And the Tudor dynasty would be saved.

With all of these precedents and arguments on his side, virtually every one who knew of the suit expected that Henry would receive an annulment. When word that Henry was considering an annulment first surfaced in 1514, a Venetian observer wrote: "The King of England intends. . . . to annul his own marriage, and will obtain what he wants from the Pope. . . . "[123] When Henry finally decided to proceed with his suit in 1527, Wolsey specifically pointed to the far weaker cases of Louis XII of France and Henry's sister Margaret. If they had received annulments, Wolsey declared, so would Henry.

But the situation was not that simple. In the years since Henry had married Catherine, the papacy had changed hands three times. Julius II, who had permitted the couple to marry, had died in 1513. Leo X, the worldly member of the Medici family who had misjudged the popularity of Martin Luther, had held office until 1521. His successor, a reform-minded native of the Netherlands named Hadrian VI, had died in 1523 after little more than a year in office. Since that year another member of the great and notorious Medici family, Clement VII, had occupied the papal throne. When Henry's petition reached Rome in 1527, Pope Clement had many precedents to give the king of England the annulment he wanted. For at least four reasons, however, he did not do so.

First, Clement was well known for indecision and procrastination. Although superior to many of his papal predecessors in character, he was so hesitant and indecisive in action that he often appeared devious and cowardly. Whatever its causes, his tendency to procrastinate caused contemporaries to mock Clement with such nicknames as "Pope-I-will-and-I-won't." Until events forced him to a decision, this trait caused him to delay acting on Henry's request for seven years.

Second, not only the popes but also the times had changed since Henry had married Catherine. Henry's request required the pope to pronounce that a predecessor, Julius II, had erred in releasing Arthur and Catherine from the law of Leviticus. To Henry and his advisors, persuading Clement to reverse Julius II's dispensation promised to be easy, for Clement had similarly reversed a dispensation of Julius II in the course of granting the annulment to Suffolk.

What they overlooked was that Suffolk's annulment occurred in a corner. No international audience watched its progress. No national interests other than those of England were involved in it. In addition, Suffolk petitioned for an annulment *after* he had already married Henry's sister (which, as it turned out, was precisely what Clement hoped Henry would do). Hence what Suffolk sought amounted to an annulment after the fact, an easier pill for an indecisive pope to swallow.

But in contrast, the king of England's petition for an annulment must have caused the pope and his curia dyspepsia. For Henry VIII's wife was not Margaret Mortimer. She was the daughter of the king and queen of Spain as well as the aunt of the powerful Holy Roman emperor. Because of the political ramifications of Henry's suit, the pope and his advisors knew that all European rulers would keep abreast of its progress through their ambassadors at the papal court in Rome. They also understood that the pope would be under conflicting pressures from the political powers of Europe — Spain, the Holy Roman emperor, England, and France, the bitter rival of Spain and of the emperor — to rule in a way that would assist their self-interest.

The Reformation added a new and complex dimension. Pope Julius had ruled that Henry and Catherine could marry under God's law. Now Henry was asking Clement to rule that they had actually not been free to marry. Did popes err on questions of faith? Did Christ's Most High Vicars substitute human opinions for divine law? Martin Luther and the other Protestant Reformers were daily claiming that they did, and Protestantism was spreading. If Clement reversed his predecessor's dispensation, the pope and his advisors feared that he would appear to confirm the charges of the heretics before all of Europe. As a result, more heads of state might lead their countries into Protestantism. Yet at the same time Clement and his advisors also recognized that denying Henry an annulment could alienate Henry and his realm from Roman Catholicism. And so Pope Clement procrastinated.

A third problem was that Catherine — who remained dignified and resolute throughout the proceedings — would not be cast aside. Calling herself a friendless Spaniard in a foreign realm, she appealed to her nephew, Charles V — Henry's rival, Holy Roman emperor, and (simultaneously, as Charles I) king of Spain — to protect her against the machinations of the English Establishment.

In response, Charles arranged the transfer of the hearing from England (where the ecclesiastical court was inevitably biased in Henry's favor) to Rome, where he could better control the proceedings. He sent a skilled canon lawyer to Rome to protect his aunt's case, and he applied steady pressure on Clement.

The pressure was difficult for England to overcome in a time when the papacy ranked among the national powers. The Holy Roman emperor possessed substantially more influence in European affairs than the king of England and had the better army. Moreover, Spain, whose population was twice the size of England, was more powerful than Henry's England.

Henry could count on the counterpressure of King Francis I of France, who did not wish a princess from his hated rival Spain to inherit the English throne and tip the international balance of power. But France had been vanquished by Charles V's troops in 1525 and obliged to agree to an embarrassing treaty. It was clearly subordinate in military might to the emperor and Spain.

Finally, at the time of Henry's suit, Pope Clement was under the domination of the troops of Charles V. In May of 1527, in reprisal for Clement's joining a military alliance against him, Charles's troops (the majority of whom, ironically, were Lutherans from Germany) burned, looted, and ravaged the papal city in the worst sacking of its two-thousand-year history. Trapped by the occupying troops for seven months in a castle overlooking the devastated city, Clement had time to ponder the earthly power of the Holy Roman emperor. "If the Pope be slain or taken," Wolsey prophetically wrote to Henry upon receiving news of the sack of Rome, "it will hinder the King's affairs not a little."[124]

The sack of Rome in 1527 had precisely that effect on Henry's suit. As the grandson of Ferdinand and Isabella and the nephew of Catherine, Charles was intent that neither pope nor English king would set aside the royal daughter of Spain. He was also vitally concerned that an annulment would remove Henry and Catherine's one child, his cousin Mary Tudor, from succession to the throne of England. And that could rob Spain of the opportunity to influence the affairs of England.

To be sure, the sacking of the holy city had damaged Charles's reputation in the eyes of Europe. But it had also served notice to the pope that he could not trifle with the emperor. If Clement annulled the marriage of Catherine of Aragon, he had every reason to fear a second and even more destructive retaliation. Hence the pope faced a far more complex situation than he confronted when he annulled the marriages of Margaret of Scotland and the Duke of Suffolk. When he had ruled against Angus and Margaret Mortimer, he had not ruled against relatives of the Holy Roman emperor. When he had given Margaret and Suffolk annulments, he had done so free of the fear that the armies of the emperor would sack Rome again because of his decision. But the case of Henry VIII was precisely the opposite. Thus when one of Henry's emissaries urged him to annul Catherine and Henry's marriage, the pope replied: "The emperor would never consent to it."

With its hearings, extensive correspondence, and pressures from England on the one side and from the emperor on the other, Henry's suit dragged on. Caught in an insoluble dilemma, and feeling too weak to withstand the wrath of either England or the emperor, Clement employed his only weapon: he stalled. For six years, from 1527 to 1533, Henry's case was heard first in England, then in Rome, then again in England, and finally again in Rome.

During this period Clement or his agents attempted various strategies. They held off Charles V's recurrent demands that the pope deliver a judgment for Catherine and excommunicate Henry for adultery. They tried unsuccessfully to persuade Catherine to enter a religious order, even temporarily, as wives of other European royalty had done when their husbands sought annulments; if Catherine had become a nun (even if she had later returned to secular life) Henry would have been free under canon law to remarry. In yet another vain effort at a solution, the pope's advisors suggested that if Henry would drop his request for an annulment and agree to return to Catherine at some future time, the pope would legitimize any children born in the meantime to Henry and Anne.

While this last suggestion may have been a ruse, Clement did make a more serious proposal. If Henry would drop his suit for nullity, the pope indicated that he would be willing to dispense the impediment of consanguinity and to allow his daughter Mary Tudor to marry her illegitimate half-brother, the Duke of Richmond. Such a marriage would have continued the Tudor line while at the same time upholding the sanctity of the marriage bond of Henry and Catherine. That it would have been incestuous apparently presented neither an ecclesiastical nor a moral problem, for during Henry's lifetime popes had already given permission for the king of Portugal to marry a wife's sister and for the king of Naples to marry an aunt.

The consensus of historical scholarship is that Clement simply wanted Henry somehow to free him from the responsibility of making a decision about the annulment. If Henry took his case to the English ecclesiastical courts, received an annulment from them, and married Anne Boleyn in England, Clement would be confronted with a *fait accompli* that he could deplore but not publicly condemn. In fact, both Clement and King Francis I of France suggested such a plan to Henry's emissaries.

Why, then, did Henry not simply go ahead and marry Anne? The answer is of a piece with Henry's actions from the beginning of his quest for an annulment: his principal concern was to continue the Tudor dynasty on the throne of England. Thus he refused to cooperate with any plan that might raise doubts about the legitimacy of the male heir he expected from Anne.

Henry had one argument that — had he used it — some scholars believe might have obliged Clement to issue an annulment. Suggested early in the discussions by Cardinal Wolsey, it involved the impediment to valid marriage known in canon law as "public honesty" or "quasi-affinity." A twentieth-century reader can perhaps better understand it as having to do with "public seemliness" or "public decency."

According to the canon law of the time, a couple who contracted to a marriage either through engagement (then known as betrothal) or through the marriage ceremony created an impediment. The impediment, which only an ecclesiastical dispensation could remove, invalidated any marriage either partner might contract in later years with a close blood relation of the other. This aspect of canon law applied absolutely to Henry's marriage to his brother's widow.

As Wolsey pointed out to Henry and to other advisors, however, Julius II had said nothing about "public honesty" in his dispensation of 1503 that permitted Henry and Catherine to marry. In Wolsey's view the pope had therefore released Henry and Catherine only from one impediment — the law of Leviticus. The second impediment to their marriage — that of "public honesty" — still existed. And since Julius's bull had not removed the second impediment, Wolsey argued, Henry and Catherine had never been validly married.

In 1529 Cardinal Wolsey fell from favor, was arrested on charges of high treason, and died of natural causes while under arrest. Henry and his advisors examined Wolsey's line of argument, found it unsatisfactory, and did not emphasize it in their nullity suit. Had they taken the "public honesty" argument seriously, they might have changed history, for in 1968 an English scholar identified Wolsey's argument as the point of canon law that could, and probably would, have won an annulment from Clement. This renewed suggestion that Henry had a valid case, but that he chose instead to argue an invalid one, has aroused strong comment.[125]

As Clement and his agents dawdled, Henry became more and more impatient. Would the pope ever act? A Cambridge don, Thomas Cranmer, argued that Charles's domination of Rome had taken away the pope's free will to arrive at a decision. On that basis Henry dispatched agents to secure opinions from the theological faculties of Europe about the validity of his marriage to Catherine. Bribery or bullying achieved a decision in his favor from the faculties of many universities. It failed to advance Henry's case in Rome, but it made Cranmer a trusted advisor.

Finally, frustrated over what he considered a wanton delay and with a growing sense that he possessed authority over both state and church, Henry initiated in 1529 a series of acts that resulted in the independence of the ancient *Ecclesia Anglicana*. Like many of the contemporary German and Scandinavian rulers who had become Lutheran, he decided that the bishop of Rome had no more ecclesiastical jurisdiction in his country than any foreign bishop. In January 1533, Henry married Anne Boleyn, who by now was pregnant. Cranmer, whom Henry had appointed archbishop of Canterbury in the same year with Clement VII's approval, pronounced Henry's marriage to Catherine invalid. By 1534, the break with Rome was complete.

The Roman Catholic Church viewed Henry's annulment as an illicit divorce lacking the authority and sanctity of annulments granted by popes, curia, or local ecclesiastical courts who spoke on earth in the place of Christ. Six months after Henry married Anne, the sacred Roman rota examined Henry's suit (or, rather, the appeal of Catherine that Charles V had arranged to have heard in Rome). After three sessions of the rota, Pope Clement — no longer indecisive — pronounced sentence. He nullified Henry's marriage to Anne Boleyn, declared any children that might result from the union illegitimate, and affirmed that Catherine was still Henry's wife. Although Clement placed Henry under excommunication in 1533 and absolved his subjects from obedience to him, the papacy prolonged the period allowed for repentance. The bull excommunicating Henry was not promulgated until 1538, five years after the king had set aside Catherine to marry Anne. Henry's turbulent and distasteful career until his death nine years and four marriages later is well known.

In the nineteenth century a history of the Christian church written by an Episcopal author for use in the grade and high schools of the Episcopal Church described Henry VIII as "a corrupt and base monarch . . . a shameless and profligate man. . . . an unprincipled and wicked king."[126] Few readers of history would quarrel with that assessment.

Yet twentieth-century readers must also view the man Dickens called a "blot of blood and grease upon the history of England" in the context of his time and not of theirs. Despite his reputation, Henry VIII was a pivotal figure and a prime mover in English history. Ironically, since his nation rose in power and prestige during his reign, he is viewed by historians as one of the "great" kings of England. Ironically, too, since he attended mass three to five times a day, crept to the cross on Good Fridays, adored the consecrated eucharistic wafers, read theology extensively, and burned many heretics, Henry was one of the more formally religious Christian monarchs of his time. And in perhaps the keenest irony of all, Parliament later adopted his papally conferred title of "Defender of the Faith" for all successive monarchs, which has meant an unbroken line of Anglican "Defenders of the Faith" from William and Mary in 1689 through Elizabeth II today.

In the context of his time, in fact, Henry's morality seems roughly the same as the morality of many leaders of medieval state and church. Precocious as a child, astute as a man, far more scholarly than the average monarch, witty, gifted in the arts and sports, for many years the handsomest of the European monarchs, yet simultaneously tyrannical, insecure, self-deceiving, and monumentally egotistical, he leaps so forcefully from the pages of history that his contemporaries and their equally reprehensible deeds go largely forgotten.

For if Henry VIII fails by the moral standards of later centuries, so do most of the popes of his time. The nephews of the unscrupulous Pope Sixtus IV (pope from 1471 to 1484), who died seven years before Henry was born, may or may not have been wrong when they accused him of co-conspiracy in murder, but Sixtus was surely guilty of nepotism, simony, and extortion. The successor to Sixtus, the worldly Innocent VIII, who was pope at Henry's birth, sold church offices to the highest bidders to pay off the huge debt left by his predecessor. Pope Alexander VI (pope from 1492 to 1503), whose death occurred when Henry was entering puberty, was elected to the papacy largely through bribery; a noted womanizer, he officiated at the marriages of two of his children in full ceremony in the Vatican and annulled the marriage of one.

Nepotism, simony, extravagance, worldliness, and worse characterized the other holders of the papal throne during the years of Henry's marriages to Catherine and Anne. The pope known as *"Il Terrible,"* Julius II — the same pope who granted the dispensations that allowed Suffolk to marry Margaret Mortimer and Henry to marry Catherine — secured the election of Innocent VIII via bribery. Although Julius initiated some important reforms and earned the admiration of Machiavelli for his warlike character, many of his actions caused gentler Christians to hold him in contempt. The pleasure-loving Leo X (pope from 1513 to 1521), who became a cardinal as a teenager, almost spent the papacy into bankruptcy, despite extensive peddling of church offices and indulgences. As Henry VIII and his court well knew, Pope Clement VII (pope from 1523 to 1534) was noted for delay and intrigue far more than for his many good qualities.

During the years in which Henry sought his annulment, only Pope Hadrian VI (pope from 1522 to 1523) appears to have exercised a papacy characterized neither by scandal nor intrigue, and frustration at his inability to reform the church seems to have contributed to Hadrian's early death. A reformed papacy lay ahead, but it did not occur during Henry's lifetime. In the Reformation period, morals were sufficiently loose that Martin Luther could advise one of the leading lay figures in the German Reformation to take a second wife while his first was still alive. What the English court called Henry VIII's "Great Matter" cannot be understood apart from this background, and in that context Henry may appear less singularly vile.

The concern of this chapter, however, is not for partial rehabilitation of Henry VIII's character but rather for historical accuracy. It is indisputable that other Christians requested annulments in the sixteenth century and received them on infinitely flimsier grounds than those the king of England presented. But Henry's plight was unique; few other petitioners for annulments before or since have been caught in such a web of complications.

For Henry VIII needed much more than arguments that would secure him an annulment. He needed a cooperative wife. He needed a decisive pope. He needed a pope who was free from the grip of the Holy Roman emperor. He needed a Holy Roman emperor who was unrelated to his wife. He needed a Holy Roman emperor who was not also the king of Spain. He needed a dispensation from a previous pope's dispensation. Finally, he needed to have been born a century before the Protestant Reformation. To depict Henry's desire for an annulment as stemming from lust, and to view Clement's failure to grant it as stemming from a higher righteousness, is to maim history.

NOTES

1. The term "Anglican," which in its Latin origins simply means "English," dates in common use only from the nineteenth century. It emerged out of the belief that the principal form of English Christianity differed from other forms of Christianity sufficiently to warrant a separate descriptive term. Prior to the nineteenth century, adherents of the Church of England used such terms as "Catholic," "Protestant," "Protestant Catholic," "Reformed Catholic," "Protestant Reformed," "Reformed," and "Orthodox" to describe their form of Christianity. This history uses the terms "Anglican" or "Anglicanism" even when they are anachronistic, for the same reason that they were coined more than one hundred years ago.

2. D. C. Somervell, *A Short History of Our Religion* (New York, 1922), 235.

3. See Margaret A. Doody, "How Shall We Sing the Lord's Song upon an Alien Soil?: The New Episcopalian Liturgy," *The State of the Language,* ed. Leonard Michaels and Christopher Ricks (Berkeley, 1980), 108–124.

4. John Booty, *John Jewel as Apologist of the Church of England* (London, 1963), 29. Readers are also directed to the criticism of Jewel's arguments by the Roman Catholic polemicist Thomas Harding.

5. G. R. Balleine, *The Layman's History of the Church of England* (London, 1913), 145.

6. Joan R. Gundersen, "The Anglican Ministry in Virginia, 1723–1776" (Ph.D. dissertation, University of Notre Dame, 1972), 88; and John F. Woolverton, *Colonial Anglicanism in North America 1607–1776* (Detroit, 1984), 270–271 n. 77.

7. William Meade, *Old Churches, Ministers and Families of Virginia,* 2 vols. (Baltimore, 1966), 1:50–51.

8. "Journal of a Convention of the Protestant Episcopal Church in Virginia . . . May 7th, 1799," in Francis L. Hawks, *Contributions to the Ecclesiastical History of the United States of America,* 2 vols. (New York, 1836), 1:79.

9. Robert Jenney to SPG, 26 October 1749, in William S. Perry, ed.,

Historical Collections Relating to the American Colonial Church, 5 vols. (Hartford, Conn., 1870–1878), 2:260.

10. Lawrence F. London and Sarah M. Lemmon, *The Episcopal Church in North Carolina, 1701–1959* (Raleigh, 1987), 14.

11. Charles Woodmason, *The Carolina Backcountry on the Eve of Revolution* (Chapel Hill, 1953), 8.

12. Quoted in Henry F. May, *The Enlightenment in America* (New York, 1976), 67.

13. May, 3–101 and passim.

14. May, 66.

15. Jon Butler, *Awash in a Sea of Faith* (Cambridge, Mass., 1990), 219.

16. Butler, 170.

17. Morgan Dix, *A History of the Parish of Trinity Church in the City of New York*, 4 vols. (New York, 1898–1906), 1:139.

18. S. Charles Bolton, *Southern Anglicanism: The Church of England in South Carolina* (Westport, Conn., 1982), 122.

19. *The Journal and Letters of Philip Vickers Fithian*, ed. Hunter D. Farish (Williamsburg, Va., 1965), 61.

20. Woolverton gives a thorough and informative survey of the colonial clergy. The book is the most complete study to date of Anglicanism in the American colonies.

21. Vestry of Caratuck Parish to the secretary of the SPG, 25 August 1710, SPG Letters, Series A, 5, no. 174, quoted in Woolverton, *Colonial Anglicanism*, 23–24. The clergyman was James Adams.

22. Quoted in Woolverton, 89.

23. May, 77.

24. The print is reproduced in many scholarly works on colonial New England. It provides the frontispiece for Carl Bridenbaugh's *Mitre and Sceptre* (New York, 1962).

25. Paul F. Boller, Jr., *George Washington and Religion* (Dallas, 1963), 24–44 and passim.

26. William White, *The Case of the Episcopal Churches in the United States*, ed. Richard G. Salomon (Philadelphia, 1954), 29.

27. "Epistle to the Right Reverend Father in God Dr. Samuel Seabury Bishop of Connecticut 1785," quoted in Bruce E. Steiner, *Samuel Seabury, 1729–1796* (Athens, 1971), 253–254.

28. James A. Dator, "The Government of the Protestant Episcopal Church in the United States of America: Confederal, Federal, or Unitary?" (Ph.D. dissertation, American University, 1959), 245.

29. Although the Episcopal Church is gradually returning to the early Christian practice of using the term "ordination" for all orders of the ministry, this book — like the documents it cites — uses "consecration" for ordinations of bishops.

30. See Nathan O. Hatch's important *The Democratization of American Christianity* (New Haven, 1989).

31. See Frederick V. Mills, Sr., *Bishops by Ballot* (New York, 1978), 304–307 and passim, and Woolverton, 234–235.

32. Woolverton, 238.

33. George Washington Doane, *Bishop Doane's Words at the Burial of Mrs. Bradford* (Burlington, N.J., 1854), 7.

34. Julia C. Emery, *A Century of Endeavor* (New York, 1921), 143.

35. *Journal of the Diocese of Kansas, 1865* (Topeka, 1865), Appendix C, 31.

36. George Kennan, "The Social and Political Condition of Russia," *The Outlook* 76 (Jan. 30, 1904), 262. Cf. Robert P. and Wynona H. Wilkins, *God Giveth the Increase: The History of the Episcopal Church in North Dakota* (Fargo, 1959), 108 n. 33.

37. C. B. Goodykoontz, *Home Missions on the American Frontier* (Caldwell, Idaho, 1939), 357.

38. Paul Lawson, "Losing the West Twice," *The Evangelical Outlook* 28 (Spring 1991), 4.

39. Phillips Brooks to Heman Dyer, 19 November 1887, in Alexander V. G. Allen, *Life and Letters of Phillips Brooks,* 3 vols. (New York, 1901), 3:252.

40. A good survey of nineteenth-century church statistics can be found in Roger Finke and Rodney Stark, "Turning Pews into People: Estimating Church Membership in Nineteenth-Century America," *Journal for the Scientific Study of Religion* 25 (1985), 180–192.

41. William H. Wilmer, *The Episcopal Manual* (Philadelphia, 1815), 49.

42. Wilmer, 21.

43. William B. Sprague, *Annals of the American Pulpit,* 9 vols. (New York, 1969), 5:516.

44. Randall Balmer, *Mine Eyes Have Seen the Glory* (New York, 1989), 171–187, gives a critical view of the work of the Episcopal Church among the Indians of the Dakotas.

45. Julia C. Emery, *A Century of Endeavor, 1821–1921* (New York, 1921), 128.

46. James Arthur Muller, *Apostle of China* (New York, 1937), 164.

47. Mary Sudman Donovan, *A Different Call: Women's Ministries in the Episcopal Church 1850–1920* (Wilton, Conn., 1986), 137–139.

48. Henry C. Potter, *Sisterhoods and Deaconesses* (New York, 1873), 87.

49. Potter, 8.

50. Thomas Jenkins, *The Man of Alaska* (New York, 1943), 244.

51. Francis Le Jau to the SPG, October 20, 1709, in Frank J. Klingberg, ed., *The Carolina Chronicle of Dr. Francis Le Jau, 1706–1717* (Berkeley, 1956), 60. The oath is also quoted in Butler's revisionist and instructive *Awash in a Sea of Faith,* 140–141.

52. Moses I. Finley, *Ancient Slavery and Modern Ideology* (New York, 1980).

53. Butler, 162.

54. *Journal of the . . . General Convention . . . 1877* (Boston, 1878), 491.

55. *Journal of the General Convention of the Protestant Episcopal Church . . . 1910* (New York, 1911), 55.

56. Normally, Episcopal dioceses elected bishop coadjutors when the bishop of a diocese neared retirement or became physically unable (as the 1910 canon declared) "fully to discharge the duties of his office." Often working with the bishop a year or more while learning the diocese, a bishop coadjutor automatically succeeded to the office when the bishop died or retired.

57. William Montgomery Brown, *The Church for Americans,* 5th ed. (New York, 1896), 305.

58. Such churches can give a false impression about what colonial worship was like. The interior of Bruton Parish Church in the colonial area of Williamsburg, Virginia, for example, represents a combination of eighteenth-century and early twentieth-century furnishings and approaches to liturgy and worship.

59. James F. White, *Protestant Worship: Traditions in Transition* (Louisville, 1989), 99.

60. George Franklin Smythe, *A History of the Diocese of Ohio until the Year 1918* (Cleveland, 1931), 261.

61. White, *Protestant Worship,* 108.

62. F. C. Ewer, *Catholicity in its Relationship to Protestantism and Romanism* (New York, 1878), 288.

63. White, *Protestant Worship,* 108.

64. Arthur Pierce Middleton, *New Wine in Old Skins* (Wilton, Conn., 1988), 17.

65. George C. Giles, Jr., *History of the Church of the Ascension, Chicago, Illinois* (Aberdeen, S.Dak., 1984), 11.

66. Henry B. Whipple, *Lights and Shadows of a Long Episcopate* (New York, 1902), 354–355.

67. John Henry Hopkins, *The Law of Ritualism* (New York, 1867), 94.

68. George E. DeMille, *The Catholic Movement in the American Episcopal Church,* rev. ed. (Philadelphia, 1950), 130.

69. William F. Brand, *Life of William Rollinson Whittingham,* 2 vols. (New York, 1883), 2:333.

70. Doody, 109–122.

71. William Lawrence, *Fifty Years* (Boston, 1923), 10–12.

72. Lawrence, 35.

73. Quoted in G. L. Prestige, *The Life of Charles Gore* (Toronto, 1935), 499.

74. Wilkins, 122. The bishop was John Poyntz Tyler of North Dakota,

who had previously been rector of the Church of the Advent in Philadelphia and archdeacon in two dioceses.

75. Lawrence, 14.

76. William Sanday, *The Life of Christ in Recent Research* (New York, 1907), 281.

77. Donald S. Armentrout, *The Quest for the Informed Priest* (Sewanee, Tenn., 1979), 181.

78. William Porcher DuBose, *The Gospel according to St. Paul* (New York, 1907), 9

79. *The Churchman*, 118 (31 Aug. 1918), 234.

80. William A. Muhlenberg, *An Exposition of the Memorial* (New York, 1854), 42.

81. William Parct, *Reminiscences* (Philadelphia, 1911), 107.

82. *The Christian Union*, 28 November 1891, quoted in Henry F. May, *Protestant Churches and Industrial America* (New York, 1967), 185.

83. See Jacob H. Dorn, "Episcopal Priest and Socialist Activist: Irwin St. John Tucker," *Anglican and Episcopal History* 61 (June 1992), 167–196.

84. Dorothy Day, *The Long Loneliness* (San Francisco, 1981), 149.

85. Richard T. Ely, *Ground Under Our Feet* (New York, 1938), 74.

86. *Discourses on the Occasion of the Decease of Adaline Haskins* (New York, 1848), 16–17.

87. Donovan, 40.

88. Charles C. Grafton, *A Journey Godward* (New York, 1914), 106.

89. Rachel Hosmer, *My Life Remembered* (Cambridge, Mass, 1991), 19–20.

90. *Journal of the General Convention of the Protestant Episcopal Church . . . 1889* (New York, 1890), 45.

91. *Journal of the General Convention of the Protestant Episcopal Church . . . 1922* (New York, 1923), 675.

92. *Journal of the General Convention of the Protestant Episcopal Church . . . 1940* (New York, 1941), 422.

93. Serving only temporary episcopal assignments in the following decades, Jones succeeded Socialist leader Norman Thomas as national secretary of the Fellowship of Reconciliation and served as a college chaplain. He was chairman of the Episcopal Committee on European Refugees when he died in 1941.

94. Quoted in Sydney E. Ahlstrom, *A Religious History of the American People* (New Haven, 1972), 884.

95. Letter of W. Hamilton Aulenbach to *The Churchman's Human Quest*, 200 (October 1986), 3.

96. *Journal of the Annual Convention of the Missionary District of Asheville . . . 1921* (n.p., n.d.), 26. Cf. London and Lemmon, 492.

97. Joseph Fort Newton, *River of Years: An Autobiography* (Philadelphia, 1946), 234–235, with language modernized.

98. J. H. McIlvaine, *Social Salvation* (Washington, D.C., 1915), 25.

99. *The Living Church Annual 1937* (New York, 1936), 8–9.

100. Wilkins, 158. The poem has been variously attributed. I have placed the titles in quotation marks.

101. *Journal of the General Convention of the Protestant Episcopal Church . . . 1928* (New York, 1929), 148–149.

102. George B. Ford, *A Degree of Difference* (New York, 1969), 164.

103. *Journal of the General Convention of the Protestant Episcopal Church . . . 1937* (New York, 1938), 577.

104. Henry Knox Sherrill, *Among Friends* (Boston, 1962), 217.

105. *Journal of the General Convention of the Protestant Episcopal Church . . . 1949* (New York, 1950), 102, 121.

106. William Porcher DuBose, *Unity in the Faith,* ed. W. Norman Pittenger (Greenwich, Conn., 1957), 21.

107. John Macquarrie, *Principles of Christian Theology,* 2d ed. (New York, 1977), 125.

108. A. N. Wilson, *C. S. Lewis: A Biography* (New York, 1990), 173.

109. *Journal of the General Convention . . . 1967,* Appendix 28:4.

110. Ibid., 2.

111. *The Christian Challenge* 23 (October 1984), 12.

112. Hosmer, 125.

113. *Journal of the General Convention . . . 1979* (New York, 1980), C–86–89. The resolution carried in the House of Bishops by a vote of 99 to 34. It carried in the House of Deputies by votes of 70 dioceses to 29 among clerical deputies and 77 dioceses to 18 among lay deputies. Eleven dioceses were divided (and so could not cast a vote) among the clergy, and thirteen dioceses were divided among the lay deputies.

114. White, *Protestant Worship,* 114; cf. 95.

115. Dean Kelley, *Why Conservative Churches are Growing* (New York, 1972).

116. Emmet Gribbin, Jr., "What is Alabama Doing Right?" *The Living Church* 201 (21 October 1990), 9–10.

117. Robert Hale, O.S.B., in *The Living Church* 192 (15 June 1986), 3.

118. In private a conservative Unitarian, Jefferson never officially left the Anglicanism of his boyhood and often attended Episcopal services.

119. Charles Dickens, *A Child's History of England* (New York, 1851), 193, 210.

120. William E. Addis and Thomas Arnold, *A Catholic Dictionary,* rev. with additions by T. B. Scannell, 11th ed. (London, 1928), 276.

121. C. Sydney Carter, *The English Church and the Reformation* (London, 1925), 42.

122. Carter, 42.

123. *Calendar of State Papers and Manuscripts Relating to English Affairs Existing in the Archives and Collections of Venice,* ed. Rawdon L. Brown, 7 vols. (London, 1871), 2:479.

124. *Letters and Papers, Foreign and Domestic, of the Reign of Henry VIII,* ed. J. S. Brewer, 4 vols. (London, 1862–1875), 4:3147.

125. In *Henry VIII* (Berkeley, 1968), 183–197, J. J. Scarisbrick confidently supports the argument. E. R. Elton's *Studies in Tudor and Stuart Politics and Government,* 4 vols. (Cambridge, 1974–1990), 2:104, supports it, Jasper Ridley, *Henry VIII* (London, 1984), 162–164, trenchantly dismisses it. A thorough discussion can be found in Henry Ansgar Kelly, *The Matrimonial Trials of Henry VIII* (Stanford, 1976), 31ff. and passim, which uses previously unknown or unused documents and focuses on the intricate procedures of canon law.

126. W. A. Leonard, *A Brief History of the Christian Church* (New York, 1891), 171, 181.

SELECTED
BIBLIOGRAPHY

Abell, Aaron I. *The Urban Impact on American Protestantism, 1865–1900.* Cambridge, Mass.: Harvard University Press, 1943.

Addis, William E., and Thomas Arnold. *A Catholic Dictionary.* Revised with additions by T. B. Scannell. 11th ed. London: Paul, Trench, Trubner, 1928.

Addison, James T. *The Episcopal Church in the United States, 1789–1931.* New York: Scribner, 1951.

Addleshaw, G. W. O., and Frederick Etchells. *The Architectural Setting of Anglican Worship.* London: Faber and Faber, 1948.

Adler, Mortimer. *A Second Look in the Rear View Mirror.* New York: Macmillan, 1992.

————. *Truth in Religion.* New York: Macmillan, 1990.

Ahlstrom, Sydney. *A Religious History of the American People.* New Haven: Yale University Press, 1972.

————, ed. *Theology in America.* Indianapolis: Bobbs-Merrill, 1967.

Albright, Raymond W. *A History of the Protestant Episcopal Church.* New York: Macmillan, 1964.

Allen, Alexander V. G. *The Life and Letters of Phillips Brooks.* 3 vols. New York: Dutton, 1900–1901.

Anglican and Episcopal History (1987–).

Anglican Theological Review (1918–).

Armentrout, Donald S. *The Quest for the Informed Priest.* Sewanee: School of Theology, University of the South, 1979.

Avis, Paul. *Anglicanism and the Christian Church.* Minneapolis: Fortress, 1989.

Ayres, Anne. *The Life and Work of William Augustus Muhlenberg.* 5th ed. New York: Whittaker, 1894.

Balmer, Randall. *Mine Eyes Have Seen the Glory.* New York: Oxford University Press, 1989.

Bellah, Robert N., et al. *Habits of the Heart.* Berkeley: University of California Press, 1985.

—— and Phillip E. Hammond. *Varieties of Civil Religion.* San Francisco: Harper, 1980.

—— and William G. McLoughlin, *Religion in America.* Boston: Houghton, Mifflin, 1968.

Bloom, Harold. *The American Religion.* New York: Simon & Schuster, 1992.

Bindoff, S. T. *Tudor England.* New York: Penguin, 1950.

Boller, Paul F., Jr. *George Washington and Religion.* Dallas: Southern Methodist University Press, 1963.

Bolton, S. Charles. *Southern Anglicanism: The Church of England in Colonial South Carolina.* Westport, Conn.: Greenwood, 1982.

Book of Common Prayer (1789, 1892, 1928, 1979).

Booty, John. *The Church in History.* New York: Seabury, 1979.

——. *John Jewel as Apologist of the Church of England.* London: S.P.C.K., 1963.

——, and Stephen Sykes, eds. *The Study of Anglicanism.* Philadelphia: S.P.C.K./Fortress, 1988.

Bowle, John. *Henry VIII.* Boston: Little, Brown, 1964.

Bozeman, Theodore Dwight. *Protestants in an Age of Science.* Chapel Hill: University of North Carolina Press, 1977.

Bragg, George F. *History of the Afro-American Group of the Episcopal Church.* Baltimore: Church Advocate Press, 1922.

Brand, William F. *Life of William Rollinson Whittingham.* 2 vols. New York: Young, 1883.

Breck, Allen D. *The Episcopal Church in Colorado, 1860–1903.* Denver: Big Mountain, 1963.

Brewer, J. S. *Letters and Papers, Foreign and Domestic, of the Reign of Henry VIII.* London: Longmans, Green, 1862–1875.

Bridenbaugh, Carl. *Mitre and Sceptre.* New York: Oxford University Press, 1962.

Brown, Lawrence L. *The Episcopal Church in Texas.* Vol. II. Austin: Eakin, 1985.

Brown, William Montgomery. *The Church for Americans.* 5th ed. New York: Whittaker, 1896.

Burr, Nelson R. *The Anglican Church in New Jersey.* Philadelphia: Church Historical Society, 1954.

——. *The Story of the Diocese of Connecticut.* Hartford: Church Missions Publishing Company, 1962.

Butler, Jon. *Awash in a Sea of Faith: Christianizing the American People.* Cambridge, Mass.: Harvard University Press, 1990.

Calendar of State Papers and Manuscripts Relating to English Affairs Existing in the Archives and Collections of Venice. Edited by Rawdon L. Brown. Vol. 2. London: Longmans, Green, 1871.

Carter, Paul A. *The Decline and Revival of the Social Gospel.* Hamden: Archon, 1971.

———. *The Spiritual Crisis of the Gilded Age.* DeKalb: Northern Illinois University Press, 1971.

Carter, C. Sydney. *The English Church and the Reformation.* London: Longmans, Green, 1925.

Chadwick, Owen. *The Reformation.* Harmondsworth: Penguin, 1977.

Cheshire, Joseph Blount. *The Church in the Confederate States.* London: Longmans, Green, 1914.

Chorley, Edward C. *Men and Movements in the American Episcopal Church.* New York: Scribner, 1946.

Cox, Harvey G. *The Secular City.* New York: Macmillan, 1965.

Cross, Arthur L. *The Anglican Episcopate and the American Colonies.* Hamden, Conn.: Archon, 1964.

Cushman, Joseph D., Jr. *The Sound of Bells: The Episcopal Church in South Florida.* Gainesville: University Presses of Florida, 1976.

Dalcho, Frederick. *An Historical Account of the Protestant Episcopal Church in South-Carolina.* Charleston: Thayer, 1820.

Dator, James A. "The Government of the Protestant Episcopal Church in the United States of America: Confederal, Federal, or Unitary?" Ph.D. dissertation, American University, 1959.

Davies, Horton. *Worship and Theology in England.* 5 vols. Princeton: Princeton University Press, 1961–1975.

Davis, John H. *St. Mary's Cathedral.* Memphis: St. Mary's Cathedral, 1958.

Davis, John W. *Dominion in the Sea: History of the Diocese of Long Island.* Hempstead, N.Y.: Georgin Foundation, 1977.

Day, Dorothy. *The Long Loneliness.* San Francisco: Harper & Row, 1981.

DeMille, George E. *The Catholic Movement in the American Episcopal Church.* Rev. ed. Philadelphia: Church Historical Society, 1950.

———. *The Episcopal Church Since 1900.* New York: Morehouse-Gorham, 1955.

Dickens, Charles. *A Child's History of England.* New York: Bradbury & Evans, 1852.

Dickens, A. G. *The Age of Humanism and Reformation.* Englewood Cliffs: Prentice-Hall, 1972.

———. *The English Reformation.* London: Schocken, 1964.

Dix, Morgan. *A History of the Parish of Trinity Church in the City of New York.* 4 vols. New York: Putnam, 1898–1906.

Doane, George Washington. *Bishop Doane's Words at the Burial of Mrs. Bradford.* Burlington, N.J.: Privately printed, 1854.

Donovan, Mary Sudman. *A Different Call: Women's Ministries in the Episcopal Church, 1850–1920.* Wilton, Conn.: Morehouse-Barlow, 1986.

————. *Women Priests in the Episcopal Church*. Cincinnati: Forward Movement, 1988.

DuBose, William Porcher. *The Soteriology of the New Testament*. New York: Macmillan, 1892.

————. *The Gospel According to St. Paul*. New York: Longmans, Green, 1907.

————. *The Gospel in the Gospels*. New York: Longmans, Green, 1906.

————. *Turning Points in My Life*. New York: Longmans, Green, 1911.

————. *Unity in the Faith*. Edited by Norman Pittenger. Greenwich, Conn.: Seabury, 1957.

Duffy, Mark J. *The Episcopal Diocese of Massachusetts, 1784–1984*. Boston: Episcopal Diocese of Massachusetts, 1984.

Elton, G. R. *England Under the Tudors*. London: Methuen, 1974.

————. *Reform and Reformation*. Cambridge: Harvard University Press, 1977.

————. *Reformation Europe, 1517–1559*. New York: Harper & Row, 1963.

————. *Studies in Tudor and Stuart Politics*. 4 vols. Cambridge: Cambridge University Press, 1974–1990.

Ely, Richard T. *Ground Under Our Feet*. New York: Macmillan, 1938.

Emery, Julia C. *A Century of Endeavor, 1821–1921*. New York: Department of Missions, 1921.

Episcopal Church Annual (formerly *The Living Church Annual*). New York, 1892–.

Ewer, F. C. *Catholicity in its Relationship to Protestantism and Romanism*. New York: Putnam, 1878.

Fairfield, Leslie P. *John Bale, Mythmaker for the English Reformation*. West Lafayette: Purdue University Press, 1976.

Finke, Roger, and Rodney Stark, "Turning Pews into People: Estimating Church Membership in Nineteenth-Century America." *Journal for the Scientific Study of Religion* 25 (1985): 180–192.

————. *The Churching of America, 1776–1990*. New Brunswick: Rutgers University Press, 1992.

Finley, Moses I. *Ancient Slavery and Modern Ideology*. London: Chatto & Windus, 1980.

Fithian, Philip Vickers. *Journal and Letters*. Edited by Hunter D. Farish. Williamsburg, Va.: Colonial Williamsburg, 1965.

Ford, George B. *A Degree of Difference*. New York: Farrar, Straus & Giroux, 1969.

Foster, Roland. *The Role of the Presiding Bishop*. Cincinnati: Forward Movement, 1982.

Franklin, R. William. *Nineteenth Century Churches*. New York: Garland, 1987.

Gallup, George, Jr. *People's Religion: American Faith in the Nineties*. New York: Macmillan, 1989.

Gaustad, Edwin Scott. *A Documentary History of Religion in America*. 2 vols. Grand Rapids: Eerdmans, 1982–1983.

————. *Historical Atlas of Religion in America.* Rev. ed. New York: Harper & Row, 1976.

Gay, Peter. *The Enlightenment: An Interpretation.* New York: Knopf, 1966.

Genovese, Eugene D. *Roll, Jordan, Roll.* New York, Pantheon, 1974.

Giles, George C., Jr. *History of the Church of the Ascension, Chicago, Illinois.* Aberdeen, S. Dak.: North Plains, 1984.

Goodykoontz, C. B. *Home Missions on the American Frontier.* Caldwell, Idaho: Caxton, 1939.

Grafton, Charles C. *A Journey Godward.* New York; Longmans, Green, 1910

Gundersen, Joan R. "The Anglican Ministry in Virginia, 1723–1776." Ph.D. dissertation, University of Notre Dame, 1972.

Hadden, Jeffrey K. *The Gathering Storm in the Churches.* Garden City: Doubleday, 1969.

Hall, Francis J. *Dogmatic Theology.* 10 vols. New York: Longmans, Green, 1907–1922.

Handy, Robert T. *A Christian America.* 2d ed. New York: Oxford University Press, 1984.

————. *A History of the Churches in the United States and Canada.* New York: Oxford University Press, 1977.

————. *The Social Gospel in America, 1870–1920.* New York: Oxford University Press, 1966.

Hatch, Nathan O. *The Democratization of American Christianity.* New Haven: Yale University Press, 1989.

Hatchett, Marion J. *Commentary on the American Prayer Book.* New York: Seabury, 1981.

————. *The Making of the First American Book of Common Prayer.* New York: Seabury, 1982.

Haugaard, William P. *Elizabeth and the English Reformation.* London: Cambridge University Press, 1968.

Hawks, Francis L., ed. *Contributions to the Ecclesiastical History of the United States of America.* 2 vols. New York: Harper, 1836.

Heimert, Alan. *Religion and the American Mind.* Cambridge, Mass.: Harvard University Press, 1966.

Hein, David. "The High-Church Origins of the American Boarding School," *Journal of Ecclesiastical History* 42 (1991), 577–595.

Henery, Charles R., ed. *Beyond the Horizon.* Cincinnati: Forward Movement, 1986.

Henry, Stuart C. *George Whitefield: Wayfaring Witness.* New York: Abingdon, 1957.

Herberg, Will. *Protestant, Catholic, Jew.* Garden City: Doubleday, 1955.

Hill, Samuel S., ed. *Encyclopedia of Religion in the South.* Macon: Mercer University Press, 1984.

Hinchliff, Peter B. *God and History: Aspects of British Theology, 1875–1914.* Oxford: Oxford University Press, 1992.

Historical Magazine of the Protestant Episcopal Church (1932–1986).

Hodges, George. *Henry Codman Potter.* New York: Macmillan, 1915.

———, and Powell M. Dawley. *A Short History of the Episcopal Church.* Cincinnati: Forward Movement, 1967.

Holifield, E. Brooks. *The Gentlemen Theologians.* Durham: Duke University Press, 1978.

Hopkins, John Henry. *The Law of Ritualism.* New York: Hurd and Houghton, 1867.

———. *A Scriptural, Ecclesiastical, and Historical View of Slavery.* New York: Pooley, 1864.

Hopkins, John Henry, Jr. *The Life of the Late Right Reverend John Henry Hopkins.* New York: Huntington, 1873.

Hosmer, Rachel. *My Life Remembered.* Cambridge, Mass.: Cowley, 1991.

Howe, M. A. DeWolfe. *The Life and Labors of Bishop Hare.* New York: Sturgis & Walton, 1911.

Hudson, Winthrop A. *Religion in America.* 4th ed. New York: Macmillan, 1987.

Hunter, James Davison. *American Evangelicalism.* New Brunswick: Rutgers University Press, 1983.

Huntington, Virginia E. *Along the Great River: The Story of the Episcopal Church in China.* New York: National Council of the Protestant Episcopal Church, 1940.

Hutchison, William R. *The Modernist Impulse in American Protestantism.* Cambridge, Mass.: Harvard University Press, 1976.

Isaac, Rhys. *The Transformation of Virginia.* Chapel Hill: Institute of Early American History and Culture, 1982.

Jarratt, Devereux. *The Life of the Reverend Devereux Jarratt.* Baltimore: Warner & Hanna, 1806.

Kelley, Dean. *Why Conservative Churches are Growing.* New York: Harper & Row, 1972.

Kelly, Henry Ansgar. *The Matrimonial Trials of Henry VIII.* Stanford: Stanford University Press, 1976.

Klingberg, Frank J., ed. *The Carolina Chronicle of Dr. Francis LeJau, 1706–1717.* Berkeley: University of California Press, 1956.

Koenigsberger, H. G., and G. L. Mosse. *Europe in the Sixteenth Century.* Holt, Rinehart & Winston, 1968.

Koenker, Ernest B. *The Liturgical Renaissance in the Roman Catholic Church.* Chicago: University of Chicago Press, 1954.

Jenkins, Thomas. *The Man of Alaska.* New York: Morehouse-Gorham, 1943.

Johns, John. *A Memoir of the Life of the Right Rev. William Meade, D.D.* Baltimore: Innes, 1867.

Journals of the General Conventions of the Protestant Episcopal Church (published triennially) (1785–1991).

Journals of the Protestant Episcopal Church in the Confederate States of America. Edited by William A. Clebsch. Austin: Church Historical Society, 1962.

Lawrence, William. *Fifty Years.* Boston: Houghton Mifflin, 1923.

————. *Memories of a Happy Life.* Boston: Houghton Mifflin, 1926.

Leonard, W. A. *A Brief History of the Christian Church.* 2d ed. New York: Dutton, 1891.

Lippy, Charles H., ed. *Twentieth Century Shapers of American Popular Religion.* New York: Greenwood, 1989.

————, and Peter W. Williams, eds. *Encyclopedia of the American Religious Experience.* 3 vols. New York: Scribner, 1988.

London, Lawrence F., and Sarah M. Lemmon. *The Episcopal Church in North Carolina, 1701–1959.* Raleigh: Episcopal Diocese of North Carolina, 1987.

Loveland, Clara O. *The Critical Years.* Greenwich, Conn.: Seabury, 1956.

Lytle, Guy F., ed. *Reform and Authority in the Medieval and Reformation Church.* Washington, D.C.: Catholic University of America Press, 1981.

Macquarrie, John. *Principles of Christian Theology,* 2d ed. New York: Scribner, 1977.

————. *Twentieth-Century Religious Thought.* New York: Harper & Row, 1963.

McIlvaine, J. H. *Social Salvation.* Washington, D.C.: Privately printed, 1915.

McLoughlin, W. G. *Modern Revivalism.* New York: Ronald Press, 1959.

————. *New England Dissent.* 2 vols. Cambridge, Mass.: Harvard University Press, 1971.

Malone, Henry T. *The Episcopal Church in Georgia.* Atlanta: Episcopal Diocese of Atlanta, 1960.

Manross, William W. *A History of the American Episcopal Church.* Rev. ed. New York: Morehouse-Gorham, 1950.

————. *The Episcopal Church in the United States, 1800–1840.* New York: Columbia University Press, 1938.

Marsden, George M. *Fundamentalism and American Culture.* New York: Oxford University Press, 1980.

————. *The Secularization of the Academy.* New York: Oxford University Press, 1992.

Marty, Martin. *Pilgrims in Their Own Land.* Boston: Little, Brown, 1984.

————. *Protestantism in the United States: Righteous Empire.* 2d ed. New York: Scribner, 1970.

Mathews, Donald G. *Religion in the Old South.* Chicago: University of Chicago Press, 1977.

213

May, Henry F. *The Enlightenment in America*. New York: Oxford University Press, 1976.

————. *Protestant Churches and Industrial America*. New York: Harper, 1949.

Mead, Sidney E. *The Nation with the Soul of a Church*. Macon: Mercer University Press, 1985.

Meade, William. *Old Churches, Ministers and Families of Virginia*. Baltimore: Genealogical Publishing Company, 1966.

Melish, John Howard. *Franklin Spencer Spalding*. New York: Macmillan, 1917.

Michaels, Leonard and Christopher Ricks, eds. *The State of the Language*. Berkeley: University of California Press, 1980.

Middleton, Arthur Pierce. *New Wine in Old Skins*. Wilton, Conn.: Morehouse-Barlow, 1988.

Miller, Perry. *Errand into the Wilderness*. Cambridge: Harvard University Press, 1956.

Mills, Frederick V., Sr. *Bishops by Ballot*. New York: Oxford University Press, 1978.

Mitchell, Leonel L. *The Meaning of Ritual*. New York: Paulist, 1977.

Moore, Paul. *Take A Bishop Like Me*. New York: Harper & Row, 1979.

Muhlenberg, William Augustus. *Evangelical Catholic Papers*. Edited by Anne Ayres. 2 vols. New York: Whittaker, 1875, 1877.

Muller, James Arthur. *Apostle of China*. New York: Morehouse, 1937.

————. *The Episcopal Theological School, 1867–1943*. Cambridge, Mass.: Episcopal Theological School, 1943.

Mullin, Robert Bruce. *Episcopal Vision/American Reality*. New Haven: Yale University Press, 1986.

————, ed. *Moneygripe's Apprentice*. New Haven: Yale University Press, 1987.

Neill, Stephen. *Anglicanism*. 4th ed. New York: Oxford University Press, 1978.

Newton, Joseph Fort. *River of Years: An Autobiography*. Philadelphia: Lippincott, 1946.

Niebuhr, H. R. *Christ and Culture*. New York: Harper, 1951

————. *The Kingdom of God in America*. New York: Harper, 1937.

————. *The Social Sources of Denominationalism*. New York: Holt, 1929.

Niebuhr, Reinhold. *The Irony of American History*. New York: Scribner, 1952.

————. *Leaves from the Notebook of a Tamed Cynic*. Chicago: Willett, Clark & Colby, 1929.

Noll, Mark A. *A History of Christianity in the United States and Canada*. Grand Rapids: Eerdmans, 1992.

————. *Religion and American Politics*. New York: Oxford University Press, 1990.

Paret, William. *Reminiscences*. Philadelphia: Jacobs, 1911.

Parker, T. M. *The English Reformation to 1558*. New York: Oxford University Press, 1950.

Perry, William S. *Historical Collections Relating to the American Colonial Church.* 5 vols. Hartford: Printed for the Subscribers, 1870–1878.

————. *The History of the American Episcopal Church, 1587–1883.* Boston: James R. Osgood, 1885.

Pike, James A. *Modern Canterbury Pilgrims.* New York: Morehouse-Gorham, 1956.

————, and W. Norman Pittenger. *The Faith of the Church.* Greenwich, Conn.: Seabury, 1952.

Pollard, A. F. *Henry VIII.* New York: Longmans, Green, 1905.

Potter, Alonzo. *Memorial Papers.* Philadelphia: E. H. Butler, 1857.

Potter, Henry C. *Sisterhoods and Deaconesses.* New York: Dutton, 1873.

Powicke, F. M. *The Reformation in England.* London: Oxford University Press, 1961.

Prichard, Robert. *A History of the Episcopal Church.* Harrisburg, Pa.: Morehouse, 1991.

————. *Readings from the History of the Episcopal Church.* Wilton, Conn.: Morehouse-Barlow, 1986.

Prelinger, Catherine M. *Episcopal Women.* New York: Oxford University Press, 1992.

Prestige, G. L. *The Life of Charles Gore.* Toronto: Heinemann, 1935.

Procter, Francis, and Walter Howard Frere. *A New History of the Book of Common Prayer with a Rationale of Its Offices.* London: Macmillan, 1961.

Raboteau, Albert J. *Slave Religion.* New York: Oxford University Press, 1978.

Rainsford, William S. *A Preacher's Story of His Work.* New York: Outlook, 1904.

————. *The Story of a Varied Life: An Autobiography.* Garden City: Doubleday, Page, 1922.

Rasmussen, Jane. *Musical Taste as a Religious Question in Nineteenth-Century America.* Lewiston, N.Y.: Mellen, 1986.

Rightmyer, Nelson W. *The Anglican Church in Delaware.* Philadelphia: Church Historical Society, 1947.

————. *Maryland's Established Church.* Baltimore: Church Historical Society for the Diocese of Maryland, 1956.

Richey, E. Russell, and Donald G. Jones, eds. *The American Civil Religion.* New York: Harper & Row, 1974.

Ridley, Jasper. *Henry VIII.* London: Constable, 1984.

Roof, Wade Clark, and William McKinney. *American Mainline Religion: Its Changing Shape and Future.* New Brunswick: Rutgers University Press, 1987.

————. *A Generation of Seekers.* San Francisco: Harper, 1993.

Ruether, Rosemary Radford, ed. *Women and Religion in America.* San Francisco: Harper & Row, 1981.

Sandeen, E. R. *The Roots of Fundamentalism*. Chicago: University of Chicago Press, 1970.

Scarisbrick, J. J. *Henry VIII*. Berkeley: University of California Press, 1968.

Schreiner, Charles F. *A History of the Bishops of the Diocese of Olympia*. Seattle: Episcopal Diocese of Olympia, 1986.

Scott, Nathan A., Jr., ed. *The Legacy of Reinhold Niebuhr*. Chicago: University of Chicago Press, 1975.

Scudder, Vida D. *Father Huntington*. New York: Dutton, 1940.

Sherrill, Henry Knox. *Among Friends*. Boston: Little, Brown, 1962.

Shoemaker, Robert W. *The Origin and Meaning of the Name "Protestant Episcopal."* New York: American Church Publications, 1959.

Skardon, Alvin W. *Church Leader in the Cities: William Augustus Muhlenberg*. Philadelphia: University of Pennsylvania Press, 1971.

Smith, Helen Smith. *I Stand by the Door: The Life of Sam Shoemaker*. New York: Harper & Row, 1967.

Smith, H. Maynard. *Henry VIII and the Reformation*. London: Macmillan, 1948.

Smith, Lacey Baldwin. *Henry VIII: The Mask of Royalty*. Boston: Houghton Mifflin, 1971.

————. *This Realm of England, 1399 to 1688*. Lexington, Mass.: Heath, 1976.

Smith, H. Shelton, Robert T. Handy, and Lefferts A. Loetscher. *American Christianity*. 2 vols. New York: Scribner, 1960–1963.

Smith, Timothy L. *Revivalism and Social Reform*. Baltimore: Johns Hopkins University Press, 1980.

Smythe, George Franklin. *A History of the Diocese of Ohio until the Year 1918*. Cleveland: Episcopal Diocese of Ohio, 1931.

Sneve, Virginia Driving Hawk. *That They May Have Life: The Episcopal Church in South Dakota*. New York: Seabury, 1977.

Somervell, D. C. *A Short History of Our Religion*. New York: Macmillan, 1922.

Spaulding, Dorothy W. *Saint Paul's Parish, Washington*. Washington, D.C.: Saint Paul's Parish, 1967.

Sprague, William B. *Annals of the American Pulpit*. Vol. 5. New York: Arno, 1969.

Steiner, Bruce. *Samuel Seabury*. Athens: Ohio University Press, 1971.

Stout, Harry S. *The Divine Dramatist: George Whitefield and the Rise of Modern Evangelicalism*. Grand Rapids: Eerdmans, 1991.

Stuhlman, Byron D. *Prayer Book Rubrics Expanded*. New York: Church Hymnal Corporation, 1987.

Sumner, David E. *The Episcopal Church's History, 1945–1985*. Wilton, Conn.: Morehouse-Barlow, 1987.

Swinford, Frances Keller, and Rebecca Smith Lee. *The Great Elm Tree: Heritage of the Episcopal Diocese of Lexington*. Lexington, Ky.: Faith House, 1969.

Sykes, Stephen. *The Integrity of Anglicanism.* New York: Seabury, 1978.

Talbot, Ethelbert. *My People of the Plains.* New York: Harper, 1906.

Taylor, Blanche Mercer. *Plenteous Harvest: The Episcopal Church in Kansas.* Topeka: Episcopal Diocese of Kansas, 1973.

Thompsett, Fredrica H. *Christian Feminist Perspectives on History, Theology and the Bible.* Cincinnati: Forward Movement, 1986.

Turner, James. *Without God, Without Creed.* Baltimore: Johns Hopkins University Press, 1985.

Tuttle, Daniel S., *Reminiscences of a Missionary Bishop.* New York: Whittaker, 1906.

Twelves, J. Wesley. *A History of the Diocese of Pennsylvania.* Philadelphia: Episcopal Diocese of Pennsylvania, 1969.

Upton, Dell. *Holy Things and Profane.* Cambridge, Mass.: Harvard University Press, 1986.

Whipple, Henry B. *Lights and Shadows of a Long Episcopate.* New York: Macmillan, 1902.

White, Greenough. *An Apostle of the Western Church.* New York: Whittaker, 1899.

White, Edwin A., and Jackson A. Dyckman. *Annotated Constitution and Canons.* Greenwich, Conn.: Seabury, 1954.

White, James F. *A Brief History of Christian Worship.* Nashville: Abingdon, 1993.

———. *Protestant Worship: Traditions in Transition.* Louisville: Westminster/John Knox, 1989.

White, William. *The Case of the Episcopal Churches in the United States Considered.* Edited by Richard G. Salomon. Philadelphia: Church Historical Society, 1954.

———. *Memoirs of the Protestant Episcopal Church in the United States of America.* 2d ed. New York: Swords, Stanford, 1836.

Wilkins, Robert P., and Wynona H. Wilkins, *God Giveth the Increase: The History of the Episcopal Church in North Dakota.* Fargo: North Dakota Institute for Regional Studies, 1959.

Williams, Peter. *America's Religions: Traditions and Cultures.* New York: Macmillan, 1990.

———. *Popular Religion in America.* Englewood Cliffs: Prentice Hall, 1980.

Wilmer, William. *The Episcopal Manual.* Philadelphia: Dickinson, 1815.

Wilson, A. N. *C. S. Lewis: A Biography.* New York: Norton, 1990.

Wilson, Bird. *Memoir of the Life of the Rt. Rev. William White.* Philadelphia: Hayes and Fell, 1839.

Wilson, John F. *Public Religion in American Culture.* Philadelphia: Temple University Press, 1979.

———, and Donald L. Drakeman, eds. *Church and State in American History.* 2d ed. Boston: Beacon, 1987.

Winter, Gibson. *The Suburban Captivity of the Churches.* New York: Doubleday, 1961.

Woodmason, Charles. *The Carolina Backcountry on the Eve of the Revolution.* Edited by Richard J. Hooker. Chapel Hill: Institute of Early American History and Culture, 1953.

Woolverton, John F. *Colonial Anglicanism in North America, 1607–1776.* Detroit: Wayne State University Press, 1984.

Wright, J. Robert. *Lift High the Cross: The Oxford Movement Sesquicentennial.* Cincinnati: Forward Movement, 1984.

————, and Joseph W. Witmer, eds. *Called to Full Unity: Documents on Anglican-Roman Catholic Relations, 1966–1983.* Washington, D.C.: U.S. Catholic Conference, 1986.

Wuthnow, Robert. *The Restructuring of American Religion.* Princeton: Princeton University Press, 1988.

Zabriskie, Alexander C., ed. *Anglican Evangelicalism.* Philadelphia: Church Historical Society, 1943.

INDEX